HOW YOU THINK AND FEEL

Changes Your Body

DYNAMIC BODY PSYCHOLOGY

Douglas Peterson, Ph.D.

3C
TRI CENTERS
PUBLISHING

PERMISSIONS

Deep felt gratitude for the following permission to reprint granted in the publication of this book.

Polarity Therapy: The Complete Collected Works, Volume One, Dr. Randolph Stone, D.C., D.O, Book Publishing Company, 1986. Reprinted by permission of the publisher.

Licensed materials from section *Book II: The Wireless Anatomy of Man* include:

- Chart No. 2 Chart of the Subtle Prana Currents in the Human Body: and Their Chakras as Whirling Primary Functional Centers of Energy (pg. 9)
- Chart No. 3 Composite Picture of the Pattern Forces of the Body and Their Wireless Circuits (pg. 10)
- Chart No. 4 Diagnostic and Therapeutic Chart of Body Areas Based on the Regional Relation of Wireless Currents of Energy Flow (pg. 11)

- Chart No. 6 Electro-Magnetic Currents and Their Proper Anatomical Relations Anterior and Posterior View of Overall Sweep Plus Polarity Centers (pg. 13)
- Chart No. 58 The Ear Canals as the Superior Centers of Gravity in the Head, Around Which Local Circuits Whirl (pg. 79)

For my Mother, Lovella Peterson,
who was a saint and now an angel in heaven.

CONTENTS

LIST OF FIGURES

LIST OF TABLES

INTRODUCTION

THE WAY YOU THINK AND FEEL transforms the body tissue into your personality made visible. This book brings to life the psychological and physical issues that become written on our bodies. The next few chapters describe the many changes in the body structure. The way we think and feel brings about changes in the body both immediately, such as with depression, and over time, such as with developing a hunched back from long-held feelings and thoughts that the world is overwhelming.

We start with a certain body then the ravages or pleasures of time make their marks on it. This book details many of those body changes. We can talk about thinking and feeling as if they had an independent existence, but all our thoughts and feelings reside in the body.

The body is like a container. We may speak of experiences, images, dreams, projections, and visions, but our comprehension of everything happens inside the body. Of course, there are thoughts about astral travel and interdimensional transformations, yet all these thoughts still occur in the brain, which is in the body. We rationalize that something is occurring outside the body, but that very act of cognitive projection is a biological process. The same occurs with feelings. They all occur inside the body, although we can act out those thoughts and feelings with our body in the environment, society, and relationships. The internal mechanisms of thinking and feeling have been studied extensively, but the effects on the body's exterior have been studied less.

We have a limited conception of psychophysiology, to a large extent, with theory and experimentation that seem to have largely overlooked the thing-in-itself, that of the body exterior, with notable exceptions. We can identify with the look of anger, sorrow, pain, and other more extreme emotions, yet the results of the external physical effects of our emotions and thinking patterns are not widely discussed. This book, *How You Think and Feel Changes Your Body: Dynamic Body Psychology*, aims to champion the often-overlooked theories and concepts of how and why the body changes as we progress through life.

Dynamic Body Psychology is a body-mind-oriented model connecting psychological processes with physiology and adaptations of tissue and the body to social and physical environments. The triune concept integral to this model may appear new, yet Plato and Aristotle taught versions of the three-centers theory, and it was found in ancient Hindu literature, among many other places (see Chapter 8 on the Three Centers Theory). This book explores the current yet ancient model of Triune Psychology, incorporating relevant psychological theories with anatomy, physiology, biology, anthropology, metaphysics, and physics.

A body of knowledge emerges that reveals ancient truths correlated to modern science. The wisdom of Aristotle, Plato, and the *Yoga Sutras of Patañjali* forms a backdrop in poetry and story that shows, in part, an understanding of a triune structure. Plato has Little Kosmos of the abdomen (appetite), chest (energy, courage, anger), and cranium (active-rational and receptive—immortal soul). Aristotle labeled the three centers as Nutrient, Sentient, and Nous or intelligence. To St. Thomas Aquinas, it was the Vegetable or Nutritive Soul, Animal Soul, and the Intellect. In the ancient Hindu *Yoga Sutras*, it was the cosmic forces of the Gunas (binding rope) called the Tamoguna (mass-stuff, matter), Rajoguna (energy, motion, change, emotional), and Satoguna (intelligence or mind-stuff). In Ayurveda, there are the dosha or body types of Kapha (heavy body type), Pitta (medium body, intense, fiery), and Vata (thin body, quick, nervous).

A theme arising from scientific research also shows a three-part course in human evolution. Paul MacLean developed a system of human development that highlights the triune brain, which houses the R (Reptilian) Complex (physical), Limbic System (emotions), and Neocortex (mental). Our body is composed of three tissue types or germ cells: endoderm (digestive system—gut and organs), meso-derm (muscle, connective tissue, heart, and circulatory system), and ectoderm (brain, nerves, and skin). Each skeletal system has three main parts: the pelvis, chest (thorax), and skull, with the arms and legs hanging as appendages and the neck and spine linking the primary three centers together. Behavior manifests physically and socially according to the three centers of the psyche: the physical life center, emotional center, and intellectual center. Arguably, Freud found the id (the it of primal matter), ego (changeable, emotional), and superego (supreme mental). Many examples of the three centers from history, religion, philosophy, and science are examined.

The body is a reflection of the thinking and feeling processes. The body tissue actually changes in size and texture from the quality, quan-tity, and periodicity of life energy flowing through it as adaptations of its DNA genetic structure. Suppressed actions or desires result in a physiological process that forms (congeals) as energy blocks on a large or minute level. Blocked energy creates rigidity in the tissue, as seen with metabolic waste and toxic residue congealing or sticking (molecular bonding) to the fascia connective tissue. This rigidity collects to become what Freud's contemporary Wilhelm Reich spoke of as body armor. Physically, a person forms their body shape from heredity and the environment. The external forces of social and physical existence adapt as tissue alterations to develop the proper defense. All psychological defenses result in physiological and tissue changes. Thus, the mind and body directly impact each other.

The body shape and texture of every part show the body-mind interaction relevant to each part's position in the body. Psychological adaptations of the body in its struggle for existence have been mapped out. Body maps begin with the psychological significance of the face, with which we "face" the world, and the head, which is the bio-orienter. As we slowly work our way to the feet, each part shows how it was treated and how it responded to the social and physical environments. Each body part tells a story of past use and abuse, as does each body section, leading to the whole person's story. The tale is of one's thoughts and emotions written over time in the body's tissue and the alignment to gravity and other energies. Out of alignment in a physical sense, such as a bad posture, can only force pressure on the psychological level.

Freud showed that the body and mind work together with defense mechanisms forming psychosomatic reactions, and now science can see the changes in body tissue. When thoroughly inspected, the view of the body-mind connection now becomes a view of "two sides of the same coin." The mind reflects on the body and the body on the mind. Body and mind are inseparable.

The types of body adaptations are presented in a mesh of physical life, emotional, and mental concepts, which form the empirical basis of the Dynamic Body Psychology Model. This integrated approach attempts to include all relevant related theories.

The drama of thought and passion plays out in the tissue of the body. A lifestyle with time and habituation also becomes a body style.

CHAPTER 1

Three Center Body Types and How the Body Changes

THROUGH THE AGES, there has been the image of an ideal body. Perhaps Leonardo da Vinci thought the *best* proportions for the human body were represented by his drawing of the Vitruvian Man in about 1487. The drawing (see Figure 1) depicts what he considered a universal design of perfect proportions, with two male positions shown to fit into a circle and a square.

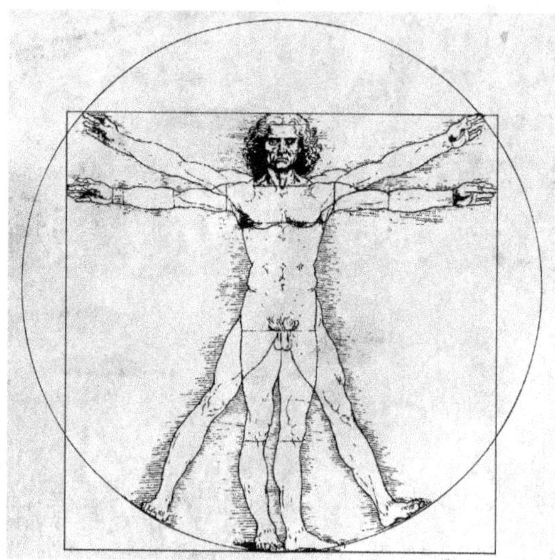

Figure 1: The Ideal Body: The Vitruvian
Man by Leonardo da Vinci

The drawing is also important because the measurements of the drawing are those of the golden mean, which provides for the measure of all things. Seeing this picture of the ideal form is nice, yet this idea of perfection is not singularly the way of nature. Perhaps every individual body is perfect in its own way. Nature gives us the muscular body, as Leonardo seems to prefer, but also the thin body, the thick body, and many variations of the three basic body shapes.

Basic body shapes follow the geometric patterns of round, square, and triangular, often more telling in the face, perhaps. Each body type—thick (round), muscular (square), and thin (triangle) has its own particular set of advantages and disadvantages, its pros and cons, its ups and downs, as does everything in life. Body types presented in the triune model (see Chapter 7) are consistent with the somatotypes but without the controversial theories of personality. The triune model includes the Physical Life Type with a rounded heavyset shape and an orientation to life, food, and family; the Emotional Type, which tends to have a square, muscular shape and focus on emotions (to emote) and movement; and the Mental Type, with a triangular or thin shape envisioning a mental focus that can bring concentration or worry.

Evidence for the triune model is abundant. Historical references abound with Plato, Aristotle, St. Thomas Aquinas, Indian Ayurvedic Body Types, Chinese Body Types, and many more. The three body shapes resemble the three primary shapes of round, square, and triangle, providing a geometric basis. Three germ cells produce all the body's cells, tissues, and organs. As simplified, the three germ cells that begin life at the start of the embryo are the endoderm, which forms the gut, intestines, and some organs; the mesoderm, which creates the muscles, bones, and circulatory system; and the ectoderm, developing the nervous system and skin.

Starting with the cellular level, we have life itself with its most basic functions of living through feeding, excreting, and reproducing. This is our physical self, which, in human anatomy, reflects as our gut (digestive system) that is living much like a one-celled animal. It is the physical reaction to impulsive stimulation. It is the animal self, the id, the uncaring survivalist. There is also the bony skeletal structure of the pelvis, allowing the stomach, anus, and genitals a place to attach. You could say that the pelvis and gut represent the physical essence or aspect of ourselves.

Chest or thorax is the second primary skeletal and physiological structure. Pelvis and the chest are connected by vertebrae. The chest center structure relates to emotion. We regard the heart philosophically, religiously, and culturally as the seat of emotion. Hormones and neuropeptides merge into the blood, and the heart pumps them all into the tissues of the body, spreading them out, enervating nerves and chemical reactions, and giving us that spreading feeling of emotion. Emotions innervate our being with the ability to move quickly when in danger, and they motivate us to bond or love deeply. To emote is to move.

The third primary bony structure of the body is the skull or cranium, which houses the brain, the physiological manifestation of cognition or simply thinking. Understanding, perceiving, thinking, rationalizing, and planning are all functions that provide significant survival value. Recognizing and acting upon seeing danger at a distance, visualizing a partner or family, building a house, and any complex pattern of behavior are all manifestations of the brain.

These three centers of life involve three anatomical centers: the pelvis, chest, and head. Thus, we have the basics of life's physical, emotional, and mental centers. These three centers of life fit perfectly with the Triune Brain Theory of Paul MacLean, which describes the animal evolution from developing a nervous system and evolving into our hindbrain, the R-complex (reptilian), the emotional brain, the limbic system developed by mammals, and the mental brain (the neocortex), which will be further described later.[1] This model of psychology minimally fits into a triangulated form. Within each of us resides the three centers of life that give us our existence. All are equally important, as life itself is physical, which involves the intake of fuel (food), the release of exhaust (waste extraction), and procreation to continue into time. Emotions are the heightened ability to quickly act and react (move, to emote) with the surroundings. The bones, muscles, and connective tissue are controlled by neurochemical processes, such as adrenaline, hormones, and neuropeptides. The mind involves the brain and nervous system to better guide the beast or organism with memory, foresight, or planning. The self relies on successfully coordinating all body systems and parts.

As presented in the triune model of life, the idea of a person genetically thin, thick, or muscular should have much supportive evidence. Yes, a wide range of evidence and supporting theories exist, and these three basic body types with combinations of the three appear generously in society. Many theories show the same three-part human system or similar body types, including Paul MacLean's Triune Brain Theory, William Sheldon's Constitutional Psychology with three somatotypes or body types, Freud and his Three Centers of Personality (the id, ego, and superego), and the Greek theories by Pythagoras, Plato, and Aristotle (see the Three Centers chart as Table 5 in Chapter 8). Pythagoras is remembered for his mathematical knowledge, especially with the Pythagorean theorem, but he also realized and spoke about the pattern of the three centers. Plato and Aristotle taught that a person had three parts to their soul-body, including Aristotle's nutrient for physical life, sentient in the chest for emotions, and nous or mental in the head. From Indian Ayurvedic tradition, these three aspects are the three doshas, including Kapha (heavyset, calm), Pitta (decisive, forceful), and Vata (thin, quick), plus various mixtures of the somatotypes. These days, you can search online and find Aristotle's three-part soul, theories by Plato, and details about Ayurvedic and begin to see the historical background of the Triune Theory.

Perhaps the best known is William Sheldon's somatotypes with the endomorph, mesomorph, and ectomorph. The somatotypes were named after the three germ cells that begin life at the start of the embryo: the endoderm that forms the gut, digestive system, intestines, and organs; the mesoderm that creates the muscles, bones, and circulatory system; and the ectoderm that develops the nervous system and skin. The endomorph has a large frame with muscle and fat, and is gut oriented, which is focused on survival, food, and enjoyment of life. The mesomorph has a medium frame and is more muscle and heart (circulatory system) oriented, which is focused on movement and action. The ectomorph has a slender or thin frame and a more nervous presentation or mental orientation. The somatotypes are shown in Figure 2.

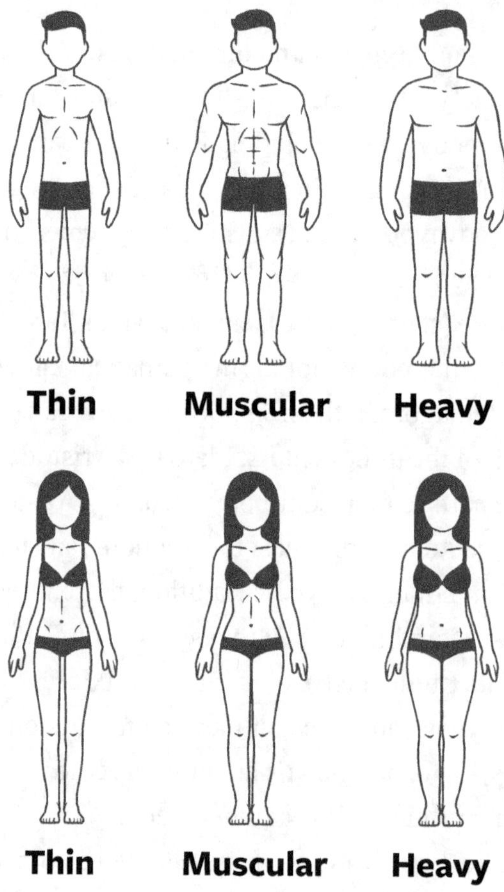

Figure 2: Three Body Types

All body types are combinations of the three centers or the three main types. A very thin person is thought of as high ectoderm (ectomorph), the medium or developed muscular person is considered as high mesoderm (mesomorph), and a thick or heavy person may be highly endoderm (endomorph). Most people are not the extreme of the three body types but instead appear to be a mixture of the three, with the more dominant somatotype named first, such as meso-ectomorph for a muscular and thin person. The sub-somatotypes also play a role in the apparent body dysmorphia described in Chapter 6 on body splits.

Yet the combinations can be even more prevalent with the hazards of life and emotional tissue changes and complications due to the environmental conditions of work, disease, accidents, stress, and trauma. Genetics provides the form, yet the environment helps to shape the form.

Although psychology moved away from the somatotypes, professionals such as athletic trainers, physical therapists, and massage therapists use and research the classifications because they fit the appearance of bodies but typically without the psychological personality theories attached.

This section discusses the physical and psychological factors of how the body changes, primarily made through emotional repression and habituation of movement, posture, and tissue position over time. This creates a body adaptation that could be considered dysmorphia, which is typically an odd shape or size of body parts.

GENETICS AND ENVIRONMENT

It is understood that genetics and the environment form a person's body and mind. Genetics creates the body composed of the three germ layers, including the physical life-oriented endoderm with the gut and some organs; emotional (movement-oriented) mesoderm with muscles, bones, and heart (circulatory system); and mental ectoderm with the brain (nervous system) and skin (epidermis). As one of the three body systems can be more developed or prominent, the physical manifestation renders the three primary body types to have many variations.

A pivotal question is about what changes the genetic body-mind form. What is in the environment that changes the genetic body? The concept of environment includes the physical environment, social environment of people and culture, and personal environment. The root causality of each aspect of the environment is primarily trauma and stress.

PSYCHOPHYSICAL CHANGES

The main issue becomes how and when these tissue alterations occur. The environmental variations largely stem from what happens to you or what you do with the choices you have or perceive. Do you have a choice in the matter? In childhood, there may be little room for individual choice until adulthood. When choice is present, do you tone your body with movement, such as exercise, work, or physical games, or do you refrain from activity except to pass another beer up to your lips and walk to the toilet while watching videos or playing games on your phone?

Actions, emotions, and thinking become habits, and these habits become your lifestyle, which alters the body. Yet the largest source of environmental change is due to trauma, primarily childhood trauma, and especially from early childhood, including infant and toddler trauma. The earlier the trauma, typically, the more impact on the psychophysical adaptation. This is why child abuse and neglect are so incredibly decisive in the formation of a person.

TRAUMA

Early childhood incidents can include injury from accidents, violence, being bullied or beaten up, rape, and verbal abuse. Aggravated hostility can occur not only in childhood but also in adolescence and adulthood. Being married to a violent person or being with controlling or violent people can subject one to a fear for life or safety. Coincidental stress stems from worry (conscious or unconscious) about the trauma happening both physically and emotionally.

Yet trauma can occur at any time. You can see it in the soldiers returning from war with PTSD or civilians suffering through mental confusion and stress as rape victims, or people suffering from severe accidents like car crashes. There are other forms of trauma, including the effects of bullying in childhood, violence or verbal abuse, and living in a cult that you got into as a social group or grew up in and thought was a benevolent religious society until you began to see through the double-speak, selfish motivations, and power grabs. Then you are ostracized and no longer welcome. There are many situations begetting violence, trauma, fear, and stress.

However, as an adult, there may be less noticeable tissue alterations than in children who are growing, as children possess more malleability for emotional tissue habituation and tissue change or dysmorphia. But the basic emotional posturing becoming habitual exists at all ages, and the adaptive tissue changes have less time to manifest, making it less severe in adulthood.

Trauma affects the mind through the thinking process, which automatically, immediately, and unconsciously has an impact on the body and reacts chemically with neuropeptides, hormones, and adrenaline. When seeing something that brings up the memory of past experiences of trauma, even as a repressed memory, an emotion could arise and the sadness, crying, stress, or fear could potentially or fully act to hide the actual memory.

Although trauma is complex, there exists a general flow in which trauma takes to manifest. Possible interventions or steps can be used to help ease the mental and physical reactions. Here is a brief overview:

1. *Talk it out:* When the trauma occurs, the discussion is critical to help work out the hurt. Typically, the first listener is the

mother. A parent can simply listen to her child, allowing the emotion and thoughts to be fully expressed with or without gentle, non-threatening guidance. If not, the trauma lingers and, over time, becomes repressed in the subconscious body as a forgotten memory. A significant friend or family member who will listen unconditionally and allow us to talk it out, that is, express our thoughts and feelings, helps us resolve and get through and beyond the trauma. Often, people do not have a safe significant person who will listen unconditionally, which then falls to therapists, counselors, or perhaps priests to fulfill.

2. *Act it out:* Our unresolved psychological issues transform into behavior. It is natural to move our body in ways to capture understanding. Perhaps you have heard someone say, "He acts just like his dad" or "She does that just like her mother." We act out our frustrations at any age and model what we have learned. Kids at school or on the playground may hit other kids, just like their parents hit them. But our attention is focused on the behavior and not the complex psychological and environmental factors underlying the motivation for the behavior. Thus, we punish the child. Yet acting it out helps recall the memory or psycho-sensory emotion. I have heard a child say, "That's how my mother hit me." Allowing the child to fully express the situation has, at times, given the child the means of looking at and naturally self-resolving the behavior. It is like the cognitive behavioral therapy (CBT) process of allowing the person to confront their mental processing. For example, when you think no one likes you, you are given the task to write down every time someone says something positive to you, and it's even better with the time and date.

3. *Dream it out (internal processing):* Dealing with or processing the residual effects from past or current trauma through dreaming can give helpful messages. Therapists, such as those who practice Jungian methods, have used dreams as material in therapy. Other internal processes may include hearing voices, creating, or identifying with different selves (multiple personalities), often due to harsh trauma in childhood. Our internal psychological process functions for our benefit in attempting to heal unresolved trauma.

4. *Embody it:* Bring it to life within the body structure with psychosomatic reactions and complications. When other psychological processes are not sufficient to ease or heal the effects of the unresolved trauma, the trauma, which is already lodged in the body, manifests in various ways that are discussed in this book. Earlier processes (talking, acting, dreaming) continue operating. It should be noted that many of the varieties of known psychosomatic adaptations (e.g., allergic, gastrointestinal) are not directly addressed in this book.

WHAT CHANGES AND HOW: BIOCHEMICAL AND PHYSICAL

Biochemical changes: blood pressure, hormone, and neuropeptide secretions.

As MacLean pointed out, emotions arise from the limbic center in the brain then send messages to the hypothalamus that signals the pituitary to activate the hormonal system.[2] The hormones, along with neuropeptides, provide the emotion to emote or to move your mind and body into certain positions, and with gravity, they change the body's energy flow (see Chapter 10 on energy).

Physical changes: the buildup of metabolic waste and toxic residue in the connective tissue occurs with similarity to the blood vessel sludge or cholesterol in the basement membrane.

Connective tissue is psychomotor susceptible, especially fascia, with the body parts that primarily attach to the joints. The connective tissue gel is fluid and increases and decreases in viscosity, affecting mobility by its flow by becoming inflamed or indurated (hardening), depending on the conditions.

INFLAMMATION AND INDURATION

These are the two primary causes of the changes in the connective tissue. Habitually repressing emotions, typically out of fear or safety, tends to project the posture and body structure into certain positions. This process may be called the emotional tissue habituation of the body position with the creation of a new or adapted psychophysical look. This process brings the evolution of tissue to a new "normal," a new psychomotor or psychophysical adjustment.

Inflammation starts out as a healing response to tissue injury with the healing complex, including white blood cells, repairing the tissue. In time through healing, the white blood cells process the inflammation and it begins moving out. It must have a small enough molecular structure to pass through the lymphatic capillaries. The remaining substances include toxic waste and residual matter. They are naturally unable to leave the cellular matrix, like human cultures bind together when in proximity, and they blend. It is happening in the connective tissue, the largest complex of structural connections interwoven with interstitial fluid that provides for feeding, the transmission of fluids, and the ability to change the thickness and thinness (viscosity) of the tissue that it has wrapped or enveloped.

The waste products or particles attach to the tissue and become indurated (hardened). This hardening of the tissue can change the body part's natural positioning through emotional tissue habituation and gravity. This occurs when the person keeps feeling, sometimes continually and consciously, but mostly unconsciously, and holding the emotionally based posture or position for an extended period so that it is an ingrained habit in the persona. The body position or posture is (re)created as a reaction to strong emotions, such as fight, flight, or freeze from fear or terror.

Thus, emotional repression and tissue habituation change the body through prolonged and chronically repeated emotions with the pathological habitual body postures reflecting the pathological habitual thinking that goes hand in hand. The primary negative emotional repression of tissue habituation patterns (or emotional re-posturing) come from fear, anticipation (worry), sadness, depression, anger, and revenge-seeking, which can be conscious, semiconscious (perhaps going in and out), or primarily unconscious, as it often is.

WHERE THE BODY CHANGES

The pectoral girdle and pelvic girdle are primary areas of psychophysical posture adjustments. Much of the postural and body formation change due to emotional tissue habituation is secured by attachments at joints, especially adjunct to the pelvic girdle (pelvis) and pectoral girdle (shoulder) due to the numerous connective tissue attachments and their crossroads structure. You can also see specific alterations in the eye orbits because of the network of connective tissue attachments. For the sake of brevity, the pelvic and pectoral girdles, referred to as shoulders and pelvis, tend to provide a visible glimpse of the individual's psychophysical outcome, habituated emotional–physical patterning. The more extreme and longer the tissue and posture habituation of the emotions and emotional reactions, the higher the psycho-physical pathological body postures or PBP index.

The pectoral girdle comprises the shoulder blade (scapula), collarbone (clavicle), and all the connective tissue that connects to the arms and shoulders and helps move the arms and shoulders. The connection allows the arms, as the doers in life, to obtain or do what is needed.

The pelvic girdle is the hip bone that attaches the leg to the body (sacrum and spine) and all the connective tissue that binds everything in place. The legs are the movers of life, as they move us with stability where we need to go. The pelvis also deals with the bowels and having an accident that could result in physical or verbal punishment and shame, and the pelvis deals with protection from spanking.

The pelvic girdle helps control not only the pelvis but the legs and, therefore, the feet, and also the stomach, to some degree, as it is attached to the torso. The alignment with gravity affects the psyche from the feet on the ground going up to the pelvis and pectoral girdle and neck, and finally the head placement.

It is fascinating how nature forms body types and how environmental stress, trauma, and fear, will pull the body into defensive positions that, over time, slowly reposition parts of the body (emotional tissue habituation). This process of tissue adaptation occurs primarily through inflammation and induration of the connective tissue. Areas with many connective tissue attachments and movement tend to become more psychoactive, such as the eyes, shoulders, and pelvis.

CHAPTER 2

Psychology of the Body

PSYCHOLOGICAL BODY MAPS

The body reflects the mind, and the mind reflects the body's energies. The body-mind connection is viewed by examining each body part and section. Each body part has a unique story due to its particular body-mind function. For example, the hands and arms are the doers of life, as they manipulate to obtain satisfaction. The legs are the movers of life, as they carry you through life where you want to go. The torso is the being or the self.

The body-mind evolved in a three-step process, starting with the physical center; next came the emotional heart center and then the intellect in the head. Each center developed out of the previous one as an adaptation for the survival and progress of the species. The three centers (physical, emotional, and mental) are also energy centers essential to the quality of bioenergy flow. Energy can become limited or blocked if the three centers are not in alignment. Emotionally based inhibitions in action or desire may cause the energy to block or minimize to some degree and manifest over time as body armor. One body part becomes over-energized and expands, while another becomes under-energized and contracts or wilts. A history of the energy blocks and suppression of thought or deed become written in tissue. Tissue shapes become remarkably similar among people with common life histories. Changes from psychological adaptations to the social and physical environment become mapped out in the tissue. This section briefly shows each body-mind part.

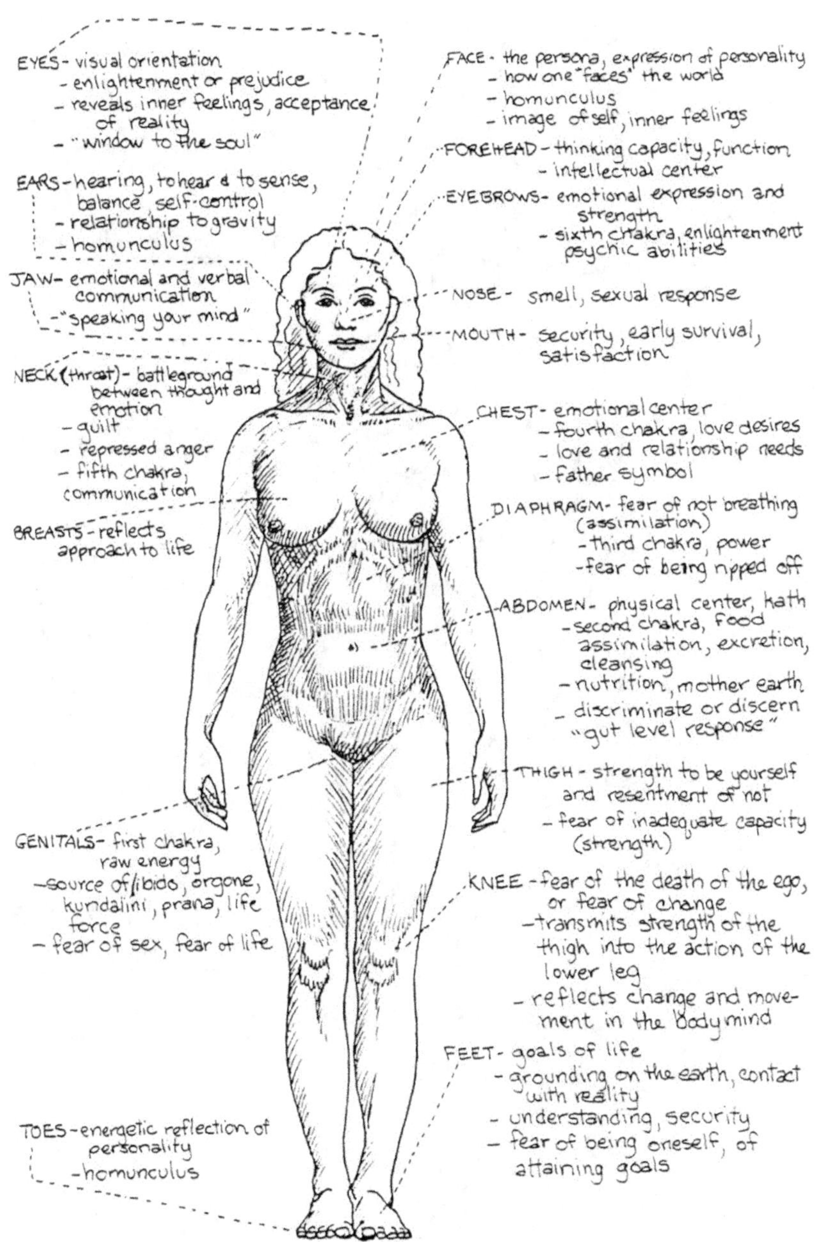

Figure 3: Body Front Map

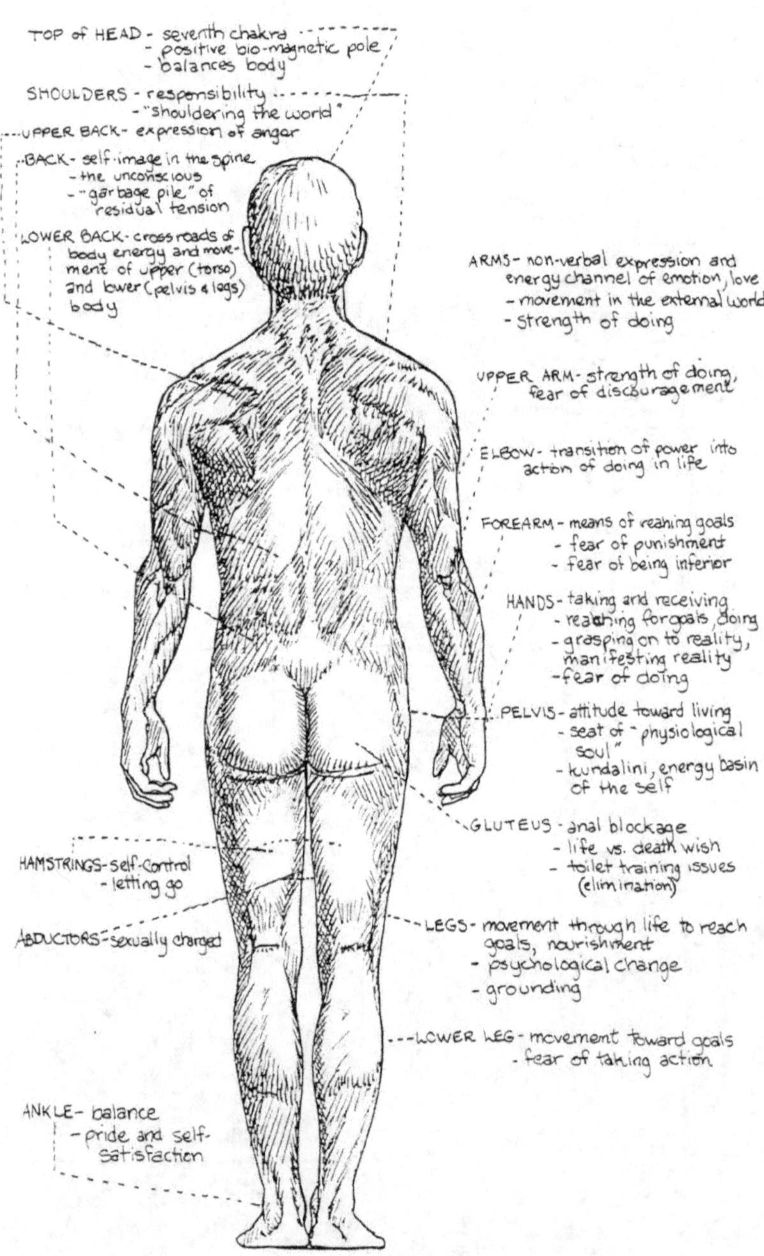

Figure 4: Body Rear Map

BODY-MIND PARTS OUTLINE

This psychophysical outline lists the body parts from the top down with a brief description of the function or action of each body part. The list is extensive, and you can skip it if you wish and go to the Body-Mind Parts.

FACE

- the persona, expression of personality
- how one "faces" the world
- homunculus
- image of self, inner feelings
  1. square face and head: mesomorphic, mesaticephalic, tends toward concave profile, shows willpower and action orientation
  2. round face and head: endomorphic, dolichocephalic, tends toward vertical profile, oriented to physical comforts, relaxation, and social interaction
  3. triangular (heart-shaped) face and head: ectomorphic, brachiocephalic, tends toward convex profile, intellectual type
  4. composite face and head: most common, a mixture of the other types, usually oval or oblong

TOP OF HEAD

- seventh or crown chakra, union
- body balancer
- positive biomagnetic pole

FOREHEAD
- thinking capacity and function
- creased forehead – thinking, worry
- smooth forehead – inner peace

EYEBROWS
- emotional expression and strength
- sixth chakra, enlightenment, psychic abilities
    1. high brow – intellectual excitement
    2. low brow – practical
    3. browbeaten – intimidated, frightened eye, pleading look, almost begging for attention and acceptance
    4. furrowed brow – intense, focused
    5. anxious brow – moving from uncontrolled tension
    6. bushy, heavy brow – strong, domineering, bullish, masculine
    7. thin, light brow – softer qualities, feminine

EYES
- ocular face segment
- emotional reflection
- visual orientation, syntony
- enlightenment or prejudice reveals inner feelings, acceptance of reality
- "window to the soul"
    1. right eye – father relationship, outgoing, yang, doing
    2. left eye – mother relationship, receptive, yin, being
    3. nearsighted – myopic, withdrawn
    4. farsighted – hyperopia, extroverted
    5. round eyes – warm, loving, innocent, soft touch
    6. deep-set eyes – withdrawn, hurt, emotional problems, study the situation before acting

7. protruding eyes – intense, anxious
8. seductive eyes – soft, manipulating, immature
9. hard versus soft eyes – control issues
10. round versus thin eyes – sensitivity versus strength
11. moving or darting eyes – anxious, paranoid of environment
12. angry eyebrows lowered, with thin, hard eyes

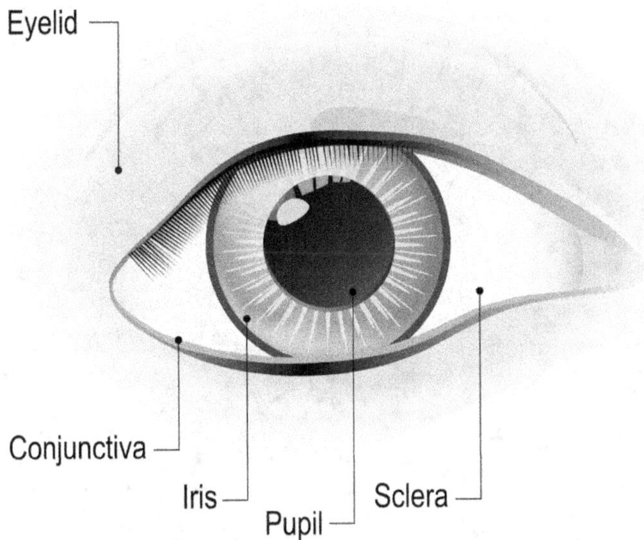

Figure 5: Sclera Chart: physical diagnosis

EYELIDS

- upper eyelash – a condition of the nervous system
- lower eyelash – a condition of sexual organs
- inward lash curl – impotence or frigidity

AREA AROUND THE EYE: BAGS AND PUFFY AREAS UNDER THE EYE

- digestion, drug use (including past usage until dissipated), overconsumption of liquid, or fate
- wrinkles at sides of eyes: expression of habitual emotions, smile lines, frown lines

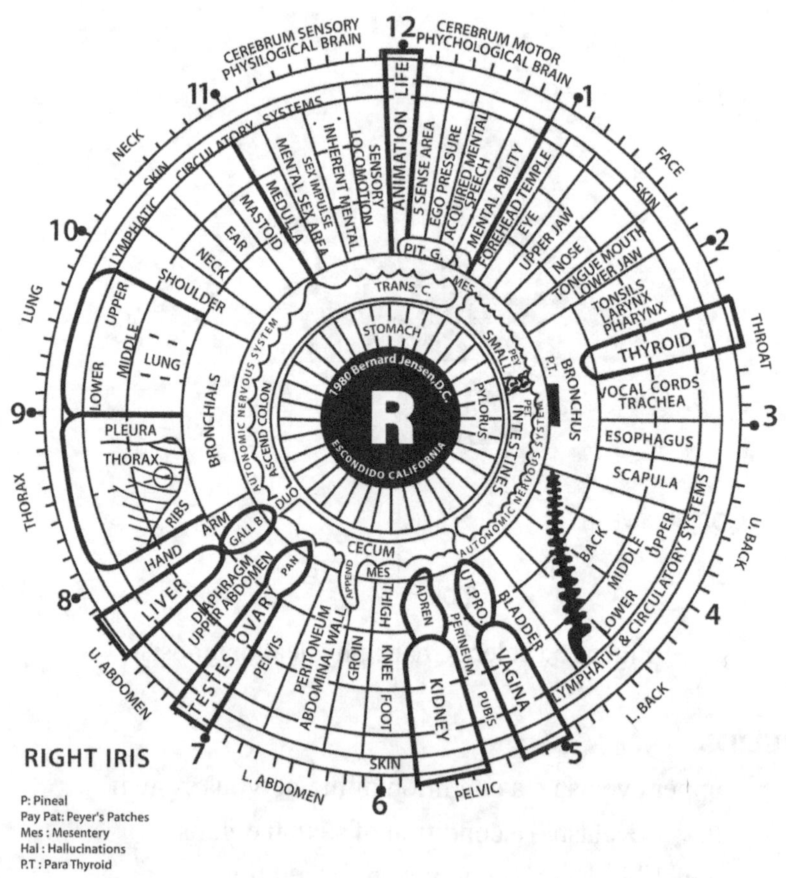

RIGHT IRIS

P: Pineal
Pay Pat: Peyer's Patches
Mes : Mesentery
Hal : Hallucinations
P.T : Para Thyroid

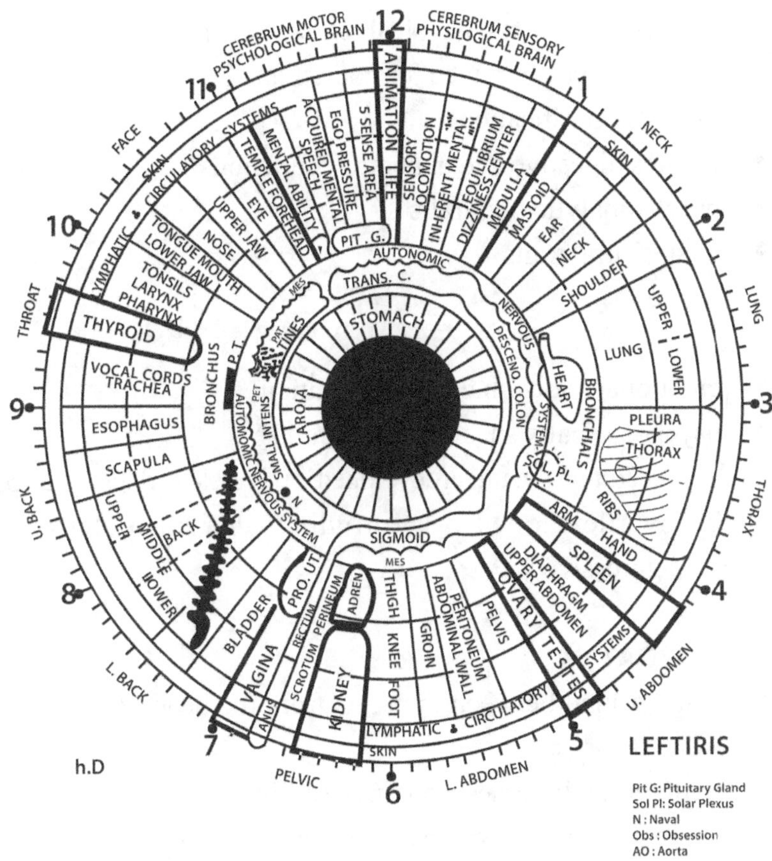

Figure 6: Iridology Chart: physical diagnosis

EARS

- hearing, attention to environment (internal and external)
- balance and self-control through space, relationship to gravity
- homunculus

NOSE

- smell, detect odor in the environment
- sexual responses

MOUTH

- oral face segment – physical reflection (map)
- early survival, entrance for nourishment
- security, gratification
- reflects digestive and generative functions
- psychoanalytic oral traits
- Eastern oral traits

JAW

- emotional and verbal communication
- psychologically speaking your mind
  1. receding jaw: underdeveloped, "withheld sadness or anger"
  2. overdeveloped or protruding: defiant, determined, aggressive

NECK (THROAT)

- battleground between thoughts from the head and emotions from the heart
- guilt, throat illnesses from inflexibility
- fear of expression, repressed anger
- fifth chakra, interpersonal communication and self-expression
  1. forward head and neck held forward – aggressive attitude, wants to "get ahead," primarily a cognitive orientation
  2. side-leaning head, and neck leaning to one side – inability to approach world directly, disorganized, perhaps schizophrenic, relates to thinking (right lean) or intuition (left lean)
  3. head bent down and forward – overburdened emotionally, defeated position
  4. tilted-back head – holding on to tension, fear of letting go, holding on to the world, high anxiety
  5. long neck – proud attitudes, gracefulness, or head-body split

6. short neck – pushed down from mental pressure, push their way or aggressive, formed through life, can have raised shoulders as well as pressure on levator scapulae, causing headaches

SHOULDERS

- responsibility, shouldering the world
    1. broad, thick, large, slightly rounded shoulders sit atop the full-bodied individual
    2. square shoulders – carries big responsibilities, can "shoulder the burden," He-Man look, usually associated with the chest expanded type (overdeveloped ego)
    3. thin shoulders: emotionally dependent, weak, unable to accept responsibilities
    4. raised-up shoulders – fear, terror
    5. pulled-back or retracted shoulders – fighting against the force of the world (gravity)
    6. hunched, rounded, or drooped shoulders –bow or droop forward from misalignment with gravity, overburdened by life, too much responsibility
    7. bent-forward shoulder: bending or wrapping of the shoulder around the body is a sign of self-protection from the fear of hurt

ARMS

- nonverbal expression and energy channel of emotion, love
- movement in the external world
- the strength of doing
- upper arm – the strength of expression, capacity to do or to be, fear of discouragement

- forearm – the final doer, means used in the doing, fear of punishment
- arm basic types are like legs—thick, muscular, and thin—showing the genetic component then the environmental-social components of emotional tissue habituation
- subtypes depending on active or passive lifestyle; underdeveloped weak, soft untoned to toned to definition to overdeveloped
    1. soft, undeveloped arms – undercharged with energy, weak feeling, unable to reach out, lacks ability, lacks drive
    2. massive, overdeveloped, over-muscled arms – overcharged from holding on, insensitive, treats others as objects, lacks grace and tact
    3. thin, tight arms – inconsistent energy charge, clutching, clinging attitude, possible joint problems
    4. weak, underdeveloped arms – thin, undercharged from the emotional drain, sluggish, clumsy

FOREARM
- means of reaching goals
- fear of punishment
- fear of being inferior

ELBOW
- transition of power into the action of doing in life

UPPER ARM
- strength of doing
- fear of discouragement

HANDS

- taking and receiving
- reaching for goals, doing
- grasping for reality, manifesting reality
- fear of doing
  1. primitive hands – short, wide, thick, and clumsy; stiff and awkward with brutal instinct and little intelligence, rarely present
  2. square hands (orderly) – practical, hardworking; seeks organized and concrete plans; strong life-force
  3. conical (artistic) – gently tapers from base to fingertips, exuberant, enthusiastic, loves social life, needs a push to activate dreams
  4. spatulate (energetic) – the spatulate shape of hands and fingertips denotes great activity, desires originality
  5. pointed hands (idealistic) – intuitive, psychic, pointed fingers in pure form, long thin hand, cultist and martyrs to own ideas or philosophies
  6. mixed hands (adaptable) – most hands are a mixture of pure types; analyze fingers, combine findings, and use the thumb as an indicator
  7. philosophical hands (old classification) – either square or conical hands with knots on all finger and thumb joints; long, lean appearance; thinker, teacher, seeks knowledge
  8. hand texture or consistency
     a. flabby hands – variable temperament, could overeat, tend toward endomorphism
     b. soft hands – avoids manual labor or provides massage therapy
     c. firm hands – determined personality
     d. hard hands – hard to convince

FINGERS AND HANDS

- reflects five elements
  1. little finger – earth element, elimination function, rectum, survival, and life
  2. ring finger – water element, genitourinary functions in the pelvis, relates psychologically to emotions
  3. middle finger – fire element, digestion and assimilation in the abdomen, vitality
  4. index finger – air element, lung, heart, desires
  5. thumb – ether, relates to throat and voice, communication, and discrimination

BACK

- self-image in the spine
- the unconscious
- "garbage pile" of residual tension
  1. upper back – an expression of anger, or lack of it
  2. lower back – crossroads of body energy and movement and of upper (torso) and lower (pelvis and legs) body

CHEST

- the emotional center
- fourth chakra, love, desires
- circulation and respiration
- love and relationship needs
- father symbol
  1. chronically contracted chest – undercharged, collapsed for self-protection, insecurity
  2. overexpanded chest – overcharged, assertive, large cage to protect injured heart

BREAST

- reflects an approach to life
- diaphragm – respiration, fear of not breathing (assimilation)
- fear of being ripped off

UPPER ABDOMEN

- third chakra, power, physical center, Kath
- food assimilation, excretion, cleansing
- nutrition, mother earth
- discriminate or discern, a "gut-level response"
  1. bloated belly – inability to absorb, assimilate
  2. tight belly – fear, terror

LOWER ABDOMEN

- second chakra, life and/or procreation, sexual needs and pleasure
- sexual organs, ovaries, testicles
- fear of sex

PELVIS

- attitude toward living
- the seat of the physiological soul
- kundalini, energy basin of the self
  1. pelvis pushed forward – sexual holding lessens sexual feelings
  2. retracted pelvis or pulled back and up – heightened sexual energy, "can't get no satisfaction"

GLUTEUS

- anal blockage, gluteal holding
- life versus death wish

- toilet training (elimination) issues
    1. squeezed gluteus – "tight-assed," holding on to feelings
    2. held-up gluteus – "corncobbed ass," insecurity
    3. tension from above – contracted pelvis, intellectual control, fear of growth, lack of drive
    4. top-bottom split – stops energy from below
    5. tension from below – extended pelvis, physical control, fear of not getting enough, survival; tend to be bottom heavy

SIT BONE

- insecurity
- fear of conservation (survival)

GROIN

- the base of the spine, between anus and genitals
- first chakra, life, survival, life-force, prana and/or sex and reproduction
- the source of libido, orgone, kundalini, prana, life-force

LEGS

- movement through life to reach goals, nourishment
- psychological change
- grounding
    1. thick legs with subtypes of soft (fat) and toned (muscular)
    2. muscular legs with subtypes of soft or toned (developed or highly muscled)
    3. thin (soft or toned or tight) legs – a go-getter

THIGH

- strength to be yourself and resentment when not being yourself
- fear of inadequate capacity (strength)

ABDUCTORS

- sexually charged
- Hamstrings
- self-control
- letting go

KNEE

- fear of the death of the ego or fear of change
- transmits strength of the thigh into the action of the lower leg
- reflects change and movement in the body-mind

LOWER LEG

- movement toward goals
- fear of taking action

ANKLE

- balance
- pride and self-satisfaction

FEET

- goals of life
- grounding on the earth, contact with reality
- understanding, security
- fear of being oneself, fear of attaining goals
    1. healthy feet – stable, secure, balanced, three-point contact
    2. flat feet – passive, surrendered, "What's the use?"

3. clutching feet – insecurity, inadequate mothering, "Am I okay?"
4. heel-digging feet – control and determination, "I will do it."
5. floating feet – unbalanced physically, cannot get centered emotionally
6. rigid high arch – inflated ego, assertive, stretching taller to be above
7. tiptoe – dreamer, out of contact with reality, "tiptoe through the tulips"
8. lead feet – weighted down (thudding step, thunder walk)

TOES

- an energetic reflection of personality
- homunculus
  1. little toe – earth element, rectum, elimination, survival, life
  2. second smaller toe – water element, emotions, genitourinary system, pelvis
  3. middle toe – fire element, vitality, digestion, assimilation, abdomen
  4. second larger toe – air element, chest, desires, lungs
  5. big toe (ether element) – communication, discrimination in relationships, head and neck
  6. straight toes – balanced body-mind system
  7. one toe partially covering another – one aspect dominating another
  8. cross toes – dominant toe (upper) cancels recessive as in water toe over fire means water (emotions) drowns out the fire (passion)

As a product of genetics and environment, the body has identifiable patterns of growth and change. The sections on body parts look at the effects of thoughts and feelings on the plasticity of the body. Social influences contain many of the environmental factors shown as the effects of emotional reactions, habitual emotions, thinking patterns, and gravity on the individual's posture and structural alignment. The body parts are divided according to the three centers of life: 1. Head or Mental Center, including the face, head, and neck; 2. Heart or Emotional Center, including the shoulders, arms, and chest; and 3. Life or Physical Center, including the abdomen, pelvis, legs, and feet.

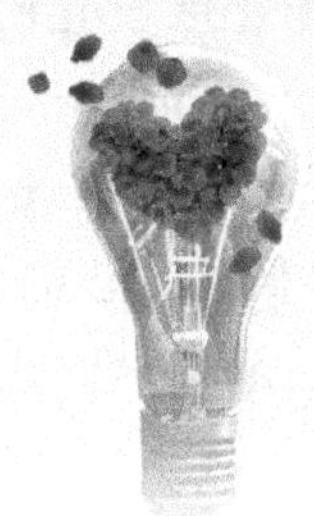

CHAPTER 3

Mental Center: Face, Head, and Neck

FACE: THE SELF: MICROCOSM, MICRO-PERSONALITY

- the persona
- how one "faces" the world
- an image of self
- round, square, triangular, heart, oval, oblong, or diamond

The face reflects the personality. It is more than just structure and movement because the face's musculature and fascia are used to express the person's wants, needs, desires, frustrations, and emotions, which we collectively call personality. The three basic shapes in the design of nature: round, square, and triangle form shapes in three dimensions that reflect the Platonic solids, which is the basis of all structure. It is not surprising that the face is composed of three basic shapes, along with the two major combinations, oval and oblong (Figure 8), and other identifiable combinations such as diamond, rectangle, inverted triangle, long, or even a heptagon shape. The three primary shapes of round, square, and triangle have combinations including oval, oblong, and diamond to make six types. With rectangle, inverse triangle, and heart basic shapes, the number grows to make nine face types.

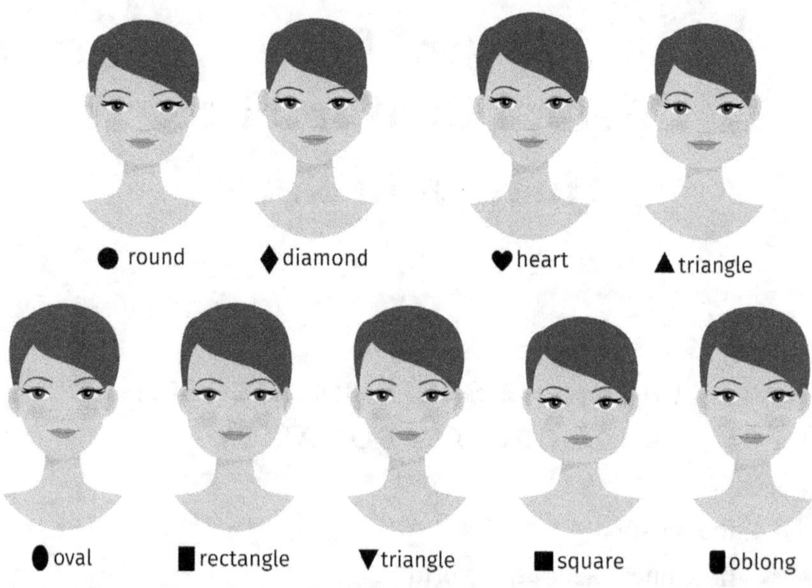

Figure 7: Face Types

Faces are not symmetrical. Ninety-six percent of all people have a more developed right side of the face.[3] This may be a Western trait due to a reliance on the rational left brain. Nerves cross over, so the right side is related to the left brain, and the left side to the right brain. The right side is usually harder, and the left side of the face tends to be softer and have a more feminine look. Kahn thinks painters and photographers mostly use the softer left side to portray people.

Much more flexibility is in the face's musculature than is generally noted. People's faces start forming according to their habitual inner feelings and thoughts, which are the feelings and thoughts you have over long periods of time. They are expressed on the face. Also, habitual feelings may involve a profession or trade that requires a particular attitude that is captured by many of the faces in that field. This has been called professional physiognomy. After years of living together, married couples often form similar facial attitudes from habitual feelings and begin to resemble each other.

Metaphysical sciences provide an intuitive perspective. Western physiognomy pioneered by the Swiss mystic Johann Kaspar Lavater was shown by Gibson and Gibson. Shapes of the faces are round, square, and triangular, which are consistent with the structure of the basic shapes. Sheldon developed a psychological theory consistent with the round, square, and triangle shapes for the face and body and defined three basic personalities based on the three germ layers that form life: endoderm, mesoderm, and ectoderm, and labeled the types as somatotypes of endomorph, mesomorph, and ectomorph.[4] Since every person has all three germ cells that grow and develop into the subsequent body parts, each person is also a mixture of the three basic types (mesomorph, endomorph, and ectomorph). Sheldon developed a rating system for the three somatotypes based on a one-to-seven scale with one being low and seven being high. Many people have a general balance of the three, but some have a higher physical structure in one of the three areas. Thus, a thin person is often referred to as an ectomorph, a muscular person as a mesomorph, and a heavier or fatter person as an endomorph.

Gibson and Gibson characterized the round-faced individual (Figure 8) as someone who is easygoing and likes to have a good time with as much comfort and luxury as possible. This description is much like Sheldon's endomorphic (viscerotonic) character, with the love of physical comforts, relaxation, and orientation to people.[5] Although Sheldon and Gibson and Gibson come from different fields and perspectives, they voice a similar observation of face types, and this persona type is visceral or gut oriented.

The (inverted) triangular face (Figure 8) is described metaphysically by Gibson and Gibson as denoting the mentality of someone quick on their feet yet able to think deeply. Sheldon considered that the over-intense mental cerebrotonia temperament type (ectomorphic) could be directed by a process allowing for the focus and discrimination of choices or inhibitory and attentional functions from the cerebrum. Essentially meaning, they are mentally oriented. The triangular or heart-faced ectomorph can also be viewed as coming from the intellectual center of Triune Psychology and the yin body type in Eastern thought.[6]

The active, emotionally oriented person may wear a squarish face and perhaps jaw, according to the typing expounded by Gibson and Gibson (Figure 8). This also appears as the exact model of Sheldon's mesomorph and the yang type in Eastern science, according to Kushi and the emotional self of Triune Psychology.[7]

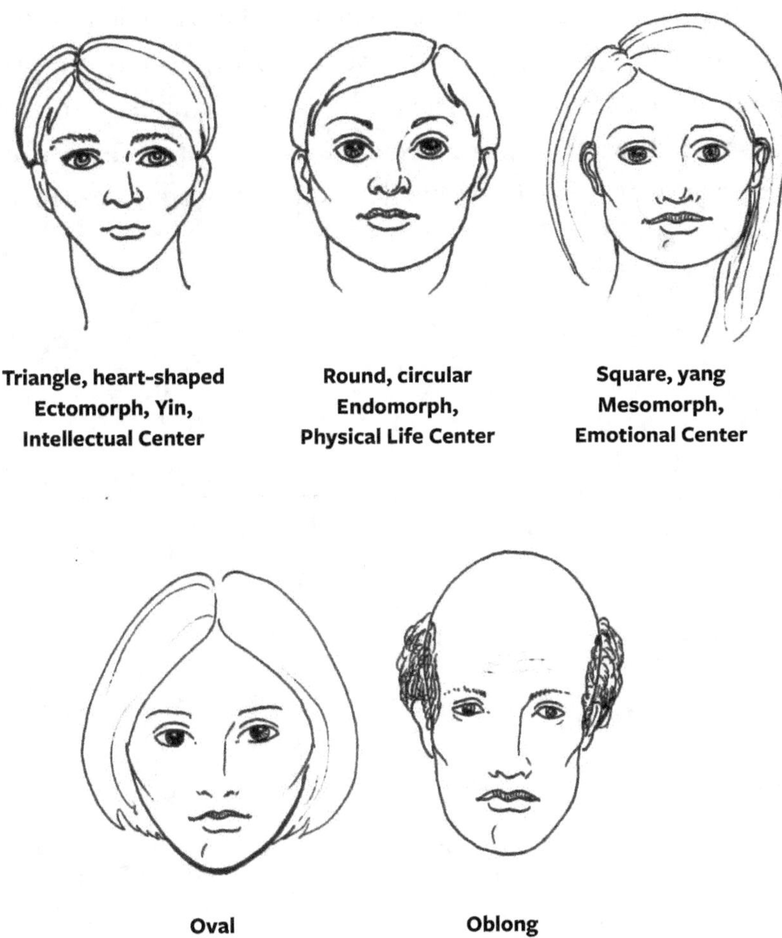

Figure 8: Triune Face Types

Ida Rolf and others show descriptions of the three head designs (Figure 9, looking down at the top of the skull) that she relates to Sheldon's somatotypes of the endomorph, mesomorph, and ecto-morph.[8] It appears that the classifications are brachiocephalic or broad-headed (endomorph); mesaticephalic, mesocephalic, or middle-width (mesomorph); and the dolichocephalic or long-headed (ectomorph).

Rolf was convinced that an adaptation in the structure followed a physiological demand and that the cranium itself had anatomical adaptations from the functioning of the physiological systems of primarily respiration and circulation. The brachiocephalic or broad-headed (short-headed) was considered more prevalent in ancient times, but it is now the mesocephalic or middle-width or moderate-headed that is more prevalent.

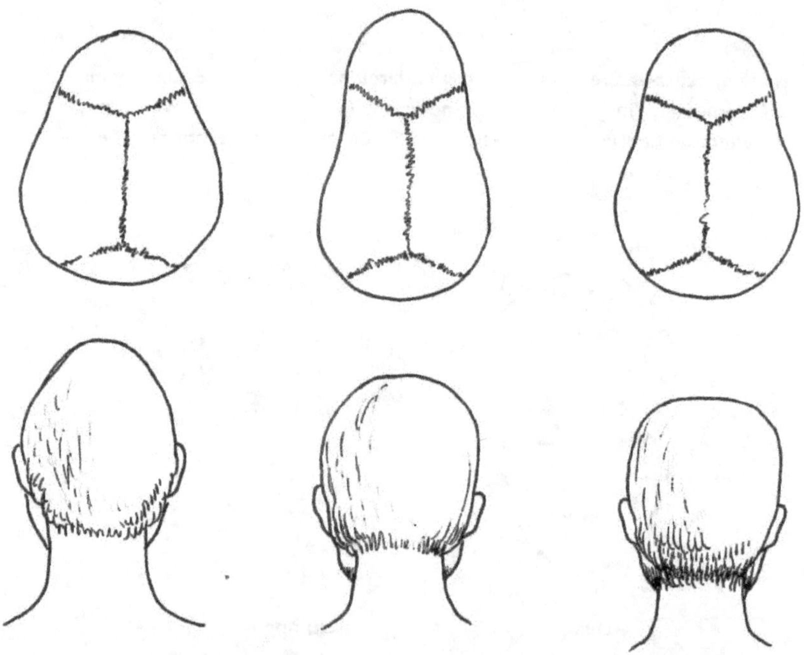

Figure 9: Top and Back of Head: pointed, round, and square[9] *(Gibson and Gibson)*

The basic human structure can be viewed from the top and back of the heads (Figure 9), the shapes of the faces (Figure 8), and the profile or side view (Figure 10). Gibson describes the backs of heads as pointed, round, and square. The top of the skull descriptions include the brachiocephalic or broad-headed, mesocephalic (mesaticephalic) or middle-width, and the dolichocephalic or long-headed.

The face profiles found in Gibson consist of convex, vertical, and concave, which follow the more extreme triune variations of the shape of the front of the face.[10] The convex as "an outward semicircle, or convex curve, consisting of frontward sloping forehead, pointed nose, strong upper lips, and receding chin. Such a profile signifies a quick mind, interested in quick results and therefore one that concentrates on practical things."[11]

The vertical is a more straight up and down profile. Gibson said, "This represents the calm, deliberate person, who weighs his speech and decisions."[12] The concave has a slight but noticeable inward curve. "Here is the person who is careful both in matter and speech, and always weighing matters before coming to a decision and then expressing a reserved opinion."[13] Gibson presents a metaphysical view that is interesting but not exactly in the scientific genre.

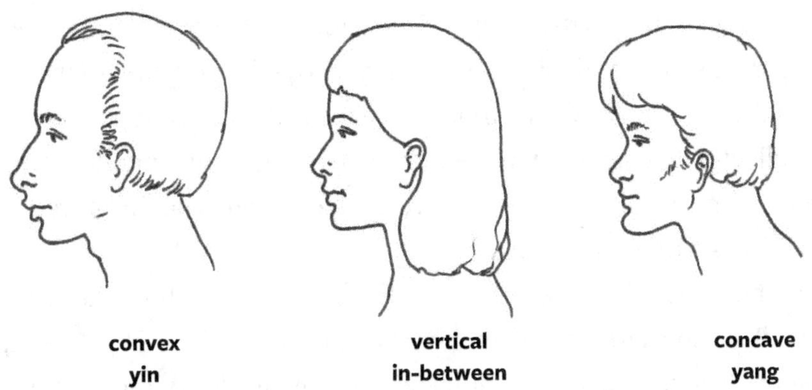

Figure 10: Head Profiles *(Gibson and Gibson)*

Aristotle's Three Centers manifests the three shapes as the Nous or nervous system and intellect, the Sentient or circulatory system and emotions, and the Nutrient or digestive system and physical. The Nous involves the brain, forehead, and eyes. Sentient involves the sensory modalities of the nose and eyes, and Nutrient deals with the mouth and chin (Figure 11).[14]

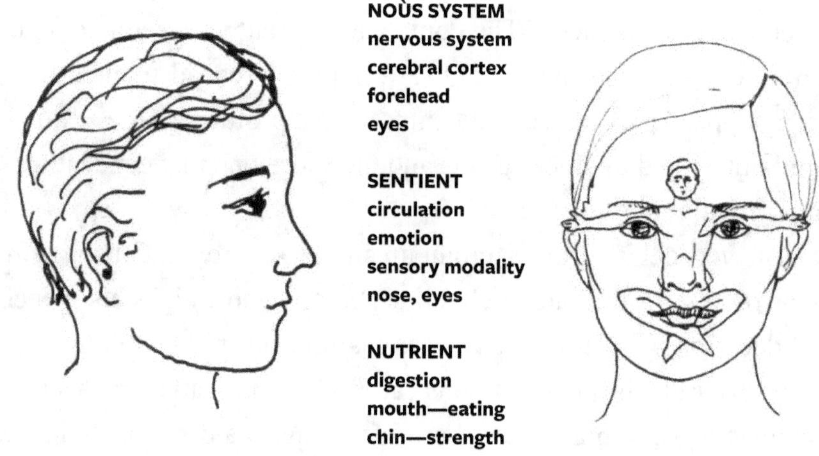

Figure 11: Aristotle's Three Centers and Face Homunculus

A square face is the "sentient" type related to movement and sensing or sensation, and this type typically enjoys the pleasures of moving and feeling the body. The triangular face is the 'nous' type, which is intellectually centered with both receptive and active intelligence. A round face is the "nutrient" type related to the physical life-force and is the basis of all the others.

It has often been said that one picture is worth a thousand words, and it is especially true with the dynamics of the face. The drawings on the last several pages indicate a strong similarity theme among various theories of facial typing. The yin ectomorph relates physiologically and behaviorally to the traits of mental orientation. The yang mesomorph and the round-faced endomorph also relate to a physical and philosophical design of emotion and being.

The theories of Eastern science, Western metaphysics, and some of Western science now point to these three basic types, although most people are composites and fewer are strikingly pure types. The idea of the entire body represented by the face is incredibly old, and the ancients of East and West expounded this line of reasoning. As Randolph Stone said about the three centers of man (generative, heart, head), putting the body in the head shows the symbolism of organic relationships and vital functions and reflects on the face as the Primordial Mind Pattern.[15] Figure 12 shows the "as above, so below" concept; the mind energy patterns show the body-mind reflecting the impression of the body on the face.

Figure 12 shows the theoretical expansion of the three centers with various geometric patterns and with astrological correspondence with the planets.

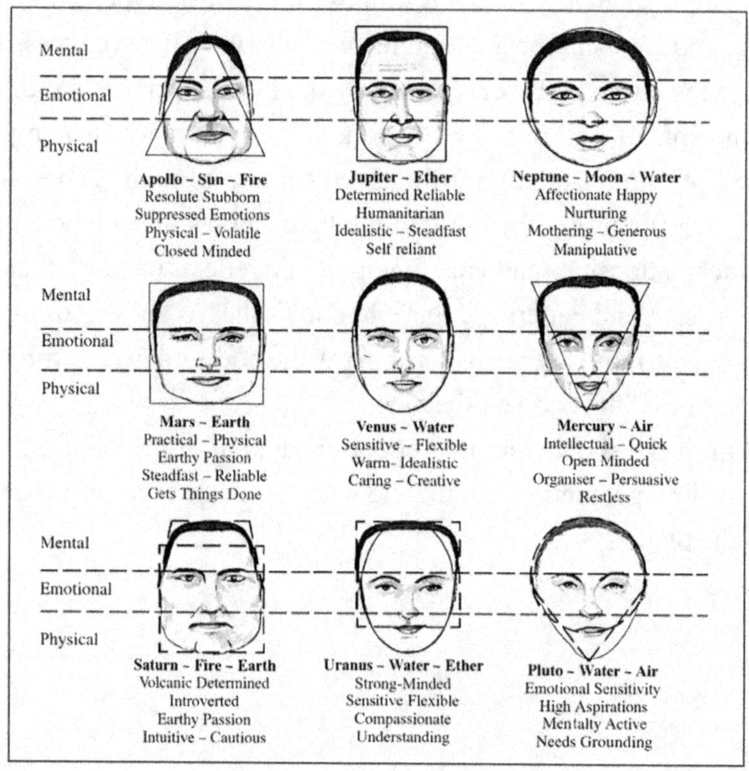

Figure 12: Asian Face Type Theory

These face types explore the round, square, and triangular faces with mental, emotional, and physical types.

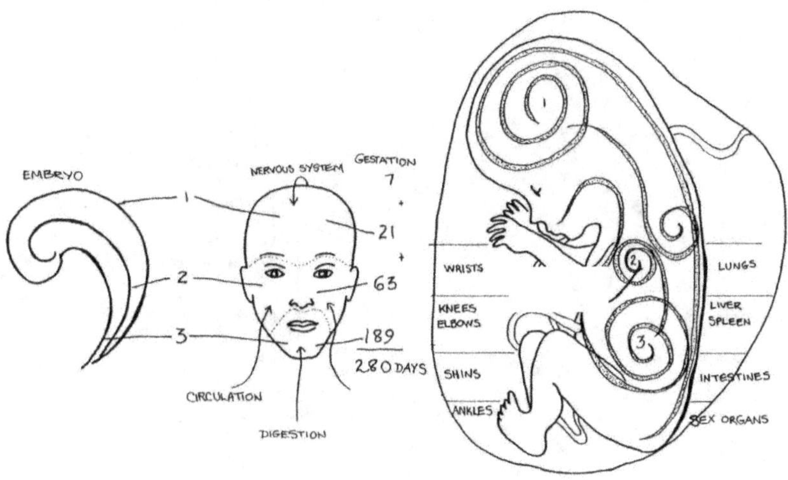

Figure 13: Embryological Development of the Three Centers

The idea upon which Sheldon expounded the three germ layers as the basis of the physiological and psychological structure was also an underlying tenet in Eastern thought, which acknowledges the three systems as the nervous, circulatory, and digestive systems, which form in the embryo, as shown in Figure 13. Western logic has struggled with the concept of Eastern meridians because it is hard to see the logic of how a point in the skin can relate to the intestine, and so on. Yet the logic becomes apparent if the meridians are energy lines forming in the embryonic stage (Figure 13).

The Eastern view of meridians and pressure points is used in healing through various methods and generally corresponds to the Three Centers approach. The charts in Figure 14 show pressure points related to many organs and bio-functions.

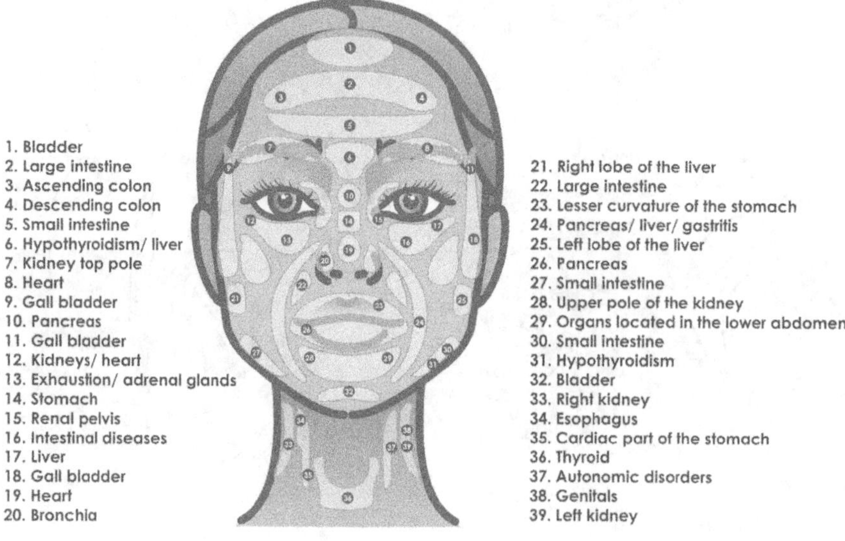

Figure 14: Acupuncture Chart – Face

Parts of a healthy face work in unity. The balance of the mouth and eyes, for instance, reflect in their manifestation of the same message or the conflict they portray. A face reflects the body's functioning, harmony, top-bottom or right-left split, and the general attitude with which we connect with the world physically, mentally, and vibrationally.

Reich viewed the living process, especially in the formative years (the younger, the more effective), as developing with a particular set of patterns created by blocked emotions.[16] The inhibited desires rage through the tissue, energizing and becoming residual, sort of like waiting around in the tissue for the opportunity to be used up, consumed, or, like an orgasm, exploded. Inhibited energy blocked during the early years but changing with the years' pleasures and pains is reflected in facial expression patterns.

Lowen speaks of how we "face" the world with the part of our body most open to it.[17] We face up to situations when responsible or hide our face from fear, sadness, or shame. Perhaps shame also causes us to lose face and then face away to escape the situation. The face shows one's self-image and self-expression, which is first examined when we face another person.

The face portrays how we feel. Dr. Ekman has developed a Facial Action Coding System (FACS) and has determined in cross-cultural studies that emotional expressions on the face, including happiness, surprise, anger, sadness, fear, and disgust, tend to be universal with rules set culturally.[18] Ekman has also shown that emotional expression, except happiness, occurs more on the left than the right side of the face, which fits into the Triune Psychology framework with the left side as the more intuitive and emotional. Losing touch with unpleasant emotional feelings shows in habitual facial muscle holding patterns. Inner feelings actually shape the face. For example, change from the tension in our facial muscles comes from our emotional outlook of who we think we should be. Emotions about things repeated over time become habituated, and the tissue forms to become this expression of you. Repetition becoming a habit or habituation of facial expressions from felt emotions that continue over time stimulate the tissue to put a hold on that pattern of emotional expression. In time, the way we face the world becomes our new persona. The unresolved conflicts begin to show in the connective tissue repatterning process.

While emotions represent the fire that sparks life into action, intellect provides meaning and purpose for that action. Our head turns energy into thoughts, and the energy of thought becomes focused as we "face up to our responsibilities." A body's energy escapes the face and head with energy leaving the feet and toes at the opposite ends of the same energy polarity. Simply put, quality and quantity of energy entering, interacting, and leaving (escaping and projecting) the face form the facial features within the context of the constitution. Quality of energy determines the effect. Some issues energize or deflate the appropriate features in the facial parts (such as the eyes, ears, mouth, and forehead) depending on the energy block in relation to the energy flow. One part may be drained while another overflows, depending on the strength and position of the dam or energy blockage.

How an individual "faces the world" is strongly influenced by muscle tension, which tells the story of the scale from chronic and tight attitudes to relaxed and unconditioned responses. The emotions blocked by inhibition or facilitated with positive regard set the tension patterns that reflect muscular, facial, and organic arrangement and functioning. The face is, in fact, the reflection of the persona. Let's "face" it. It is the "person-a."

TOP OF HEAD (CROWN CHAKRA)

- Seventh or crown chakra; union
- Enlightenment
- Body balancer
- Positive biomagnetic pole

The top of the head comprises the seventh chakra, Sahasrara. This crown or coronal chakra relates to the pineal gland. The meaning of the seventh chakra is the union with nature, which occurs when all the chakras are aligned and the bioenergy or kundalini smoothly flows up the back. At this point, the person evolves to a state of consciousness known as cosmic consciousness.[19]

Stone depicted the top of the head as the positive end of the biomagnetic body system with energy flowing up and out of the crown or top of the head.[20] Rolf was concerned with the head placement so that the energy flows consistently with gravity from the pelvis to the crown. The skull itself consists of an aggregate of individual segments with sutures connecting these bony parts. According to Rolf, the sutures will slightly adjust even in adulthood due to the mechanical demands of an increasingly erect posture.

Spino mentions the cranial motion discovered by Dr. Sutherland, an osteopathic doctor in the 1920s, who observed that the brain was not static but breathes in and out while it pulsates and secretes hormones.[21] When you inhale, the brain expands and contracts with the exhale. Thus, there is a cranial motion necessary for appropriate regulation. The cerebral spinal fluid flows from the brain down the spinal cord to the sacrum with the breath. The brain is built to allow for motion that aids in the brain's regulation.

The head is the primary balancer of the body and works in conjunction with the pelvis. Any misalignment of the lower body directly changes the position of the head.

It is of miscellaneous interest to note that the head is penetrated with air pockets, which Rolf suggests may have an effect on the weight of the head in relation to gravity. In even more of a theoretical light, the skull consists of an organic matrix with deposits of inorganic salts. This structure may have an energy function much like Reich's orgone energizer with layers of organic and inorganic materials that possibly produce a type of energy Reich called Orgone, the energy of the organism.

FOREHEAD (THINKING CAPACITY AND FUNCTION)

- thinking capacity
- thought
- creased forehead – thinking, worry
- smooth forehead – inner peace

The forehead is the top of the quadrant of the face that manifests the direction of thought with the power of emotion. In the Face Homunculus in Figure 11, the "little man's head" fits at the point of the sixth chakra, Ajna. This seat of mind consciousness, also known as the third eye, relates to wisdom. The creases in the forehead may stem from an overused mental capacity that tends to favor the cortex's convolutions. The deep forehead creases may signify a lifetime of worry, anxiety, or fear about the self and the world's problems. A forehead without deep crevasses may reflect a manner of peace and an alliance with reality rather than a battle with life.

EYEBROWS

- emotional expression and strength
- sixth chakra
- psychic abilities

All movements of the expressive eyebrows affect the forehead. Anger, fear, pain, pleasure, surprise, puzzlement, and concern are displayed, with the forehead and brow playing different instruments in the same concert. Much of how we face the world reflects on the forehead and eyebrows. Creases in the forehead are called worry wrinkles for a good reason. The forehead and eyebrows provide us with our expression of our experience of reality as we see it moment by moment.

Gibson and Gibson adapted the following types of eyebrows.

1. Highbrow: The constant look of amazement as if a mad scientist has raised his brow to show his interest level. This brow could come from an intellectual constitution. It also offers a happy, excited, or lively way of being in the world, which

may also show a large, round, and loving eye. It depicts little resentment and hostility. Metaphysically, the highbrow was a person of social and intellectual refinement.

2. Lowbrow: The lower brow is weighed down by the realities of the world and distinguishes an individual with a practical nature. Traditionally a "coarse person" was thought to have a low brow as part of their constitution.

3. Browbeaten: Along with downcast eyes, drooping head, and a look that says "kick me," this type looks intimidated. The brows are not pushed down with anger; instead, they droop down from chronic sorrow and self-pity.

4. Furrowed Brow: This person is intense. This type maintains a contraction inward on the brow from anger, skepticism, or urgently figuring out how to control or manipulate others. This narrows the vision and presents a more limited view of life.[22] When angry, this type cannot see beyond their emotions and usually cannot take on another's point of view.

5. Moving Brow: The brow moves up and down with a sense of urgent nervousness. The look of "anxious surprise" shows an inability to focus on an intellectual matter for any length of time.

6. Bushy, Heavy Brow: A strong, domineering nature characterizes this very masculine type. The "Oscar Madison" body type can be blunt in their manner and usually oriented to a male attitude.

7. Thin, Light Brow: The pencil-thin brow can demonstrate a fussy nature with a softer, more feminine quality.

Figure 15: Eyebrow Types *(Gibson and Gibson)*

EYES (VISUAL ORIENTATION)

- enlightenment, wisdom, or prejudice
- reveal inner feelings
- "window to the soul"
- microcosm of the total person

The eyes reflect the psychological and physical functioning of the body-mind more than any other single part. The eyes see with the enlightenment of the sixth chakra or the hatred and negativity of prejudice. Misunderstanding, an inability to see the truth or accept reality, creates the psychological complex of resentment. Resistance to change comes with the fear of looking at the facts.

As the only visible part of the brain, the eyes form an extension to get a firsthand view of the world. Eyes reveal inner feelings of fulfillment and rejection. They show the inner you. Metaphysically, the eyes have long been known as the "windows of the soul."

Many thoughts and emotions reflect through these mechanisms of environmental contact. As the most-used sensory modality, the eye directs the concert of syntony or one's orientation to the environment and to the self. Reich's ocular segment relates to the attachment to mother, which centers on trust versus mistrust, to use Erikson's words, as the infant uses the eyes to see and keep contact with mother.[23] In adulthood, people maintain the use in "meeting the world." The ocular segment includes the eyes, ears, forehead, and cheekbone areas and is located above the oral segment of the throat, jaw, and mouth.

Ajna, the sixth chakra, is located just above the eyebrows, like a third and middle eye. This energy vortex represents enlightenment, psychic sight, or increased awareness.

As extensions of the brain, the eyes reflect the rational and intuitive functions of the right and left hemispheres in action. The left mirrors the person's essence or being. This image concerns the intrinsic receptive side, which is a picture of the core self. The opposite or right side is concerned with "doing" in the world and outwardly projects the energies of expansion (yang). The right is the father, and the left is the mother. Right-eye energy shows the father-son relationship. A glowing eye comes from a deep sense of making our way in the world, which developed as a father who guided us in understanding how the world works. If the guidance is inadequate, relating to other people may be difficult. The shine in the left eye describes one's self-worth, anxiety, and ability to receive.[24]

The pyramidal shape of the eye orbit allows the eye to be pulled forward and back.[25] A nearsighted or myopic person focuses on objects and activities close to him, reflecting an inward quality of shyness and high rationality. Early childhood traumas forced them to withdraw their sight inward for safety. The opposite condition, hyperopia or farsightedness, is an ability to focus outwardly. Extroverts think of the future and rationalize it as a mechanism to avoid inner self-development.[26]

The Japanese have a term, sanpaku, meaning "three whites" of the eyes. Sanpaku is a condition identified by three white areas around the iris.[27] Higher sanpaku, which appears most often, relates to farsightedness from a very yin vertical eyeball expansion. A horizontal expansion of the eye creates nearsightedness and the lower sanpaku look. The general condition of the nervous system may be seen in the area or boundary of the pupil and iris or white of the eye and iris. When eyesight is becoming less capable, the area between the white and iris may seem less bright and differentiated.[28]

EYE TYPES

Many eye types can be found in the literature and on the internet. Protruding eyes are eyes pushed forward in the eye socket. Deep set eyes are larger and pushed back in the eye socket. Round eyes seem large and fit well in the eye socket. Hard eyes seem to show a hard life. Soft eyes are sometimes called seductive eyes, and almond eyes are the mesmerizing eyes. Almond eyes are big eyes with smaller eyelids. Upturned eyes have a slight lift in the outer corner while the downturn has a lowered outer corner. Monolid eyes have an eyelid without the double lid's arc shape crease. Hooded eyes have an extra layer of skin as a layer placed over the crease, causing the lid to appear smaller. Close-set eyes are less than the eyeball width apart, and wide-set eyes are more than the eyeball width apart.

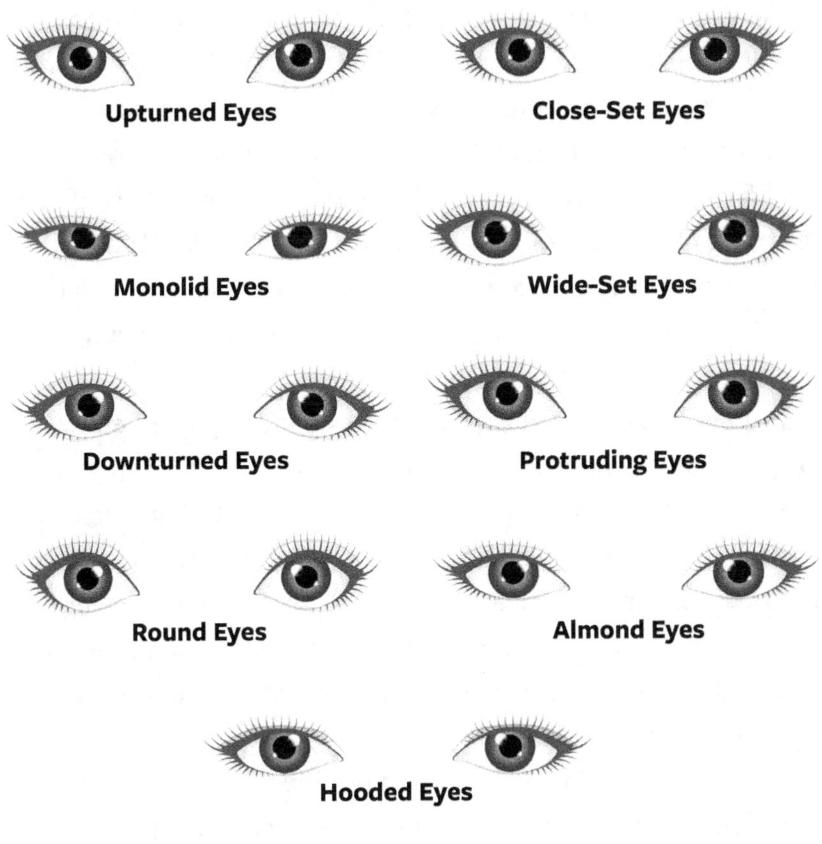

Figure 16: Eyes

In looking at various eye shapes that are of genetic origin, some eye types appear to be more vulnerable for emotional tissue habituation given that the person continues a high level of emotional experiences over a significant time. These high-level emotional experiences tend to last for extended times and, when repeated, become an emotional habit or emotionally tissue habituated, which tends to alter the structure of the tissue. The focus in this section will be on the eye types that tend to embody tissue changes due to psychological influence, including the protruding eyes, deep-set eyes, round eyes, and seductive eyes.

Psychologically, the eyes can show marked differences according to their degree of openness, closedness or balance, cloudiness, level of protruding, or level of receding. These characteristics, if habitual, tend to form character armor, and the tissue becomes cast in perfect character. The orbital cavity allows the eye to adjust to various positions. Grief may cause the eye to withdraw within, and excitement may bring the eye out to get a good look at the world. However, not all shifts of the eye are expressions of pure psychological changes; blows to the sphenoid bone (eye socket), jaw, nasal structures, and dental work can shift the facial expression.[29]

In general, the eye shapes that have more psychoemotional changes result mainly from the connective tissue in the eye orbit, allowing the eye to move primarily back and forth. This can clearly be seen with the protruded and deep-set eyes. Protruding eyes bug out to keep watch over what is happening. In the same way, deep-set eyes want to create distance from being hurt and to separate the person from the dangers out there, thus the emotions can help to keep the eyes pulled back in the socket.

Various authors throughout time have offered eye types representing psychosomatic derivations and personality characteristics. The following eye types of round eyes, deep-set hurt eyes, protruding eyes, and seductive eyes are thought to represent distinct psychoemotional changes and personality characteristics offered by various authors (Figure 17).

1. Protruding eyes or bugged-out eyes: These indicate a need to keep watch over what is happening because the world could be perilous, which has the effect of pushing the eyes forward in a straining effort to see and determine. The eyeball looks like it is bugging out at you with a penetrating glare that feels laced with anxiety. The person seems to push out the eyeball to get closer to ensure that what they are looking at is really there. Many people do not feel very comfortable having those bugged-out eyes eyeing them all over. Thus, the anxiety someone feels with bulging eyes seems to transfer to the other person, and the desired warm connection may not be returned if the other person feels uneasy.[30] However, Ida Rolf contends that this position is more to watch the outside world with a sense of excitement or curiosity. Perhaps it could be either or the effects of an accident or a medical condition.

2. Deep-set or recessed eyes: These eyes reflect a life of withheld sadness that guards and protects us against the hurts and worries of the outside world.[31] This critical observer depicts years of prolonged unhappiness by withdrawing and projecting the self—the rejected, dejected self, deep inside. This eye position creates a change in their chemistry, increases apathy, and produces less mobility.[32] The pyramidal shape of the eye orbit allows the eye mobility in length and position, such that emotional anxiety tends to accompany the drawing inward of the eyeball with less structural space to allow for movement. Kushi, describing the Eastern view, related a yin condition of thin eyes signifying a stronger and more active condition. The deep-set eyes pushed back as protection against seeing the unpleasantness of reality may become thin for the same dynamic reason.

3. Round eyes: This person usually emits a loving and warm feeling. People generally enjoy being around this person. A very

soft, feminine woman or a sensitive, artistic male wears these eyes, which, according to Kushi, relates to a more yang condition. The expression of well-being also expresses physically in the eye's fit in the orbit.[33] Round eyes fit softly and gently.

4. Seductive eyes: These are the innocent, wide-eyed, or baby eyes. Like all body parts, the eye functions as a unit in concert with the eyebrows and face. These immature-looking eyes tend to accompany a baby face. These eyes have a wide-open, seductive look that may look pleading, which may come about from the person's strategy for survival or to get needs met, as parents stifled development, and the child may have been known as mama's little boy or daddy's little girl.[34] There is a type of seductiveness about these eyes. The person learns to manipulate parents with a soft and sensual look and later in life uses the same approach to draw in another person to close proximity so they can manipulate them. This manner of interpersonal interaction is not necessarily negative; instead, it exists because it remains the learned method of survival during early childhood.

5. Small or squinty eyes: These eyes might look sneaky, and this person appears to be sneaking around looking for something. I've had friends who would complain about certain people who had a sneaky look as they looked around when entering their house.

6. Hard eyes: These eyes appear hard like the person has a hard life. The activities/events of life can harden the eyes. The eyes seem to show little remaining empathy from their harrowing experiences in life.

7. Soft eyes: Eyes like these, with a cloudy appearance, may indicate little desire or ability to control others or their own life.

Michio Kushi identifies the rounder eyes as more yin, which, in a woman, reflects a soft, feminine quality and, in a man, a gentle, sensitive, and artistic side. The thin or yang eyes are a masculine sign of activity and strength. Kushi claims that excessive yang foods cause the cross-eyed condition.

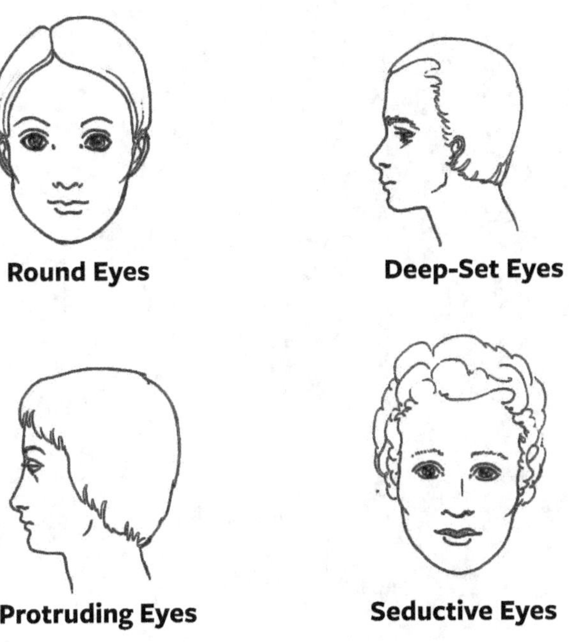

Figure 17: Eye Types

The eyes have long been known as the key to one's inner nature. The positioning of the eyes and irises, in context to the proportion of the face, reveals something about the inner self. It has been suggested that the eye and the iris, if in different positions relative to each other, may indicate a schizophrenic person.[35]

Iridology has become a popular form of physical diagnosis in alternative medicine. By looking at the markings of the iris, the iridologist can diagnose various physical diseases. The map of the iris forms another homunculus, much like the palm of the hand and the sole of the foot (see Figure 29). The iris has specific geographic locations where various organs and body parts correspond (Figure 18).

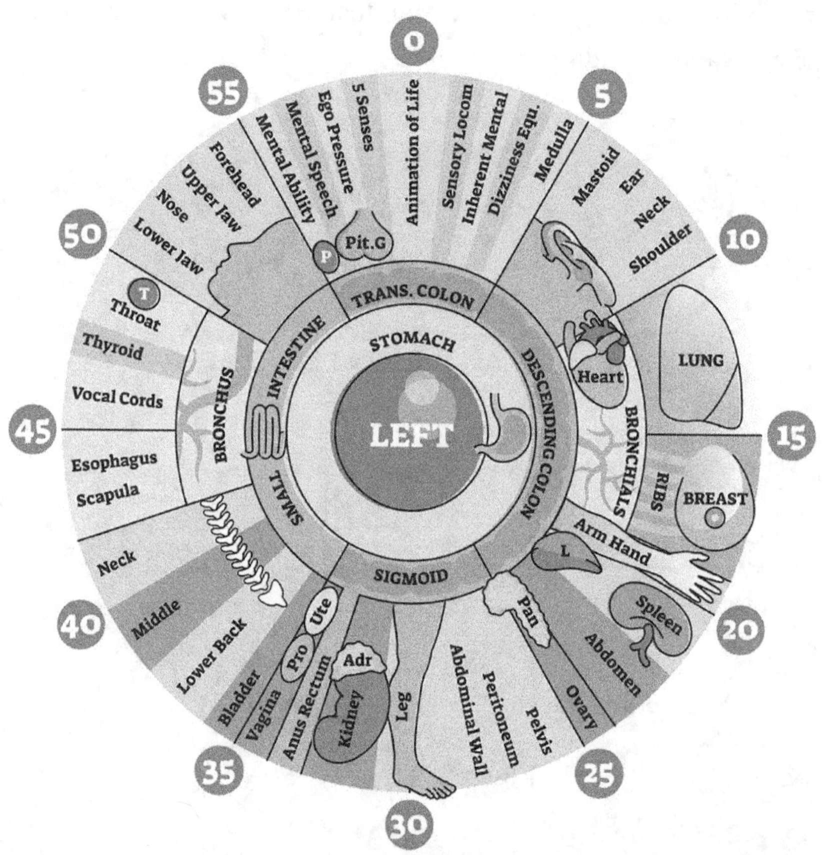

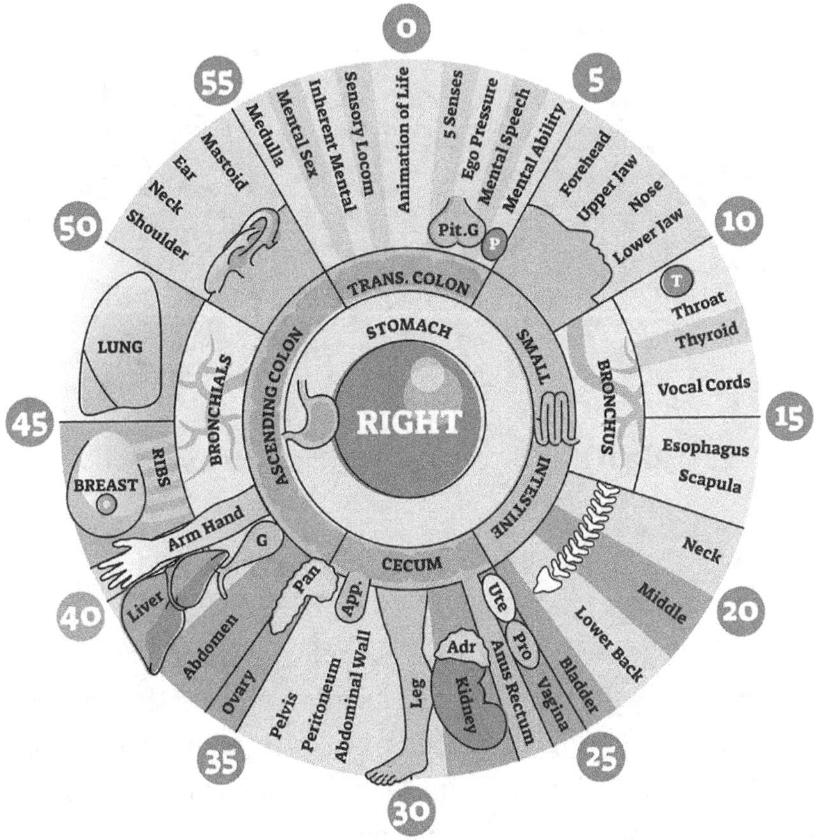

Figure 18: Iris Diagnosis Chart

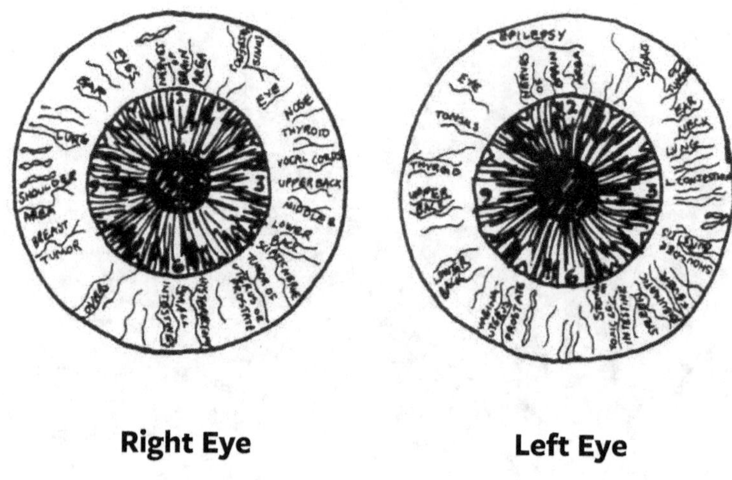

Right Eye   **Left Eye**

Figure 19: Sclera Diagnosis Chart

Another eye map comes from sclerology, which diagnoses the body by reading the lines and discolorations of the sclera, the white part of the eye. See Figure 19 for a comparison with other eye maps on that page. As shown in Figure 19, the eye homunculus presents a macrobiotic view of the body-mind relationship.[36]

EYELID REGION

Kushi claims that the upper eyelash gives the condition of the nervous system and the lower lash the functioning of the sex organs. The normal slant of the eyelash is inward, and an outward curl indicates sexual problems, impotence in men, and frigidity in women.

Area Around the Eye

The area under the eye can accumulate liquids and fat, which, according to Kushi, form hard or soft bags. These bags come from drinking an excess of fluid or overconsumption of fat. The eye bags also reflect one's lifestyle with manifestations from the overuse of drugs, functioning of the digestive system, and overconsumption of liquids.[37] In one case known to the writer, an individual encountered a puffing-up of the skin just under the eye bag on the right side. The psychological meaning was discovered as the inability to express tears (emotions). This physical problem stemmed from the father-son relationship in which crying was negatively reinforced. The unexpressed tears blocked up and developed an overabundance of histamine, which spilled over into the loose skin below the eye. The weight of gravity pulled down the substance until it uniquely resembled a tear blocked inside the skin. An emotional release allowed the tears to come out and diminished the subcutaneous tear's size.

The wrinkles at the sides of the eyes reflect the expression of habitual emotions. The lines form from the cheeks and mouth movements and are referred to as smile lines and frown lines.

EARS (HEARING, ATTENTION TO THE EXTERNAL AND INTERNAL ENVIRONMENT)

- balance and self-control through space
- relationship to gravity
- homunculus

Through the ears, we hear the happenings of the world. How we feel about the world and our relationship with it often affects hearing competency. Balance materializes as the fluids in the semicircular canals move back and forth, telling the brain which direction is up and which is down. When there is an imbalance in the canals, a person can lose their feelings of equilibrium, making them feel less secure. It isn't easy to feel secure in the world when your sense of balance with the world is out of synchronicity.[38]

The ears are a homunculus of the entire body, like the face, hands, feet, brain, and spine. Stone developed the chart shown in Figure 20 for his Polarity Therapy. He wrote:

Figure 3 [my Figure 20] gives the representative areas of the body on the ear. Redness or discoloration in any one area can be a diagnostic clue, like a white or yellowish discoloration in the lung area for pneumonia and other lung diseases. The abdomen is represented in the middle area of the ear. The pelvis is represented below the ear canal. A large lobe below it shows great vitality and reserve energy. It is equivalent to buttocks tone which is the negative pole and the wrist bracelets which are the neuter pole and indicators of vital force. A person who has both can go through illness with more energy and react better to therapy than those who do not have that inherited share of vitality. This simple observation is of value to the doctor. Earlobes, wrist lines, buttocks tone spell reserve energy.[39]

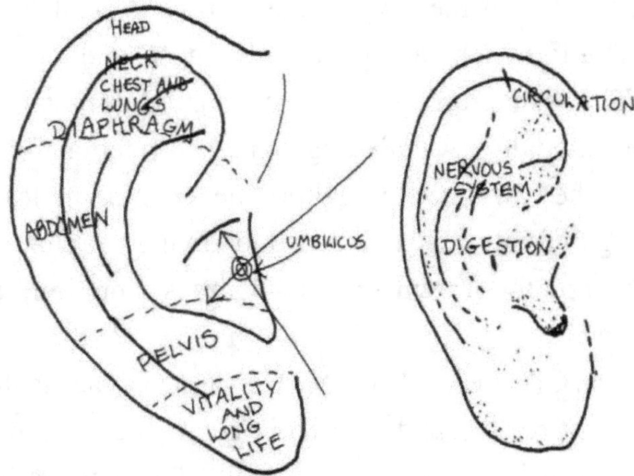

Figure 20: Ear Diagnosis
(Reprinted by permission of the publisher)

Kushi claims ears represent the three major body systems (digestion, circulation, nervous) due to their central location in the embryo. The protruding middle of the ear is yang, and the indented part of the ear is yin, which, according to Kushi, tends to show the mother's diet during pregnancy.

Rolf pointed out that with the ear, we both hear and speak, which was instrumental in the development of our human culture. Paul MacLean agrees that hearing development was required for the mother-child bond to be maintained over time and for social groups to keep together.

NOSE (SMELL; DETECT ODORS IN THE ENVIRONMENT)

- sexual responses

The nose consists of the structure that evolutionarily was pushed up into the cranium as the physical matter used to create the neocortex. This is partially why a dog has a long nose, and a person has a short one. The sexual response in most animals has much to do with this sensory modality. A male dog can smell a female in heat and line up with the rest of the neighborhood's canine males howling and moaning in front of the female's door. In the search for the right smell, the market for perfumes and colognes is a multimillion-dollar sales industry.

Gibson and Gibson detailed a metaphysical approach to the nose. A big nose was aggressive, and a small one quiet. The thin nose showed nervousness; a wide one was more casual; a long one was a careful, worried person; and a short one was a cheerful person who paid little attention to consequences. These nose types are based on metaphysical tradition rather than scientific study and thus are not listed as actual types in this study.

Like all other facial and body features, the nose tends to fit together in forming the genetic, emotional, and intellectual history of the person written in tissue.

LIPS

The lips are significant in traditional Asian diagnoses. Kushi presented an assorted collection of relationships for the constitution of the lips.

1. upper lip (mustache) reflects sexual organs (generative system)
- upper lip reflects the stomach, digestive system
- corner of the lip reflects the duodenum
- lower lip reflects the intestines

- swelling of the lower lip shows constipation
- dual dark spots or recurring sores on lips indicate ulceration and stagnation of blood

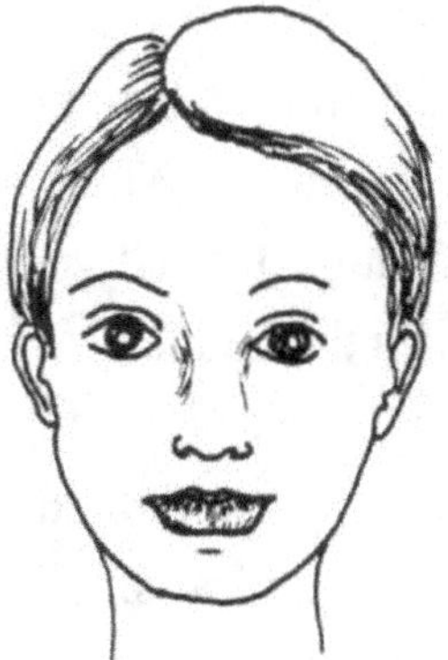

Figure 21: Swollen Lower Lip

- whitish lips show weak intestinal blood and poor absorption
- tightness in the mouth reflects tight intestines (and vagina), too tight from poor absorption

MOUTH

- early survival, the entrance of nourishment
- security, gratification
- reflects digestive and generative functions

The mouth must be considered psychologically as part of the jaw and Reich's oral segment. Verbal communication comes through the mouth, going out with the exhaled air. All the energies of expression energize the mouth and reflect patterns, especially in the jaw's shape. Yet the mouth is more than verbal expression; the mouth as the entrance for nourishment, psychologically and physically, means early survival. The infant's mouth knows what to do to survive: suck!

The oral process typically becomes the first area to reflect problems. Physical and psychological functioning of parent and child motivate the behavior that becomes their history of interaction and their relationship. Early frustration from inconsistent gratification of needs creates a sense of insecurity. Will food be here or not be here for my survival? The amount of trust versus distrust in Erikson's first stage of life forms with the incidents of continued or interrupted gratification of needs. It is about how each of us was cared for.[40] A mother who cared for our needs facilitated our sense of security and ability to perform. As an infant, if satisfaction was not present, it was beyond our ability to obtain the desired gratification. In adult life, the frustration may become the fear of not being able to do or perform what they want to do in life.[41]

Freud initially developed the issues arising during the oral phase in his psychosexual stages. Kurtz and Prestera and others have expanded on Freud's work. When the oral trait is related to emotional deprivation in infancy concerning food, the adult may present with oral behaviors, such as over- and under-eating, smoking, talking loudly, or talking nonstop.

Oral traits related to dependency through early childhood experiences of parental control versus growth and independence. Oral traits may be associated with the experience of insecurity and discomfort from events where security or comfort were threatened. Idealistic or dogmatic behaviors may characterize a need to control the environment. Oral traits are associated with a lack of physical contact with tenderness, control, and affection. The glue for the mother-infant bond is touching.[42] Due to the child experiencing a lack of tenderness or affection that feels like insufficient love, the mother-child relationship becomes impaired. The child feels unloved and insecure on a deep inner level and has a vacuum of love to fill. The desperate need for love and touching may host indiscriminate sexual behavior, or the opposite with sexual timidity.

JAW

- chewing food, physical intake
- emotional and verbal communication; speaking, laughing, biting, smiling, crying, fear of expression, biting down hard, "chew on that for a while"

The quality of verbal expression reflects in the jaw's structure. The energy of expression becomes actualized by the motion of the jaw, and the throat, mouth, and chin, which comprise Reich's oral segment. Any emotion or expression inhibited can become lodged in the armor of the jaw and throat.

A small child's chin quivers when tears are prematurely held back. Shaking comes from unleashed energy, which must settle for internal vibrations without an exit. Trauma may end, but this residual tension sets into the chin as armor, layer upon layer, from experience after experience. Tension layers into the tissue just as it layers into the subconscious.

When children cannot speak freely to their parents, especially for fear of punishment, the expression of the repressed speech involves the jaw. They learn to prevent making the sounds that the mind is saying. The child holds back from speaking by holding back on the jaw muscle, which, in turn, pulls back the lower jaw. The frequency of this behavior could be so chronic as to lead to an overbite that is commonly known as "buck teeth." Changing the muscular structure of the jaw from chronic repression of speaking the thoughts of the mind can also throw off typical speech patterns by creating a lisp and making it difficult to say the "s" sound, as the upper and lower teeth are not together.[43]

In describing how the ego can control the voluntary muscles, Lowen contends a person will inhibit the impulse to cry by controlling the jaw to constrict the throat and, at the same time, holding the breath that seems to tighten or restrict the abdomen. In the Arica system created by Oscar Ichazo, the chin represents the fear of inferiority or the feelings of being inferior and separate.[44]

The masseter or jaw muscle holds the bulk of the tension. This muscle holds anger from "biting inhibitions." This anger can readily show up in dental problems. Excessive grinding (bruxism) comes from repressed anger, especially when one has to "chew it over." The muscle tension puts a strain on the base of the skull, which will release if the jaw is released. From the writer's experience, for example, the masseter's tension from unvoiced conflict or desire can cause tension headaches. An energy release with massage or trigger point therapy in and around the jaw will often reduce episodes of head pain.

Face structure largely determines that of the jaw with the generic round, square, and triangular or thin face that appears as pointed. Round jaws come from a face that is round, oval, or long. Square jaws indicate a square-shaped face, especially if the cheekbones, jaw, and forehead have widths that are about equal. Jaws having a little less of a square end might be part of a diamond-shaped face. Pointed chins may accompany an inverse triangle or heart-shaped face or a diamond shape if the forehead is narrow but the cheekbones are wide.

The jaw is a complex of the face, neck, shoulders, and chest. The individual psychophysical-pathological types have been identified by Dychtwald, Kurtz and Prestera, and others, including overdeveloped or protruding, tight or clenched, and receding. These jaw types stem from the emotional habituation of the tissue, which gives them form.

1. Overdeveloped or Protruding Jaw: This overdeveloped jaw projects aggression rather than withdrawal as the first type of inhibition response. This person behaves with defiance and determination in their manner of fighting for their life to make themselves in the world. The jaw almost appears to project him forward as he leads with his chin, and the degree of forwarding placement increases the defiance and arrogance.[45] Like two ends of a magnet, emotional charges at both ends of the torso can become bound together. A block in the pelvis can also create a block in the jaw; the chin and the feet are also related.[46]

2. Tight or Clenched Jaw: Tight jaws clench down as if biting on a problem. Hurt or pride cannot be swallowed. The mind gains control and does not allow the jaw to say what the unconscious wants to say. Jaws hold on to have control of the thought or situation. Jaws do the work of the brain by holding on and not letting go out of fear of the outcome of the thought, emotion, or situation. Tight jaws form an attitude of self-control. Holding back expressions of anger as a child from abuse, fears, or threats can lead to TMJ and cause tightness of the jaw.

3. Receding Jaw: This undercharged body-mind part looks weak, as if it lacked assertion. The person projects so much buried sadness and anger that they cannot bite onto, sink their teeth into, or hold onto it.[47] This person may have trouble expressing what they think to offer their opinion in a group or when pressured by others.[48] It is precisely that repressed urge to cry or scream that this jaw desires and fears but needs psychological and physical release.

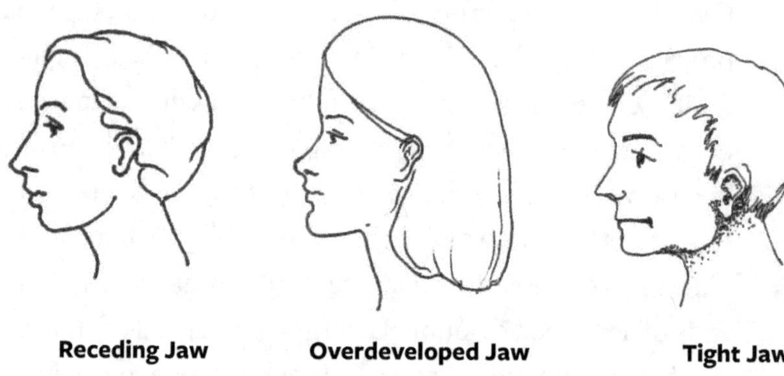

Figure 22: Jaw Types

A good way to understand the psychosomatic issues with the jaw is to hold the emotional position for a few minutes and allow yourself to pick up on the imagined emotional intensity. You can stick out your face in defiance with the overdeveloped or protruding jaw. The tight jaw can be experienced while thinking of biting down on a thought or feeling, as if to stop the expression of the feeling or thought. When you pull the jaw back, the receding jaw has the feeling that you are withdrawing or hiding from social interactions and life in general.

As interesting as the idea of emotionally based tissue alterations with the jaw, the natural body types cannot be ruled out. Suppose you look at the face profiles presented earlier by Gibson. In that case, emotional complexity is listed as convex (devoid receding), vertical, and concave (overdeveloped or protruding), which also follows the more extreme triune variations of the shape of the front of the face.[49] The convex as "an outward semicircle, or convex curve, consisting of frontward sloping forehead, pointed nose, strong upper lips, and receding chin. Such a profile signifies a quick mind, interested in quick results and therefore one that concentrates on practical things."[50]

The vertical is a more straight up and down profile. Gibson said, "This represents the calm, deliberate person, who weighs his speech and decisions." The concave has a slight but noticeable inward curve. "Here is the person who is careful both in manner and speech, and always weighing matters before coming to a decision and then expressing a reserved opinion."[51] Gibson presents a metaphysical view that is interesting but not exactly in the scientific genre.

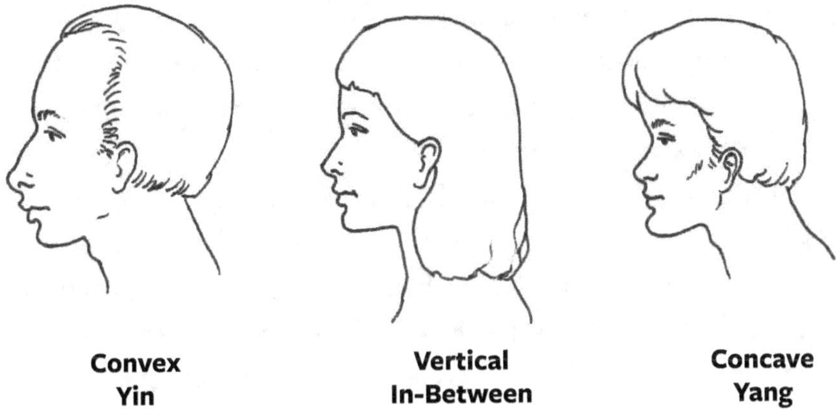

Figure 23: Head Profiles to Compare with
Jaw Types *(Gibson and Gibson)*

NECK, THROAT

- the battleground between thoughts from the head and emotions from the heart
- guilt, neck illnesses (from inflexibility)
- fear of expression, held breath, repressed anger
- fifth chakra, interpersonal relations, self-identification

Necks assume the crossroad where the head and heart meet. Vital energy amplified by the emotional flow in the heart raises up through the throat in its attempt to produce sounds of the heart-mind.

Downward flow of thought energy from the intellect meets this heart energy and, in the throat, transforms the energy synthesis into words. Any conflict or imbalance between the desires of the heart (and the instincts of the belly-mind) and the rationale of the head literally turns the throat into a battleground. It becomes at either pole the graceful flow like a long swan's neck or the battleground between thought and emotion or love and expectations.

In Eastern wisdom, the throat represents the area of the fifth chakra, vishuddha, which is responsible for hearing, listening, and speaking or expressing oneself.

The throat-voice process can be likened to musical instruments in which the vibrating reeds push through the life-force and emotional content into sounds and work much like the musical instrument plays out music.[52] Rolf contends that the speaking process has a psychospiritual function. The modern man's entire social and intellectual culture rests on his ability to give and receive communication. The vocal apparatus to speak and the auditory system to hear form this system's larger order of functioning. To support Rolf's contention, it may be pointed out that the rise of heightened hearing, according to MacLean, was a mammalian evolution necessary for mother-child bonding and interpersonal interaction.

Tensions in the neck may come from more obligations or responsibilities than can be handled. The additional stress physically comes in the form of inflammation or induration stimulating the pain sensors and, as such, becomes the proverbial "pain in the neck." Stress may come from the inability to express what you need to say. Fear, anger, resentment, and shame may be the source of the stress or tension that renders a person consciously, but usually unconsciously, unable to express what needs to be said. Emotional expressions are blocked by a repression of feelings and the mind rationalizes an acceptable story. Tension in the neck forms the primary body-mind separation of the head-body split, which is discussed later, but presents as a major factor in the play of the thoughts and emotions molding the shape of the body. Physical and emotional tension make the neck rigid and inflexible, as if the person became stubborn by his refusal to look at all sides.[53]

Throat muscles hold on to emotional expression, and the breath assists by becoming shallow. Guilt forms a primary factor in locking the throat and "squeezing out" the emotional energy. Perhaps the main reason the emotional flow becomes blocked has to do with the myth that it is not okay to express emotions. The anger becomes repressed, and the person swallows the emotional hurt.[54] It may be that the suppressed tears and screaming tightly clamped in the throat can be associated with an underactive thyroid. Body therapists often note the importance of the voice in body-mind diagnosis. The quality of the voice's expression has a considerable link to throat tension and verbal expression. Ida Rolf points out that a person's voice and speech provide serious clues to their physical and mental health.

The head's position is directly associated with the person's evolved perception of the world. According to Rolf, the key to the position of the head is the axis (second cervical vertebra). With this anatomical point, it is interesting that the Arica system splits the fifth chakra into communication relating to the throat, and coordination and balance dealing with the atlas (first cervical vertebra).

NECK TYPES

It starts with the anatomy of the typically slender, muscular, and stout body structure. Slender people tend to have a longer neck than the other types. The stout (thick) structure and, to some degree, the muscular body tend to have a shorter neck.

Leaning forward or to one side or back often involves adapting to the environment. These adaptations may be from the embarrassment of being too tall and wanting to get down to the level of other people in order to fit in. Other adaptations may be from depression or an abusive childhood, so they do not want to look up or make eye contact with others easily.

A thin-structured body frame with the typical long neck may be more susceptible to psychological adaptations of neck hunched over, neck leaning to the side, neck forward, and the Bioenergetic oral type.

Other body types present with these positions for the same psychological reasons, but the thick or endomorphic body may be more likely to exhibit a short neck, stuck back or down, and more akin to the Bioenergetic masochistic type.

The following psychophysical head-neck positions are adapted from the classifications indicated by Dychtwald, Kurtz and Prestera; Lowen; Rolf; and Green:

1. Forward Head with the head pushed forward (but not down): The head reflects an attitude of aggression as if this person is determined to "get ahead in life." This head stance reflects a person who stays in his head; his primary mode is head or rational consciousness with lesser body or emotional or right brain consciousness.[55] The cognitive orientation of the head thrust forward, leading the body, denotes someone who plans what he wants out of life.[56] However, with the advent of the computer, the forward posture of the neck also poses an occupational hazard.

2. Side Leaning Head: Many people slightly lean their head to one side while thinking (usually on the right) and planning (to the left) while feeling or creating. Slight spontaneous temporary leaning of the head is natural. A dog might perk up an ear

and rotate the head slightly in response to a noise. Humans also evolved with this reaction to the sensory modalities, especially hearing and vision, to orient the being to the energy realities of the earth.

A more constant lean to the side may represent more than orientation behavior, especially if the leaning is habitual, which shows, for instance, with a continuous leaning when lying down. The head and neck tilt may manifest tissue in the psychological battle of making it in the world and avoiding fears of interaction. This displays an inability to approach the world directly.[57] Conflicts may result in the disorganization of body parts, in body splits, or in body-mind disassociation, which Lowen believed was a condition of the schizoid or schizophrenic.

3. Head Bent Down with the head bent down and forward: It may appear as someone with his attention focused on the ground. Fear, failure, and defeat are expressed in this overburdened position. The individual may be caught up in the daily demands of living and have trouble dealing with everything.[58] The position of defeat is a statement about emotional exhaustion. As with any unbalanced position, this head orientation indicates a head-body split. Any misaligned body part causes physiological difficulties. Ida Rolf insists that the head-forward position has numerous causes. The misalignment could be from holding the head forward, stemming from sitting in an office chair, feelings of depression or fear, or even residual effects after an accident. Over time, the forward head position affects blood circulation as the artery narrows, as is also evident in most postural misalignments. Gravity, chemical breakdowns, hardening of arteries, and deposition of calcaneus matter on vessel walls all limit the blood flow, which can also

be associated with the creeping on of senility. Changes in the fascia from habituation of posture misalignments will tend to trap the habitual posture over time, and the person begins to think that is how they are made.

4. Tilted Back Head: The back of the neck was referred to by Green as an anxiety barometer, which one can check out as an indicator of the level of tension, physically and psychologically (which are the yin and yang of the same Tao). The head tilts back, contracts, and the chin juts up. As is typical with the emotional holding of connective tissue, the tension is created from a need to hold on to particular anxieties as a defense from dealing with past emotional issues. An emotional discharge will usually follow the release of the muscles in the neck and jaw so long taught to hold on; "Don't lose your head."

5. Long Neck: The long neck is often a characteristic of a very thin or highly ectomorphic person (see Chapter 7 on body types). The neck's length seems graceful and defines an air of proud attitudes, according to Dychtwald. Kurtz and Prestera contend that the long neck can also signify a head-body split. The energy from the head-heart battleground assists in extending the neck, trying to physically separate the two battling warriors, and placing the head with as much distance from the heart as possible.

6. Short Neck: The short neck may embody someone with a high endomorphic body type. This short turtle-necked position almost looks like a turtle holding in its neck in defense of life. Tight neck muscles put pressure on the vertebrae, reflecting an induration of interstitial tissue, which limits muscular movement and blood and lymph flow.[59] A certain mental attitude may become one of a limited but aggressive position in dealing with life situations.[60] Necks might be pulled or weighted

down from the pressures of the head if the head demanded too much.[61]

Often there are adaptations lower in the body for which the neck compensates. The lower adaptations restructure the body from the bottom up. The myofascial tissue from the body adaptations puts pressure on the vertebrae, blood vessels, lymph vessels, and nerves.

The dowager's hump that often accompanies this position physically shows the top built up from the layering of tissues to cap off the flow of energy rising up from the spinal cord. The head seems bent over so far that it sits in front rather than on top of the body, producing a physical energy block. Rolf points out that the condition involves a maladaptation at the cervicodorsal junction, and in which case, a leg reacts or compensates through its hyperextension. Lowen was convinced that the widow's hump was caused by a lifetime of frustration and unexpressed anger from a conflict between the submission to society's values and sexual frustration.

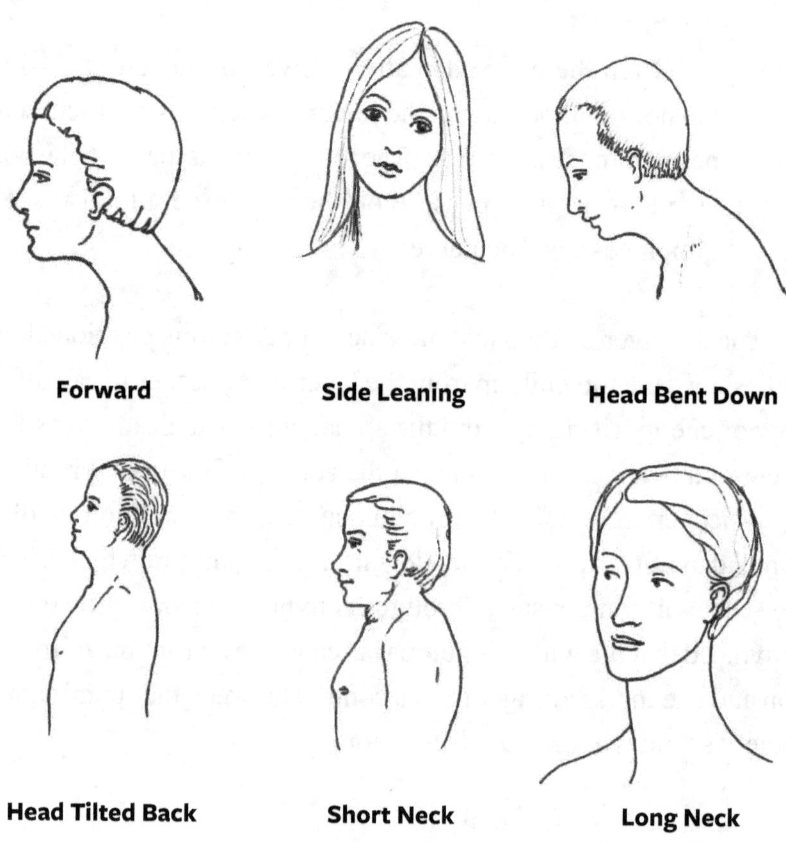

Figure 24: Head and Neck Types

CHAPTER 4

Heart or Emotional Center: Shoulders, Arms, and Chest

OUR ADAPTATION TO THE WORLD gives us the lessons we learn, initially from parents and caregivers. Did they treat us with love so we would learn to love ourselves, others, and the world? Hate works the same way, and we learn to hate ourselves, others, and the world. Indifference works the same way. Then there is the mixture of all three, as there are extremes around love, hate, and indifference, but it's usually a mixture given that parents have different issues that skew the basic pattern.

The entire pectoral girdle guides the upper body as the pelvic girdle guides the lower body. Balance, positioning, posture, and the emotional habituation (change in tissue from emotions) of much of the body are primarily controlled by the pectoral (shoulder) and pelvic (pelvis) girdles. The pectoral girdle connects through the shoulders and neck (cervical vertebrae) to the head, just as the pelvic girdle connects with the pelvis and back through the (lumbar and thoracic) vertebrae.

Thus, the shoulders and pelvis control and coordinate the body's movement, posture, and balance. These girdles are connections of bones and tissue through which the connective tissue of fascia, tendons, ligaments, etc., react to emotional stress and trauma with the natural processes of inflammation and induration.

Chronic inflammation can lead to chronic induration, as the toxic fluids bind to the connective tissue. Induration is the natural process of the hardening of the tissue, which acts over time to help stabilize the body when emotional habituation from traumatic or stressful events is stimulated by an emotional reaction occurring frequently and repeatedly over time. This process causes the body to "freeze" or harden into a new posture or body (habitually) position, much like the posture or position of the emotional reaction. Wilhelm Reich called the process "body armoring." The induration process occurs throughout the body, which is the physiological basis for variations evident in body psychology.

The musculoskeletal systems of the three basic types of bodies—thin, thick, and medium—or in between, also have variations or adaptations to their needed psychophysical adjustments. The thick-bodied, heavy-set person will naturally move his arms and body somewhat differently than the thin person.

The entire pectoral girdle works so closely together that the upper back, shoulders, and arms cannot be separated in their physical or psychological function.

Ida Rolf identified the pectoral and pelvic girdles as pivotal for the body's motor ability. When the person wants to move these two girdles at the shoulders, moving the arms, and at the hip, moving the legs, the person's thoughts move into action.

SHOULDERS

- responsibility
- "shouldering the world"

Contained within the shoulder girdle, the muscles of the spine's thoracic region hold anger. This anger is most often expressed in the rhomboid muscles. According to Green, the building up of muscles and rigid holding of the scapula shows inadequacy in the expression of anger. Although a lack of muscle tone in the scapula also indicates inadequacy in the expression of anger but with a "giving up" rather than a holding-on attitude. Holding on builds up the muscles and the anger until it explodes in rage. At the other extreme is the "lack of rhomboids," with the underdeveloped muscle seeming lifeless, as if it cannot hold on (to the scapula). Behaviorally, it reflects helplessness or waiting to be a victim. Rhomboids may be seen as a socioeconomic class indicator for the basic middle- and upper-class people who were taught not to express anger.

The shoulders psychologically stand for responsibility, and they carry the load. The psychic symbol for the shoulders is traditionally exhibited as Atlas carrying the world on his shoulders. This symbol represents a load to bear, which shows the responsibility for the self or others in tissue.

Big, overdeveloped shoulders denote big responsibilities with the person capable of doing too much. The big shoulders were the prize for "shouldering your burdens" and working hard until the shoulders enlarge from the strain of work. Growing large shoulders has evolved as an ego ideal of male achievement. Conversely, the traditional female ego being told that she will be taken care of desires small shoulders. Small shoulders (in body proportion) signify an inability to take on significant responsibilities. The feeling is one of defeat or "I can't do it."

The shoulders act as a mediator or gateway for the power of love and emotion. The energy comes up from the emotional center in the chest and flows out through the arms and hands. An individual's emotional experiences reflect in the shoulder's positioning. The interstitial tissue in the muscle, tendon, and ligament complex indurates or hardens and gives the look that it has frozen the habitual thoughts and feelings into the body structure, which then is the character we become.

The shoulders held forward or back denote the position of the heart (emotional self). The hyperextension of the back shows a holding back of the heart from a fear of making an emotional connection. Shoulders held up rigidly show a history of internalized fear or terror.[62] The right shoulder raised signifies a need to obtain external, worldly work approval, whereas the left shoulder raised means approval for internal work. Similarly, the right and left shoulders are often related to male and female principles. A lower right shoulder predominates in men and reflects the primarily male orientation of being assertive and controlling in their behavior. The left shoulder remains lower in the feminine sex role (receptive, soft, yin). Actually, either side that is lower shows an imbalance of the male and female or the internal and external.

The position of the shoulders contributes to a person's well-being by its connection to the relationship of the head to the body through the neck. When the bioenergy flow is disrupted by the shoulders, neck, and head being out of alignment in any direction, it creates the physical dynamics conducive to energy blockage. The type of shoulders is considered in relation to the rest of the body.

Shoulder positions are hard to separate from the neck and chest, as the same basic body types with variations and adaptations to trauma, stress, and gravity all play a significant role in the habituation of the structure (such as depression with the neck leaning down, shoulders folding forward and down, chest somewhat collapsed). It is atypical for these anatomical parts to have a separate psychophysical reaction and habitual sustained structure. So, when we look at them, we can see the structural adaptation of the body, typically upper body and lower body or the whole body participating in the pathological adaptation.

The three basic types of shoulders correspond to the three basic body types (thick frame, medium, and thin frame) and various variations. Some are natural or genetic, and some are environmental or psychological due to stress and trauma that bring on physical adaptations from emotional habituation. Some environmental adaptations can derive from work, such as the developed shoulder and arms on a carpenter's right or dominant side, perhaps before the advent of electronic nail guns.

1. Broad, thick, large, slightly rounded shoulders sit atop the full-bodied individual. The thick, full-bodied individual can typically be identified as endomorphic and gut-oriented, which is really to say life-oriented, as our first priority for life is self-sustaining, and that comes primarily through digestion, elimination, and procreation. Often, they have weight issues from tendencies toward eating and lack of movement/exercise. But those who rise to their potential can monitor weight and fat and show their beautiful, full-shaped body in a healthy mode. Some bodybuilders with a heavy endomorphic body can develop large muscles, but overdevelopment may pose an issue with each of the three primary body types (see overdeveloped shoulders in #2).

   These large shoulders can be weighted down and sometimes look like they are sloped, hunched, or overburdened, although their body type seems made to carry the burden; they feel big and strong and can do it even when it gets tough to do.

Their size rarely allows for the visible raised shoulders of the slender frame or ectomorph showing fear. Yet, it may be that they are obstructed by the size of the big-boned person, and perhaps the padding from extra weight covers up the emotional intent. Endomorphs naturally have the rounded shoulders, and when there are psychoemotional issues, they become more rounded and can be pulled forward until they look like the masochistic of the Bioenergetic body classifications.

2. Square, muscular shoulders appear strong and powerful, and this mesomorphic structure seems self-assured, like they can handle what they need to do. This look of strength forms the "ego ideal" in Western culture. This epitome of masculinity represents what every young Charles Atlas aspirant desires with big, powerful, strong-looking, square shoulders.

   Depending on the mixture of mesomorph, they can be muscular to heavy or muscular to thin. Similar to the endomorph covering (with fat) the psychoemotional signs of fear, the mesomorph likewise disguises the raised shoulders with the look of muscles. Fear helps promote exercise and development of muscles, which then, to some degree, acts as a coverup of the emotion, as the shoulders look more developed and raised up. Muscular shoulders can become pulled forward, but that tends to pull the whole body forward and thus makes the overburdened look less likely to be as noticeable as with the heavy body type. Difficulty with the muscular type may be in becoming overdeveloped to hide their fears, social inadequacies, or ego issues.

   Large, powerful shoulders often form in conjunction with the overexpanded chest. Psychologically, the attitude of over-self-confidence relates to the development of an overexpanded ego.

3. Thin shoulders appear narrow when they are compared to thick or muscular shoulders. The thin shoulders are the natural type of shoulders for the thin-framed individual often described as an ectomorph. The thin shoulders typically house thin arms and chest. As with all body types, fitness plays a significant role in development. Unfortunately, many thin-shaped individuals have not gotten into exercise as a life priority, as they don't think of themselves as fat, so why exercise? In time, the body may become soft and weak.

   The undeveloped thin or ectomorphic-framed individuals with narrow, thin shoulders, arms, and chest appear like they may need help, as they do not have the built-up muscle of the mesomorph or muscle and fat of the endomorph to hide their emotional reactions. Without the extra padding, their shoulders can more easily be pulled forward, especially if the thin person is tall, in an unconscious effort to bring themselves down to the shorter size of peers and not look out of place. Just like early-maturing girls who pull their shoulders forward and down to hide their breast development, they sometimes become self-conscious.

   All body types may experience situations that leave them angry and, as a reaction, have emotionally habituated to have their shoulders pulled back and chest pulled forward in a defensive posture. Raised shoulders form out of the fear of hurt, pain, or verbal abuse. Everyone may experience a hurt or broken heart and pull their arms forward and down over the heart to protect themselves emotionally. We all can feel the weight of the world on our shoulders like the ancient Greek Atlas. Yet every person shows their emotional response somewhat differently, and thus, their emotional tissue habituation will also be different, which may be in degrees as everyone has all three bodies (three in one) inside that differ only in degrees.

After the three basic body types of thick framed, medium or muscular, and thin framed, there are some natural variations related to body type, and the psychoactive alterations based on stress, fear, and trauma, primarily. The emotionally based alterations include raised-up shoulders (fear), pulled-back or retracted shoulders (anger), hunched or drooped shoulders (overburdened), and bent-forward shoulders. Dychtwald, Kurtz and Prestera; Lowen; and Rolf have talked about the psychoadaptive shoulder types.

4. Raised-up shoulders or hunched-up shoulders symbolize fear and terror. Shoulders naturally rise as a gesture displaying thoughts, such as "Who knows?" or in a state of fear, like a cat with shoulders and back pulled up. After the fear passes, the shoulders relax and lower. If sufficient fear resides in the child's life, the shoulders freeze into the habitual defensive stance.[63] This frozen posture can be seen in dogs who were terrorized or beaten into submission when young.

   A person living in a state of fear reacts by raising the shoulders, and over time, the connective tissue attaches to the emotionally reactive position. The body exposes the drama from the habitual fear that has become a defense mechanism by shortening the levator scapulae muscle.[64] The person with raised shoulders will usually behave with a tone of fear or may act out fears that have become internalized over time and perhaps have repressed the actual cause of their dilemmas. Yet the fearful state may continue, bringing new situations, objects, or people into its rationale of caution and fear and turn into a paranoid state of mind.[65]

5. Pulled-back or retracted shoulders are fighting against the force of the world (gravity), ready to strike. People with pulled-back

or retracted shoulders face the world in an off-balanced position. Nonalignment (out of alignment) with Earth's force, gravity, actually thrusts the person into a defensive attitude of fighting against the power of the world because pushing against gravity is literally fighting the strength of the world. Lowen related retracted shoulders as the habitual sign of anger that expressed itself as striking out. Shoulder girdle muscles are contracted, and the shoulders are pulled back. The emotion can usually be felt by the mere pulling back of the shoulder and arms while thinking about something causing anger.

With a usually constricted back of the neck and pushing or thrusting of the self into reality to satisfy needs, the person finds himself continually off-balance with a forward thrust. It is no wonder this person who holds on to his temper and from his fantasies of hitting someone may feel upset or unsatisfied with what they see happening to them and feel like striking out at something or someone but cannot. This very habitual emotion of anger and readiness to fight or somehow strike out sets the connective tissue in the muscles to form the position as a frozen history of the emotive cognitive adaptations. Through experiencing the constrictions from habitual emotions and thoughts of striking out and then not striking out, the muscles and joints can develop arthritis in the shoulders, arms, or hands.[66]

6. Drooped-rounded shoulders appear rounded as they droop forward. A common test looks at the position of the hand with arms down to the sides. Rather than the typical palms facing the legs, the hunched shoulders will result in palms facing toward the rear. Numerous causes exist, from computer time and office work to the burdened or hurt psychoactive tissue modifications. The overburdened shoulders are more apt to

be found with those of a thick frame or endomorphic or what the Bioenergetic masochistic character type seems to portray. These shoulders feel overly responsible as if they have a heavy burden in life and are overburdened. The world's weight is psychologically and physically resting on its bowed surface. This, out of alignment with the requirements of gravity, makes the overburdened feelings a physical reality. In essence, in terms of gravity, the entire world is pulling down on top of their misaligned body.[67]

When a person bows or raises their shoulders, especially due to emotions of sadness, depression, or fear, the shoulder muscles change shape to accommodate the habitual expression of feelings. Muscles may shorten, but like other emotionally based body alterations, muscle disuse and overuse bring strength to some but degeneration to others through its lack of use. The fascia plays its physical connection role in the redesign of the muscle attachments. Once ongoing heightened emotional responses habituate with their postural or body expression, the fascia binds the muscles together in good order to maintain that habitual expression of round shoulders, raised shoulders, etc.

This person may feel that they must be responsible. Perhaps they fear they must keep it together and hold on to whatever mental story they are telling themselves. The person may fear that they must hold on and not let go of their mental resolve, bringing them an overburdened feeling. When the shoulders are out of alignment with gravity, it adds to the pressure of feeling overburdened with whatever is their fear or concern.

7. Bent-forward shoulder is a bending or wrapping of the shoulder around the body as a sign of self-protection from the

fear of hurt. This shoulder position most often goes with the thin-framed or highly ectomorphic individual who also has a constricted chest, which psychologically holds the same significance to the body. A common test looks at the position of the hand with arms down to the sides. Rather than the typical palms facing the legs, the hunched shoulders will result in palms facing toward the rear. The shoulders curve progressively as a defense mechanism around the front to enfold the heart with protective strength. Often, the left shoulder has more forward rotation in a physical attempt to cover the heart. These shoulders reflect a person who has lived or is living in fear of being hurt. Over time, the shoulders seem to move themselves over to protect the heart as a way of self-protection.[68] The connective tissue obliges by forming the bent-forward shoulder structure to protect the heart.

Shoulders are pulled forward as the chest contracts back, as can be seen with thin-framed individuals. This upper chest collapse comes from the chest's almost constant feeling of emotions.[69] The sense of a need for protection makes the person feel vulnerable, although he looks pretty defensive, perhaps armored. Emotionally, the person has heightened sensitivity and overreacts to confronting situations by withdrawing. Shallow breathing, characteristic of this type, stems from an emotional holding of the abdomen and diaphragm, which will lead, with chronic use, to a top-bottom body split.

Kurtz and Prestera saw that society's restrictive sex roles hampered early large breast development in young women. The unfortunate young woman constricted her back and hunched her shoulders in an attempt to hide the evolving signs of sexuality out of a confused reaction of shame and embarrassment.

8. Contracted-narrow shoulders reveal one who is emotionally dependent, weak, and with a limited or narrow ability to handle life. Although genetics are involved to a degree with the slim ectomorphic body type, the mind-style of the person can significantly exaggerate this shoulder type. These shoulders have quite a narrow look to them. The contracted narrow shoulder look is different because the shoulders do not typically have a bowed look and are not raised, denoting fear, or retracted, showing anger. The shoulders look as if they have been squeezed together. Contracted narrow shoulders indicate a limited or narrow orientation or ability to deal with life's interchanges or interactions.[70]

Contracted-narrow shoulders from the thin body type may lack the strength to deal with the world's situations if the person does not exercise or do hard manual labor, which would go a long way in making them strong. This shoulder, chest, and arm type would be considered the weak or underdeveloped type.

Contracted shoulders seem to be a defense to withdraw the self-inward, not into the heart as a more classic contracted chest but inside and down to the physical center. The top-bottom split occurring here is the small top with the large bottom. The top is virtually robbed of vitality. Shoulders cannot handle the responsibility of pressure from daily life, and the breath becomes controlled to protect against stirring up too much emotion.

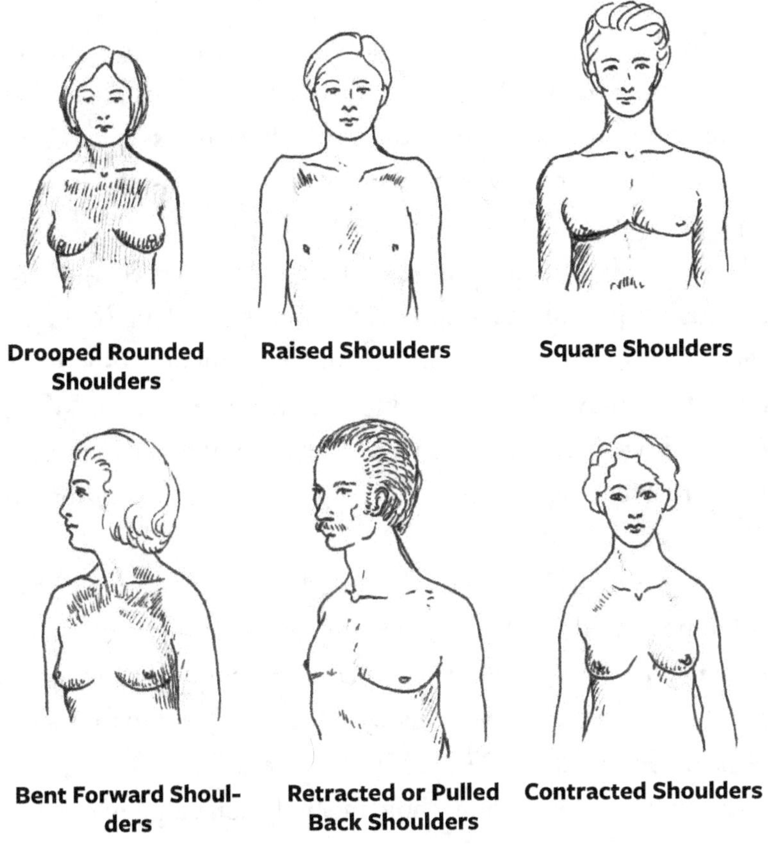

Figure 25: Shoulder Positions

ARMS

- nonverbal expression
- movement in external world
- strength of doing

The vital energy or libido flows up through the gonads (propagation of the species) for generative functions, rises to the stomach to mix and swirl with nutritive power (food), rises (unless blocked) to the diaphragm for airpower, and then to the heart for circulation throughout the body. At the heart, this "orgone" substance, charged with emotion, rushes up the throat for verbal expression and out the hands and arms for nonverbal expression. The arms and hands thus become an energy channel for nonverbal expression.[71]

People with psychic abilities penetrate this heart energy through the hands for psychic healing, laying on of hands, Jin Shin Do, and Shiatsu.[72] This vital energy vibrates from the Kauf or one-point (physical center of gravity) with tingling and warm sensations. When the energy is blocked or cut off, a fear of love's emotional expression is noted, which can be seen in undeveloped arms and torso-limb body splits.

The upper arm shows one's "strength of expression" or the capability to be or to do. If traumatized, the upper arm can become very heavy. The psychological picture becomes that of discouragement, as in, "I can't do that." The arms will then fall down to the sides and appear lifeless or energy-less when in movement.[73]

The elbows, like all joints, hold the body parts together and play a unique role in one's flow of movement. As we move through life, our joints give us the ability to move freely and easily or can present us with some sense of awkwardness or ill at ease with the way we interact with others and the world.

The forearm has in common with the lower leg the role of acting as the final doer of an action or movement. They are the way and means of our doing. They act out the intent from the intellect motivated by the impulse or passion of the emotions. The action from the forearm can be flowing and happy with the involvement of doing, for it makes action happen.

As the final actor in the quest of doing, the forearm can be locked or bound up in psychological trauma from punishment, criticism, and judgment. These reactions can stem from the fear of not doing things "right" or correctly. Fear of punishment in the forearm is exemplified by the mental picture of a person expecting a blow or when forming the "ward-off" position in Tai Chi.

There are three general types of arms that describe how they look: thick, muscular, and thin. There are two subtypes of each type categorized according to a lifestyle that is passive or active. Thick arms subtypes are soft (fat, underdeveloped) or toned (muscular, although may have a layer of fat on top of the muscle). Subtypes of the muscular arms are the soft (underdeveloped), often covered with a layer of fat, and the toned (defined development to highly developed muscular). Thin arm subtypes are soft, weak (underdeveloped), and tight or toned (strong muscular). Just like the arms, the types in the three centers of round, muscular, and thin have subtypes of the body parts with numerous variations.

A muscular person with a high level of mesomorph may be active and show their muscles and even aggressively body-build to bring out muscle definition or even have created a highly muscled body (over-muscled). The individual could also decide (consciously or unconsciously) to be passive and gain weight that results in a more fatty underdeveloped look. Similarly, a thin person could exercise or work to maintain a fit, thin, but muscular body or be passive and have a thin underdeveloped body with saggy skin.

There are six categories based on having two subtypes (active and passive) for each of the three body types.

Table 1: Arm Types With Active or Passive Lifestyle

Thick body	Muscular body	Thin body
Active: muscle with fat	Muscular to highly muscled Developed to overdeveloped	Thin tight with muscle
Passive: fatty tissue abundant	Muscular covered with fat	Thin, loose tissue w/o muscular appearance Undeveloped to highly underdeveloped

The following categories of arm types are more specifically focused on psycho-emotional considerations of the basic arm forms listed earlier.

1. Soft, underdeveloped arms that are large: Typically, the sign of a large-framed person or endomorph who does not choose to stay in shape or has life situations that preclude exercise or work. When the soft, underdeveloped arms are small, they are from medium- or thin-framed individuals. These arms typically stem out of issues like depression, fear, and stress. They primarily seek quiet and have as little as possible movement in life. Softness from fat in the underdeveloped body may underscore the issues of this unevolved arm. In this way, the arm, like the body, suffers from a lack of sufficient energy. Although energy is there, the psychological issues of the heart drain the power for its emotional use. A person feels such emotional intensity that their energy remains in the emotional

body center, which decreases the energy flow to the arms, making actions hard to initiate. Fat arms usually denote an overweight person who feels weighed down by their body, making movement and clear emotional expression difficult. Layers of fat serve as insulation from feelings, and they learn to stay deeply buried inside the body for their safety, which is then also self-defeating.[74] Drained energy is underscored in the body by its lack of vitality and action and the uncoordinated movements.

2. Massive, overdeveloped, over-muscled arms: The overdeveloped muscular arm can be most easily developed from a medium-framed or mesomorphic body but is also present in the large-framed or endomorphic body that has focused substantial energy on muscular development. This massive piece of tissue has been chronically overcharged because, in some way, the body-mind was concerned with the strength or the ability "to do." Perhaps being held back could bring a body-mind directive to over-energize or overexpand the arm. The yin reaction of the body-mind was the undercharged, weak arms, as compared to this very yang expansive, perhaps aggressive, arm. Both overcharged and undercharged arms reflect insufficient maternal care. The infant may have felt the need to hold on, to grasp on for dear life to that which satisfied the needs—sustenance or nourishment. But need satisfaction was not very precise, and the infant literally learned to hold on for "dear life." The body-mind is overcharged for strength. But in the intensity of survival, the person feels the need to reach out and grab what they want with force and hold on to it for fear of losing what they want.[75]

The issue became holding on for dear life, and holding on somehow meant life. Softer qualities were not developed, not when the yang issue of survival remains a high priority. Massive arms typically have little knowledge of grace or tact, with their movements forceful like a bull and awkward in their balance. This type acts with insensitivity. They treat others as objects because they lack the necessary experience to understand or orient toward personality or interpersonal sensitivity. The way one treats the environment in all respects directly reflects how we've learned to treat ourselves. The evolving story of how we were treated is written on the tissue and the psyche as the drama of life unfolds.[76]

3. Thin, tight arms: These arms may indicate an individual with a thin body frame who has found the drive to be strong, or someone with a mighty body-mind conflict elsewhere in the body (probably upper body) who creates a strong and vital energy flow from which the energy becomes cut off for reasons the arm cannot comprehend. This usually strong flow of vital energy becomes redistributed to other parts, such as an expanding chest, as a reaction to trauma. Afterward, the energy returns to its normal flow down the arm. But the arm, sensing the loss of energy, immediately blocks off any further loss, creating a muscle rigidity that manifests in a tight arm. The person has an unconscious reaction of panic as they grab on to life with a clutching hold that renders the person with a clutching-like attitude that looks consistent in terms of the arms doing what they can to contain as much energy as possible.[77]

    Sadly, the clutching and grasping psychologically and physically are a losing battle. The person reaches out and grabs what they want, but holding on to it over time becomes difficult. Focusing and maintaining attention become issues. Dychtwald believes this person has many joint-related problems such as strains or injuries, especially in the hands.

4. Thin, underdeveloped arms: These arms typically stem from a person with a thin (ectomorphic) body who does not work or work out to develop the arms. Undercharged and over-charged body parts can result from a displacement of the bioenergy from core to periphery or body to arms and legs. Thus, the underdeveloped arms usually result in an under-charge of energy in the arm, which may be due to the energy being held back through fear or because another body area is chronically overcharged. This energy overcharge or hold-ing is most often found in the chest, belly, or shoulders. This syndrome, over time, when chronic and extreme, can be the bioenergy mechanism resulting in the limb-torso body split. The person with energy blocked from the arm feels that the arms are not providing the strength that the mind wants and naturally complains about not having the strength and vital-ity they want in the arms. This weakness or lack of strength reflects in their restricted ability to make their way out in the world by grabbing on to life and their desired relations.[78]

The cutting off of vital energy to the arms also changes the temperature. The cold, clammy hands are due to the vital, healing warmth from the heart energy dribbling down in small supply. Cold hands and feet are constant complaints from people whose undercharged limbs yearn for the heart's warmth. The undercharged arm, robbed of strength as a psychic defense for another issue in another body part, cannot possibly have the full strength necessary to do the "doing" or embrace the world with "doing" as it was genetically designed. On a genuine basis, the person lacks initiative or drive, for the arms physically lack the strength to do the bidding of the mind.

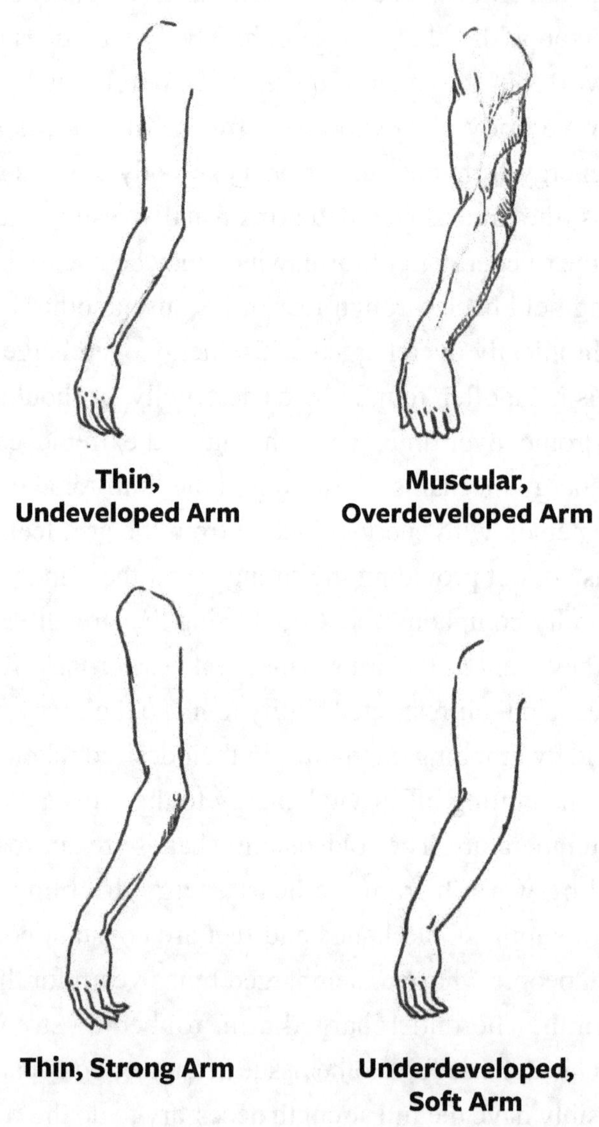

Figure 26: Arm Types

HANDS AND FINGERS

- taking and receiving
- reaching for goals
- grasping on to reality
- fear of doing

Hands are made for doing. They are the actors of the brain in manipulating the world to satisfy needs by obtaining nourishment and desires and manifesting reality. The hands reach out for the goals, consisting of the triune basic needs, Maslow's hierarchy of needs, or the chakras as reviewed in the section on Triune Holistic Theory. In their effort to manifest reality, the hands grasp out to bring the intent of the mind and the heart's desire into existence through the movement of the hands.

Randolph Stone illustrated Polarity Therapy, in which he designated particular physical, organic, and psychological processes to the various areas of the hands and fingers. As the section on toes and feet also explains, the energies flow up and down the body. The toes and the fingers are the last parts of the body that energy goes through, the last place for residual residues to be left behind. The residual tension attaches to tissue in the area and interacts with the tissue in various ways according to the dynamics of the energy flow. Thus, the feet, hands, toes, and fingers are manifestations in the material form of vital energy. And it is the manifestation of this energy flow in behavior that becomes the personality.

The hand and finger personality diagnosis system that Stone created presents physical and psychological ailments. Although Stone utilized much of Eastern Ayurvedic medicine as a theoretical basis for Polarity Therapy (in the five element theory as related to the digitals—fingers and toes), he chose the Greek or Hermes system rather than the more widely used Chinese five element theory. The elements of fire, earth, water, air, and ether were used in potent conceptual design with modern thought toward physiology and anatomy.

Toes reflect the energy of moving through life while fingers tell of the doing or manipulating elements in life to gratify basic needs and aspire to enlightened understanding and choice of lifestyle. To a lesser extent than toes, fingers are crossed over one another or have splits enlarging the more normal digital spacing. The significance of these defensive manifestations is also listed in the section on toes.

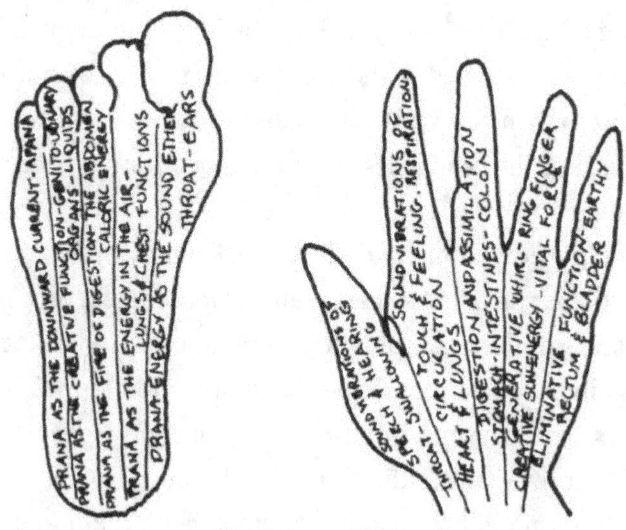

Figure 27: Hand and Foot

Stone developed a system showing the psychological and physical significance for the fingers, which is basically the same for the toes.

1. The little finger, like the little toe, represents the earth element and the eliminative functions through the rectum. The psychological representation is survival or life.
2. The ring finger shows how the person functions emotionally.

It is interesting to note that the ring finger has a link via the wedding ring to the emotional issues of relationships. Physically, this finger reflects the functioning of the genito-urinary system in the pelvis.

3. The middle finger has the fire element represented by digestion and assimilation in the abdomen, which physically and psychologically brings vitality.

4. The index finger brings out the air element of the lungs and chest, representing the heart's desires.

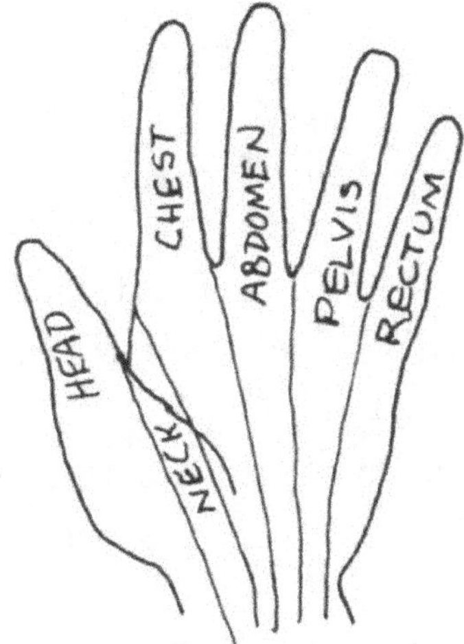

Figure 28: Body-Finger Relationship

5. The thumb, represented by ether in the throat, gives rise to sound vibrations of speech and hearing, communication, and discrimination.

Stone developed a system for relating the fingers and hands along with toes and feet to the contour of the body. Enlargements or curvatures in the fingers signify a related problem in the head or neck.

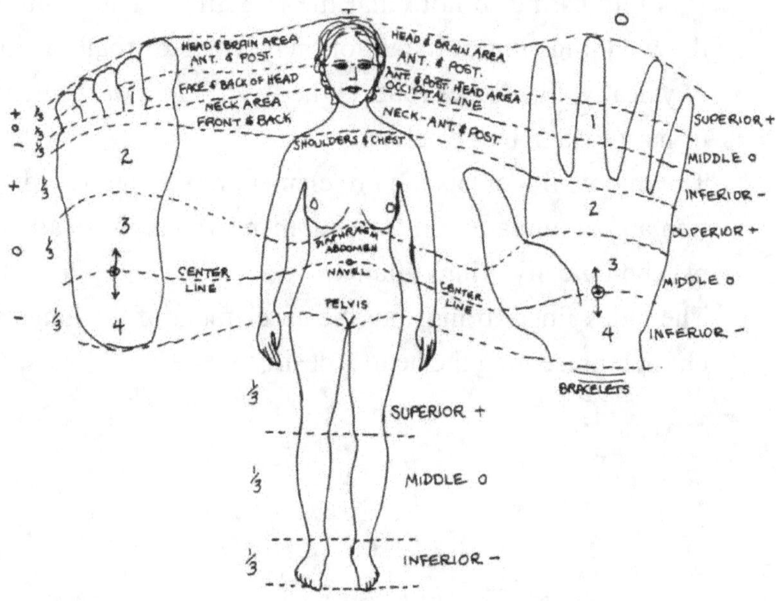

Figure 29: Hand and Feet Homunculus
(Reprinted by permission of the publisher)

The Hand and Feet Homunculus shows its relation to the body from R. Stone.[79]

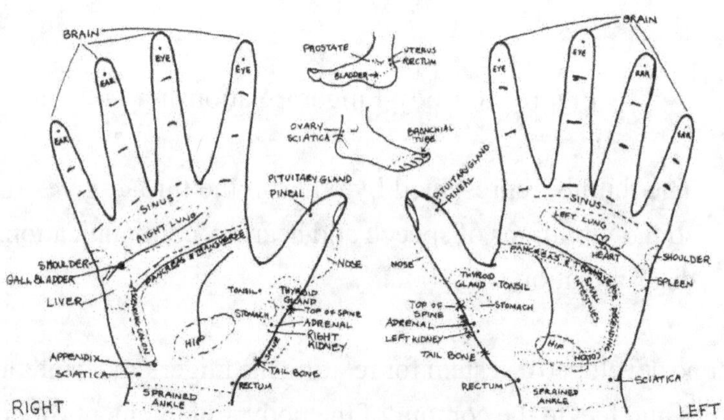

Figure 30: Hand Reflexology
(Reprinted by permission of the publisher)

The hand, a homunculus (little man) like the foot, ears, brain, spinal cord, head, and face, reflects the body-mind physically and psychologically.

Gibson and Gibson mentioned another system of hand classification. Due to its metaphysical flavor as opposed to the scientific method, this particular system may not withstand the tests in a clinical study, yet it cannot be ignored. The ancient history of Western humanity is woven into the metaphysical view of the hands.

Each hand, like each arm, is a part of the whole and holistically related. Hands that fit structurally reflect a smoother transition into the adult world of doing, rather than the proportionately enlarged (overdeveloped) or restricted and underdeveloped as a reaction to the interchange of societal encounters.

The hand could not do without the forearm, nor the forearm without the elbow, nor the elbow without the upper arm, which lastly rests upon the shoulder. This indicates a relationship that each carries to the other.

Metaphysical hand classifications have been proposed throughout time. The following hand classifications have been in the metaphysical literature and espoused by Gibson and Gibson and others.

HANDS

1. Primitive hand (rarely present): These hands have a short thumb with a wide palm. The fingers are short but thick. This hand looks elementary and stiff with awkward and clumsy movements. A kind of brutal instinct with little intelligence wears the hand of an almost pre-human look,

2. Square hands (orderly): This hand shows order in everyday life and, through its practical application and hard work, denotes

a strong need for organization and concrete plans. A strong life-force comes through the hands.

3. Conical hands (artistic): The artistic hand structurally shows a gentle tapering from the base of the hand to the fingertips. This enthusiastic person loves to have fun and enjoys an exuberant social life. Because the artist is often up in the air (not grounded), they need external motivation to actualize the constant flow of dreams.

4. Spatulate hands (energetic): The energetic hand has a spatulate shape for the hands and fingertips. This person is characterized as producing a tremendous amount of activity and highly desiring originality.

5. Pointed hands (idealistic): The pointed hand denotes a very intuitive person who may have strong psychic abilities. In pure form, the hands appear pointed, but the fingers look pointed as well. This long, thin hand has often been esoterically associated with people who become cultists or martyrs to their own ideas.

6. Mixed hands (adaptable): Most hands are not the pure types listed but rather combinations of these pure types. In deciphering the mixed hand, which is the most common, one needs to analyze the shape of the fingers and hand and combine the findings, and use the thumb as the indicator, especially when the hands have a highly mixed shape.

7. Philosophical hands (knots on joints): The philosophical hand category was used in the distant past with either square or conical hands and fingertips with knots on all fingers and thumb joints. This long and lean structure has been associated with teachers who "weigh every question" and become motivated to seek knowledge.

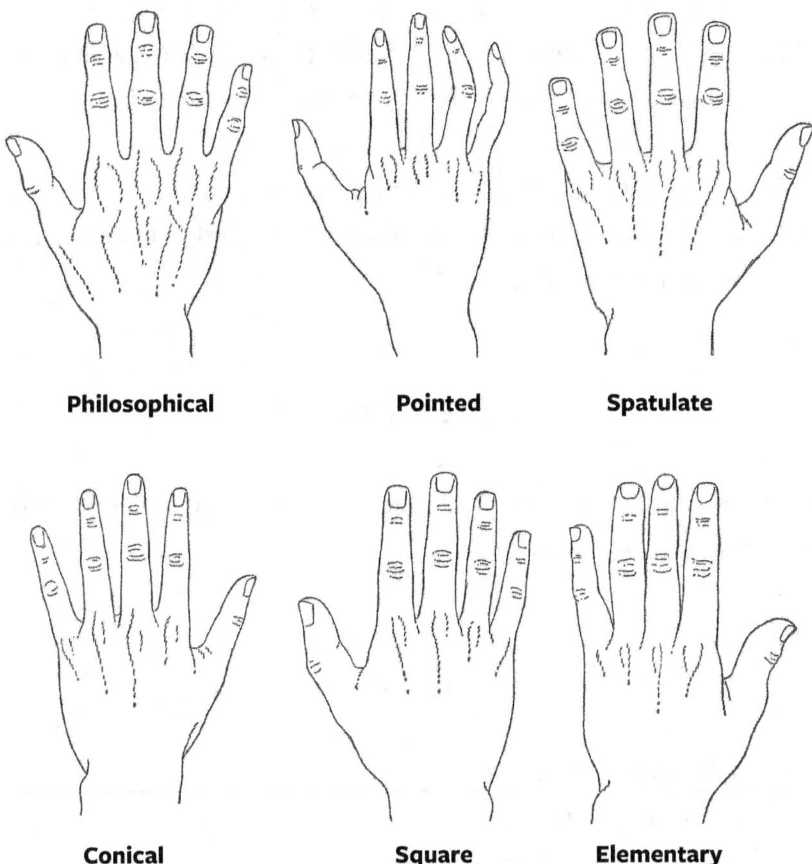

Figure 31: Hand Types *(Gibson and Gibson)*

HAND TEXTURE OR CONSISTENCY

Gibson and Gibson described a system of understanding the personality from the hand texture. However, as noted with the hand categories, these classifications are metaphysically rather than scientifically based and need to be acknowledged as such.

1. Flabby hands: These feel swollen and loose-skinned and denote a variable temperament from kind to irritable.
2. Soft hands: A limp feeling belongs to these hands, which may detest manual labor yet often become quite successful through other endeavors.
3. Firm hands: Denote a determined personality.
4. Hard hands: These stiff hands reflect a rigid personality that is hard to convince.

UPPER BACK

Expressions of anger perhaps enraged by or through the connection with the shoulders and upper arms.

BACK

- self-image in the spine
- the unconscious
- "garbage pile" of residual tension

The spinal cord and adjacent muscles comprise the back. The back must support the shoulders, chest, rib cage, solar plexus, abdomen, genitals, and anus. Esoterically, the spine represents a coiled serpent whose power flows up from the spine like the caduceus (Figure 63), which is the symbol of ancient medicine. Physicians of old understood the meaning of energy in terms of qi, kundalini, energy centers (chakras), and the triune body-mind (three centers). Egyptians viewed the spine as the "link between the upper and lower heavens," and Tansley talks about linking the three courts of the body temple with the spinal column. Rosicrucians correlated the "planets" with the seven cervical vertebrae—from upper to lower: Saturn, Jupiter, Mars, Sun, Venus, Mercury, and Moon. Twelve dorsal vertebrae represent the twelve signs of the zodiac, and the five lumbar are the five elements of earth, water, fire, air, and ether. The five-segmented sacrum contains the kundalini power.

Metaphysically speaking, the spine is the link connecting spirit in the head and matter in the sacrum. A threefold fire of kundalini refines the energy and regenerates the human through this link. The refining energy or fire ascends through the astrological guidance of the three fiery signs. The ritual purification begins in the Outer Court, symbolic of the generative center under Sagittarius. Though refining, the energy of fire rises up to the Inner Court or the heart under the sign of Leo, and finally, the purification of fire ascends to the Holy of Holies in the head under the guidance of Aries.[80]

Ida Rolf discovered that a person's spinal stability was reflected in the individual's worldview or outlook. This was seen in the spine's ability to give the person an accurate perception of where it was in time and space. Spinal stability also provides the psychological capacity to bring meaning to special patterns.

The back psychologically represents the self-image, and the balanced back has a solid feel with an uplifted self-image. One can do this because of the strong back, or the opposite type, the unbalanced back, in which one suffers from weak back muscles and an incapacity, as in the "I'm sorry" person.

The back forms a closet where unexpressed emotions or residual energy are dumped when undigestible to the front (genitals, abdomen, diaphragm, chest). Any inhibition of psychic energy in terms of physical movement, emotional expression, thought, or vibrational patterns creates residual tension in the nervous system and toxins in the chemistry of the emotional and physical apparatus. The repressed energy charge lingers around the body part area of restricted intent and along the appropriate spinal area(s). The tissues adjacent to the electrochemical charge become energized (vibrationally, chemically, or electrically), and the energy becomes deposited in the tissue.

From *Bodymind*, Ken Dychtwald:

As a result, the spine becomes the "garbage pile" for these unwanted feelings and unresolved conflicts. By locating themselves along the spine, the emotions become temporarily blocked from view, and as they continue to accumulate, congestion in these muscles increases and the feelings begin to grow into anger and then rage. If unexpressed, this rage will translate itself into spite and bitterness, which will seep into all the expressive aspects of the bodymind in an attempt to release some of the accumulating tension and conflict. When this happens, the individual is no longer consciously "in control" of his angry passions. Instead they have become blocked from consciousness and from this new place begin themselves to control all his actions, motions, and expressions.[81]

According to Green, the energy moves out from the stomach. It circulates up and around the chakras until it finds an attachment to the appropriately emotionally charged area in the back. The back takes energy in and hides it. The theme becomes, "What you don't see, you'll never know." On an unconscious level, the "front," which "faces" people, is open, soft, and gentle, but the back becomes charged and left to harden like a rock and feel tense and sore. The body assists the front in keeping its good looks by dumping the energy. Or, perhaps from another perspective, trying to allow the energy to flow as it naturally should up the main flow or chakras along the spinal cord.

LOWER BACK: CROSSROADS OF BODY ENERGY AND MOVEMENT

The lower back functions as a crossroads between the respiration and digestive systems, between generative and visceral, and even between the legs and the torso. It is a psychosomatic mediator between the top and bottom halves. Alexander Lowen saw the conflict as having pressure and feelings from above and below. He saw the tension and feelings from above as requirements, feelings of guilt, and physical and psychological burdens. From below, they represented a force moving upward through the legs, physically contending with gravity and erect posture, and psychologically with feelings of sexuality and the control and stability of the self.

The lower back manifests, in tissue tension, the degree of balance between the physical and emotional centers. Muscle tension chronically held tends to misalign the spinal column, which can pinch nerves and otherwise be painful. Abdominal tension pulling on the great network of angled fibers can frequently be unbearable if the stomach is contracted and rigid. Muscles and associated emotions chronically held for long periods of time can predispose the area to injury.[82]

CHEST: EMOTIONAL CENTER

- love and relationship needs
- circulatory and respiratory systems
- fourth chakra, love

The chest area, diaphragm, and heart all compose the emotional center. The energy from the nutritive and generative physical center will rise through the diaphragm to be refined by the heart and fired up by oxygen. Whereas survival is the instinct of the physical center, feelings of love, emotion, and social relationships satisfy the heart's instinct.

Like other body parts, the chest embodies the thoughts and emotions habitually held through the function of the myofascial tissue. The hyaluronic acid in the interstitial tissue/fluid raises and lowers its viscosity based on the timing of holding the emotional, cognitive body position, temperature, and other factors. The chest area houses the heart, which spews out the blood to the body. Blood is a life-force responsible for continued life by providing its nutritional load to tissues, which contain necessities such as oxygen and vitamins. The hormones and neuropeptides give the body-mind the spreading feeling of emotions, including happiness, sadness, excitement, and depression.

When life presents us with traumatic situations that cause us to block our loving, soft emotions, we tend to replace those feelings with those of rejection or anguish, which are also expressed as sorrow, sadness, self-pity, depression, anger, wanting, and heartbreak. Thus, the feeling of love becomes mixed with those of despair or anger, changing their form depending on the emotional, cognitive stimulation. The expression of each emotion or mixture of emotions is often not immediately understood by the thinking self, but the body naturally forms the posture for its expression. Thus, the habituation of expression shapes the body based on the DNA or initial body form.

Dychtwald found the chest represents blocked feelings. The chest was:

…primarily a feeling focuser, amplifier, and translator. All the different aspects of human be-ing, such as emotions, thoughts, reactions, and expressions, mix and swirl in the chest, continually changing form and direction as they proceed from creation to expression.[83]

The chest has a natural variation from the thick-framed individual, the medium or muscular, and the thin-framed. Apart from the natural genetic variations, stress and trauma from the environment and social relations contribute to the psychoemotional adaptations through the physiological process of emotional tissue habituation. The chronically contracted or collapsed chest is the adaption of the thin ectomorphic structure, and the overexpanded chest stems from the muscular or thick body frame.

Physically shaped by biology, the chest integrates all the swirling energy of emotions. Like any body part, too much or an overcharge of energy tends to expand or enlarge the tissue, and an undercharge or "not enough" energy robs the tissue of matter and tends to contract inward. The psychoemotional chest types are also described by Dychtwald and Kurtz and Prestera.

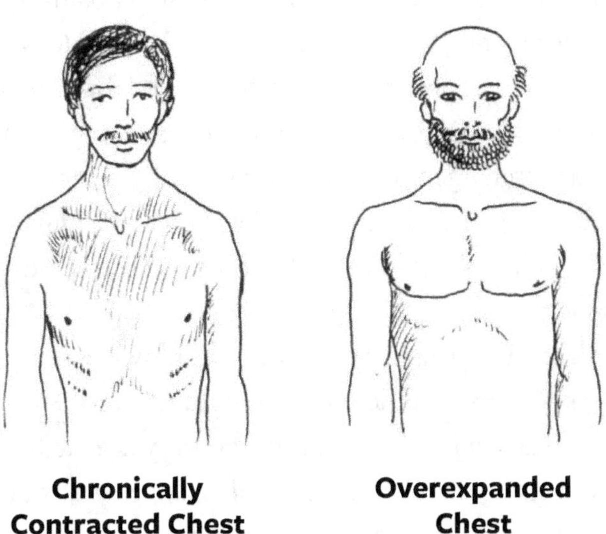

Figure 32: Chest Types

1. The chronically contracted or collapsed chest is typically seen in the thin body or high ectomorphic body type. It seems the collapsed or chronically contracted chest was somehow robbed of energy or refused it out of fear of survival. The slight, delicate chest with its immature pectoral muscle looks collapsed with a sunken posture. This body type was formed due to a dynamic relationship with another center, usually the physical center. The undercharged feeling becomes habitual, making any additional charge an emotional crisis. This deeply hurt chest looks like a blow was received onto the center, and the heart sank in and closed off.[84]

2. Overexpanded chest tends to occur with the mesomorphic and endomorphic subtypes of the meso-ectomorph subtype and the endo-ectomorph subtype (see Chapter 7 on body types for details). The overexpanded chest has similarities to the chronically collapsed or contracted chest, which is held tight in a highly contracted or collapsed position, as the overexpanded chest is held tight in an inflated position. In energy displacement, the chest can rob the pelvis and legs, and sometimes the face and chin, of matter needed for its enlargement. The overcharge of energy in the chest expands matter, and the undercharged parts, usually the belly center and legs, are undercharged and thus underdeveloped. The image is of the man with a big, burly chest and little, tiny, spindly buttocks and legs.

   This type usually reflects an overblown ego, as the person hides his heart in the enlarged columns of the rib cage. An emotional center always has the primary need to be loved, and any chest deviation always involves love or lack of love. Our heart always strives to be in the loving, "blissed out" state.[85]

Fear of hurt in social interactions represses the verbal expression of self or love, and the person defensively compensates by performance and success. Soft, tender aspects of the self are cut off as the belly tightens and the diaphragm rigidifies. The person reacts by feeling tough and powerful.

In the expanded chest, receiving energy or feedback is difficult, although they can give it. The big ego matches the oversized chest, and anything in word or deed that challenges the mindset is not received well. It is just as difficult for someone with an oversized chest to receive feedback as it is for the collapsed or constricted chest type to give feedback.[86]

The hallmark of this type may be the absence of tears. Soft emotions have been hidden by layers of bulging muscle and have turned into anger and yelling. This strong person longing for freedom from his front of power, control, and strength needs to learn the expression of softer emotions and the relief of sharing true feelings. Physical problems may include hypertension, high blood pressure, chronic anxiety, and a tendency for tuberculosis and heart problems.[87]

The collapsed chest portrays insecurity, depression, and shallowness of breath (see gasp effect in diaphragm section), with feelings of not enough air to breathe or energy to do what they dream of doing. The person seems to have constant fears about self-protection, perhaps due to the less-than-adequate air supply. This image seeks energy or charges through another person's inspiration (motivation or energy regeneration). On an interpersonal level, the role of the taker becomes more portrayed than that of the giver.

Using muscle tension to block the energy flow upward from the abdomen and diaphragm is motivated by a sense of fear and inferiority. At best, they find it difficult to move with self-assured action through the world. The chronic fear of self-protection stems from a lack of sufficient air, and thus the lessened life-force projects into anguish and despair.

When a person has habitually withheld emotional expression or thoughts, the chest becomes more and more congested. The congestion, in turn, can assist in a complex of chest-oriented ailments, such as asthma and breathing disorders, and chest colds, along with chronic anxiousness, hypertension, and high blood pressure.[88]

The ripped-off child feels to blame because they were not good enough and so rips off the self internally—the inside structure of tissue changes. With great heart energy never able to flow outward, the chest begins to sink slowly, as if by an inner vacuum of hurt feelings. Tissue expands into a formation where the energy is in overstock and, on the other end, will stagnate growth from a lack of energy. Energy and potential tissue development are siphoned to another body part, usually the belly center.

The body even forms the shape of energy siphoning down. Chests collapse with the upper ribs flattened down and in. Energy flares out at the bottom ribs, and the ribs stick out like an inappropriately yet defensively necessarily placed ski jump. Bottom ribs roll out or turn out to express the energy's force to avoid heart issues.

The chest sunken from repressed pity and sorrow may appear as a deep cavern running to the heart. A hole going through the sternum may be created as the heart attempts to pull in its energy and hide.

The shoulders may tuck forward into an "I'm so sorry" self-pity position, making his reality seem so withdrawn. By the very action of the pulled-over shoulders and the energy vacuum pulling in at the chest, the heart is tucked away in a cage all its own. The energy in its cage sanctuary becomes hardbound to escape or enter. The hard-to-touch (emotionally) person slowly transforms into physical and psychological rigidity from lack of loving.

The defensive reactions (the polarity) could include: 1. poor me and 2. hostile. Both are reactions to not getting love. Although still angry, the "poor me" defends with the safer passive-aggressive stance. The more assertive "hostile" stance would be to throw back the shoulders, attempting without success to expand the chest and say, "I don't need your love." The entire chest and rib cage area exist to protect the heart, which is always felt as the longing for love.[89]

BREASTS: APPROACH TO LIFE

Women naturally tend to have one breast smaller or higher than the other. Breasts reflect one's approach to life. Because their firmness relates to the pectoral muscle development, the developed or expanded chest will tend to have firmer breasts than the undeveloped, contracted, or collapsed chest.[90]

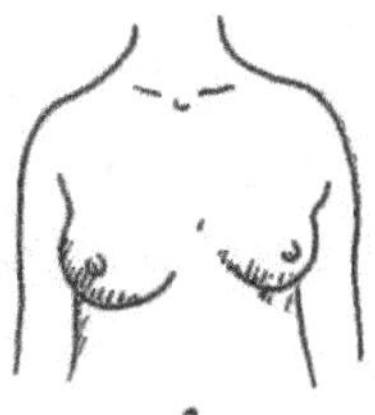

Figure 33: Right-Left Breast Split

Our bodies are asymmetrical due to the brain's right and left hemispheric functions, which, at the body level, reflect in the right-left body split. The right side of the body (left brain) has assertive, rational functions, while the left (right brain) finds intuitive, artistic endeavors. The more developed and usually larger breast shows the primary way in which life is approached. A larger right breast signifies an assertive lifestyle, the left a more receptive but creative behavior style, and a balance of breast size indicates a balanced personality.

DIAPHRAGM

- fear of being ripped off
- respiration (fear of not breathing)
- third chakra, power

The diaphragm is a thin, flat-like skeletal muscle that sits below the lungs and separates the abdomen from the chest. The diaphragm contracts when a person inhales, which creates a vacuum that pulls air into the lungs and releases it during the exhale.

This critical junction between the belly-mind and the heart-mind functions for the assimilation of air. Respiratory motions displace the viscera and allow air to rush into the solar plexus and the area of respiratory assimilation and energy production. Oxygen going in can be compared to the damper on a wood stove. The more open the damper, the more air comes in to fuel the fire in the solar plexus.[91] The third chakra pertains to power. The solar plexus symbolically mixes the energy of the belly-mind (food) with that of the respiratory system (oxygen) to power the body. All the emotions (chest), groundedness (security) from the legs, and sex from the pelvis mix together and become powerful.

The diaphragm represents the gateway of marital bliss between the heart and the ground center and further represents the coexisting of the male and female within each of us.[92]

The chest and heart are emotional, and as the male principle, they symbolize heaven or father above. In contrast, the abdomen/belly constitutes the nutrition and generative functions as the female principle of earth or mother below. Psychologically, the diaphragm functions to integrate the male and female principles.

The heart-center and belly-center connection may be, at least partially, through the psoas muscle. Rolf demonstrated the function of the psoas as being a bridge between the upper body and the legs. Through events in life, especially emotional trauma or deep-set emotions, various muscles, such as the psoas, tend to become bound together through the work of the myofascial tissue. This connective tissue can use its fibrous consistency to bind muscles and inhibit a person's ability to breathe normally, and it can even affect walking.

Each breath expands the diaphragm from side to side and front to back. The spinal cord can lengthen and shorten, which may especially be felt during breathing. The breath brings in oxygen to the lungs, which is moved to the blood and transported to the cells.

Each breath should move as a wave starting at the bottom of the abdomen and flowing, as an incoming ocean wave, up to the top of the chest and ending in the clavicle. Each breath charges the nervous and circulatory systems. The heart needs air to stoke the fire and bring a feeling of aliveness, and the energy needs continual stoking by the air to vitalize the system.

The air feeds the fire as the emotions swirl around in the belly. As seen from the energy flow pattern of the chakras, the swirling action tends to ground emotions together. Ungrounded feelings can manifest as the laugh in an uncomfortable situation or as anger or hysteria.[93]

The diaphragm functions as a gateway for the sensations or "belly feelings" to pass through in route to full emotional expression. The air from the diaphragm's action fuels the fire of emotions. A person cannot breathe slowly and be enraged. If an emotion is limited, the breathing is restricted. Reich theorized that a person could defend himself against having feelings of anxiety or misunderstood pleasure through the limited movement of the diaphragm, as the diaphragm could move as a defense against the feelings. Not to breathe is not to feel emotions. Shallow breath keeps the belly-mind (instinctual energy) under control. The armoring against unwanted feelings holds the muscles tight and rigidifies the diaphragm and solar plexus. These largely unconscious body movements or lack of movement are part of a process of survival used to stifle the emotions.

Barry Green reported the gasp effect. This psychological and physical occurrence takes part in the parent-child interaction. A child receives feedback that it is not okay "to do" or "to be" whatever is received by a child. The parent gives a severe reprimand, and the child cries. The parent says to "shut up," and the child's diaphragm becomes rigid in an attempt to follow orders, but a few gasps or small expressions of emotion and hurt dribble through. Feelings emerge of being ripped off, and the shoulders, in time, weld over forward as if to protect the fragile, energy-less heart. The gasp effect is like a "psychic hammer," which then becomes increasingly easier to touch off by reassuring emotionally backed stimulus. In a body sense, the emotions can be digested and understood or blocked and not assimilated, as can food or thought.

A chronic blockage at the diaphragm grows into the major top/bottom or belly-center/heart-center split. If the gasp effect becomes chronic, the sternum may be pulled inward toward the creation of the contracted chest type. The pressure to block off the pelvis pushes out and can, in some instances, put enough tension on the ribs to rotate the bottom ribs outward, making it look like a ski slope. These tension disorders in the diaphragm and in the muscles underneath create symptoms of disorders leading to a nervous stomach or ulcer with a tendency for liver and gallbladder conditions or diabetes.[94] In order to release the diaphragm, it must get exactly what it fears by the inability to breathe. It needs the charge of air to be complete emotionally and vitalize the belly to integrate with the primal, instinctual self within.

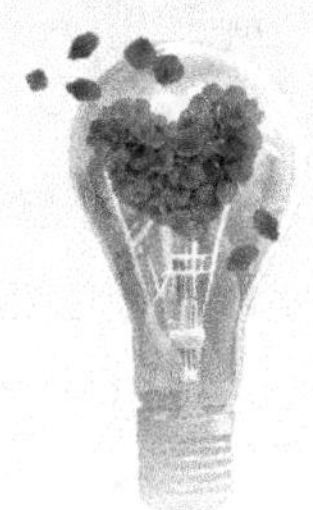

CHAPTER 5

Life or Physical Center: Abdomen, Pelvis, Legs, and Feet

ABDOMEN

- physical center
- nutrition, mother earth
- discriminate or discern
- second chakra, food assimilation, excretion, cleansing

The abdomen provides the ability to discern and discriminate. We use our "gut-level" response from a situation's "gut-level feelings." The gut tells us what is nourishing and what is waste or poison, as if "I know it as I feel it."

The entire physical center strives for internal nourishment, from the feet to the abdomen. The pelvis is the transmission and the perineum is the boiler that put the legs as wheels into motion.

The psychology of the belly represents discernment and discerns the quality of moving energy. In the gut, the good and the bad, the pure and the toxic, are separated. The Chinese five element theory has the gut separating the pure from the impure.[95] As the final digester, the small intestines take out what is nourishing and discard what is not. Such begins the beautiful act of elimination.

The abdomen represents the physical self or the belly-mind, which is the physical center's instinctual drives involving hunger, satiation, and sexual urges. It represents our gut understanding of ourselves, others, and the environment. When people have difficult experiences, they try to absorb them psychologically by putting the energy, residual tension, or emotional charge inside the self. They stuff it in right down to the gut so it can churn around and become a "gut-level experience."

The physical center holds the bladder belt, in which its tension has the psychological function of control. The belt chokes off and thereby controls the genital area, the source of raw energy. Socially, it manifests as "controlling yourself." The parent retorts, "You're not supposed to get angry at the dinner table with grandmother." The repression of control, represented by the bladder in the five element theory, could come from being told to "control yourself," and hence, always being "in control."[96] This repression of vitality, cutting off from raw earth energy, produces an anti-life mechanism (death wish) because to be "in control" and to be "quiet" is equal to being "dead."

Green related the following psycho-adaptive abdomen types, the bloated belly and the tight belly.

1. Bloated Belly: The energy, libido, orgone, vital force, or kundalini becomes "swallowed," as it were, down to the stomach. If this energy is not digested, worked out, resolved, redirected, and able to be eliminated, it becomes "psychic shit" or psychological material that never gets processed. As a result, the belly bloats.

An example of this is the counterphobic who becomes a mountaineer while afraid of heights. The climber continually strives for that experience as if it were an unfulfilled or unresolved passion. Yet, in this reaction formation, there is no release. Because of the underlying fears, they cannot absorb or digest it, and the belly becomes increasingly bloated.

2. Tight Belly: This abdomen type evolved from the continual experience of fear or terror. The high emotional content or charge makes it difficult to discern toxic from pure or, in another sense, from a physical or psychological level. The tight belly wants to be open for breath to come in and give it life. But the shallow, tight breath has too much fear to allow in the fire-fanning breath. The tight belly finally learns not to express emotion.[97]

PELVIS

- kundalini, energy basin of the self
- seat of the physiological soul
- attitude toward living

The pelvis, the bone that houses the nutritive center, was known to tantric physiology as the spring of kundalini and to Rolf as the seat of the physiological soul. The pelvis is the basin that is the foundation for the entire upper body, connecting the legs and feet with the spinal cord and torso. Green suggested that because any pelvic distortion cuts off the vital energy, the pelvis syndrome always says, "Don't be alive; don't fully feel or fully be."

Rolf viewed the pelvis as a key to personal well-being because the pelvis connected us to the earth and its gravitational field. For women, the pelvis is seen as the container of the feminine qualities of nourishment and support.

As the pelvis goes, so do the buttocks, belly, and genitals. All these body-mind parts so interrelate that a change in any one proportionately affects the others. The pelvic and pectoral girdles give the body the ability to move (legs) and manipulate (arms), and any alteration of these will affect the quality of movement. Just like the pectoral girdle controls the position of the head, neck, jaw, shoulders, and chest, the pelvic girdle controls the lower body movements.

Dychtwald and Kurtz and Prestera discuss the pelvis regarding pelvic tilt and anal blockage, although different words are used to identify the positions.

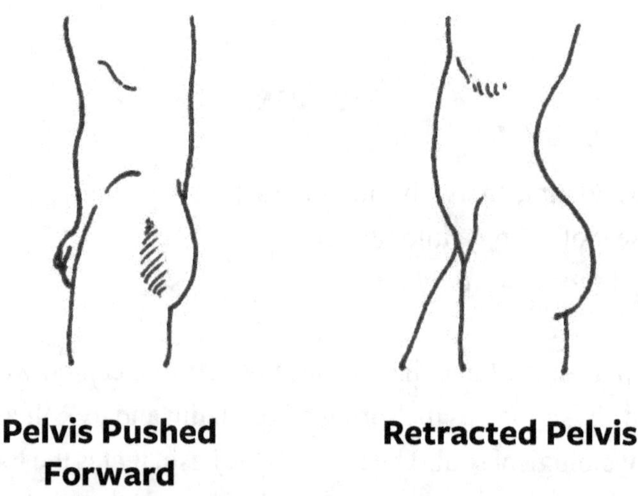

Figure 34: Pelvic Positions

PELVIC POSITIONS

1. Pelvis pushed forward or tucked under and forward: This position is typically accompanied by the gluteus muscles of the buttocks squeezing together as a "tight ass," which forms as

a position of anal blockage (see Figure 34). The tight gluteals have maintained over time this cognitive-emotional position resulting in the chronic tension necessary to shift and keep the pelvis rotated out of alignment.

The pelvic rotation down and under flattens out the lower back and rigidifies the area from constant holding on. The body is off-balance due to the rotation and physically must hold on or maintain a degree of chronic tension. This habitual position undermines the free flow of energy and, consequently, feeling, especially sexual feelings and sexual energy.[98] The physical center is cut off energetically from the emotional and intellectual centers and receives less energy. The lessened energy means more energy and growth in another area, usually an overdevelopment in the chest (expressing and controlling) as in the top/bottom split. But the legs and pelvis lose out. The legs become rigid or underdeveloped, and the pelvis tends to be trim and immature.

Dychtwald claimed that this type might be prone to injuries related to localized anatomy, such as injuries of the lower back and legs, tension in the abdominal area or bladder, or hemorrhoids. Tension could also be referred up to the head for headaches. Kurtz and Prestera spoke of the sacral bone pushed forward, tending to spread the pelvis. Females acquire a motherly look with the widened pelvis and tend to add extra weight.

2. Retracted pelvis or pelvis pulled back and up: This pulled-back and up position has usually been associated with the anal blockage of pulling in and up or the "corn-cob ass." Either the pelvis pulls the gluteals up and back, or perhaps the gluteals and perineum chronically pull up, leaving the pelvis in the retracted position. This curving of the lower spine seems to enliven sexuality and bring attention to sexual

needs from the over-congested sexual energy in the pelvis. The positioning of the pelvis and containment of the sexual energy results in feelings of wanting release and sensuality with an obsessive desire to have sex.[99] But the person has a difficult time with the sexual release. As Kurtz and Prestera insist, this person is ready for a sexual experience yet afraid of totally letting go and allowing it to happen. Rolf contends this pelvis tip caused by an imbalanced pubococcygeus muscle could be a psychophysical instigating sign of deep-seated emotional problems.

The other aspect of pelvic rotation relates to unresolved anal conflicts. These unhealthy survival reactions come from punishment, severe abuse on the buttocks, or too-early toilet training requirements before the development of anal sphincter muscles. During the too-early toilet training, the child learns out of necessity to contract the muscles necessary for control, such as the buttocks, thighs, and area around the pelvic floor. This contraction both tends to retract the pelvis and create a further inhibition of the breathing process. This unconscious response to the demands for toileting before the muscles are sufficiently developed is a type of body armoring that Wilhelm Reich alluded to. The armoring decreases the experience of pleasurable sensations or more natural feelings from the pelvic area.

GLUTEAL HOLDING POSITIONS

- anal blockage
- life versus death wish
- toilet training (elimination) issues

Dychtwald, Green, and others identified types of gluteal holdings. These included Squeezed Gluteus (Tight-Assed), Held-Up Gluteus (corn-cobbed ass), and Tension from Above Gluteus (constricted pelvis).

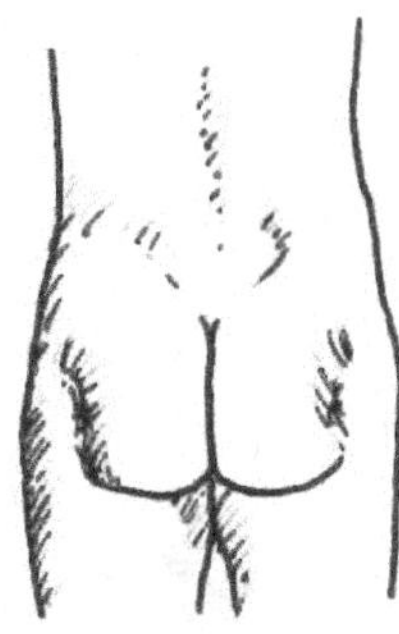

Figure 35: Squeezed Glueus

1. **Squeezed Gluteus:** "Tight-assed," or pinching in of buttock or gluteus maximus and the rotators, leaves the usual mark of a little dimple on either side. This contraction usually has involvement with the pelvis-tucked-under type of pelvic rotation. The defense mechanism reflects the fear of life, the fear of sex, and holding in emotional content inside the body.[100] The chronic habitual muscular holding pattern becomes compatible with a person developing a mindset of holding on to their emotions and feelings and even their inspirations to create something, contends Dychtwald.

   This condition is more likely to develop hemorrhoids and lower back pain from the over-contraction of the anus muscles and lower back connected to the buttock.

   Often, the pounds of padding (fat) around the buttocks stem from fear as a way of providing (physical) isolation. Frigidity in women is associated with the clamping down on the vagina, especially the bulbospongiosus muscle.[101] When this muscle, which influences the erection of the penis and clitoris, tightens, the entire pelvis contracts. This state of tension manifests by a restrained movement of the pelvis and associated areas.

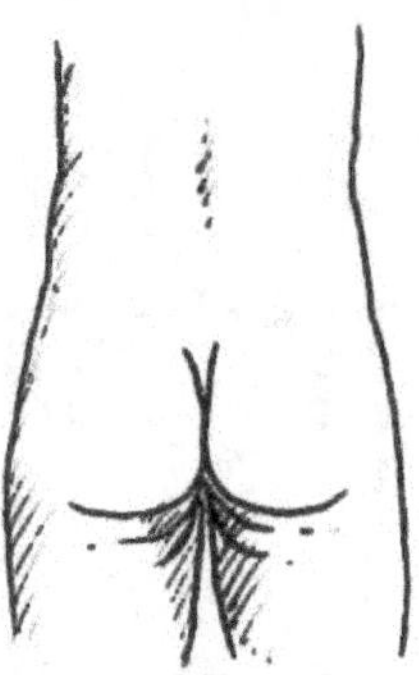

Figure 36: Held-Up Gluteus

2. **Held-Up Gluteus:** The pulling in and up of the pelvic floor, often termed as the "corn-cobbed ass," reflects the tension of maintaining a closure in the perineum.[102] When the perineum closes and the pelvic floor goes into a state of chronic tension, there is no relief from contraction. This closure significantly inhibits the flow of energy from the human's root. Feelings associated with the physical action of the perineum blockage psychologically become insecurity. Instability of trying to form a state of homeostasis (balance) with a significant energy block is near to impossible experientially, and frustrating at the least. Balance continually alters, thus allowing no sense of real balance, which cannot build a sense of security.

Figure 37 Tight Perineum

The tight perineum uses muscle supports from the rotators and the buttocks to assist in the formative struggle to close. The physical look is like someone rammed a corncob right up the anus, which swallowed it and held on to the cob with intent (so as not to lose it).

The physical insecurity of the base part of the energy system closed or limited reacts to the insecurity with paranoia. In the television series *Kung Fu*, Master Po tells Grasshopper, "Where fear goes, danger follows," which may have some bearing on this anal type.

The fundamental issue at the initial infant or oral stage is that of survival. Can the child survive? The fundamental insecurity with this trait is the fear of not getting enough. Not getting enough food, love, or life sustenance to survive, the infant "decides" (or is directed or motivated) to trust the world, but not based on its feelings of security from the environment, which can be measured by the degree of need satisfaction.[103]

One negative expression of this situation is the "mother's dried-up breast." The hard realities out in the world, the really dangerous entities, somehow come out to get you, and the developing child adapts with cunning, suspicion, and paranoia. The reaction could be a cynical, all-pervasive doubt of everything pertaining to the self and the world, a gloomy, apocalyptic outcome, whether short or long range.[104]

Another response would be the counterphobic belief in mysticism. The insecurities might be placed at the whim of the astrological signs or in the fate of the cards, numbers, or religion. This is not to say that mystics have a tight perineum. Rather, the need to know cannot be grounded by someone who cuts off the energy flow from his body at the anus. They cannot have a real sense of the body, which is reality. Hence, this person is attracted to explanations or rationalizations from out of this reality or another world.[105]

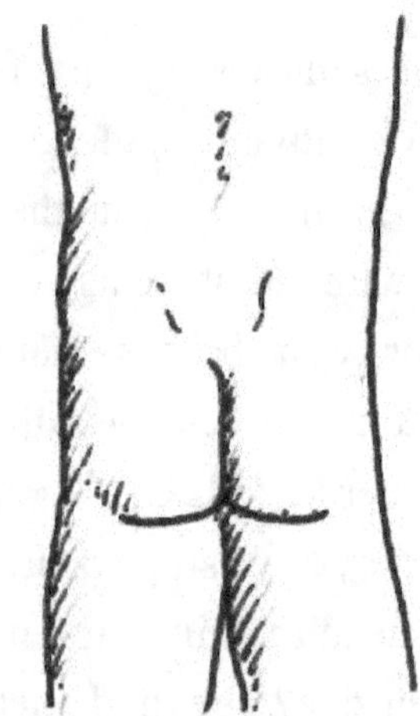

Figure 38: Contracted Pelvis

The corn-cobbed buttocks protrude from the second corn-cobbed crease, which is the holding pattern of the levator ani. Rolf, using the new muscle name of pubococcygeus, claimed that this muscle, if unbalanced, was involved in the pelvis tip (retracted pelvis) and was responsible for many deeply rooted emotional problems (from a muscle-skeletal imbalance).

According to Green, this blockage involves the not-enough syndrome. The perineum cuts off energy, making the limited energy into the body never enough. Especially never enough sex! With never enough energy to do or to succeed, there is always a sense of psychological insecurity. One tries to limit energy expenditure to create a comfortable life position by controlling as many environmental factors as possible.[106]

Overprotective mothers or rigid parental rules may highly influence this syndrome. The parental message becomes "don't," "don't do," so in order not to "do," the energy is blocked off at the perineum.[107]

3. Contracted Pelvis (tension from above): This is the most difficult to detect as the tension blocks are in the belly and the lower back. Tension originates in the belly. Suppressed emotions render the backside to look undeveloped, often with lower back pain or discomfort. This contorted position more often leaves the person with intellectual control and unresolved blocked feelings and sexual issues.[108]

GENITALS

- life-force
- sex and reproduction

Heaven above
Heaven—the uplifting heart
Heart energy is the energy of heaven

Earth below
Earth—genitals
Earth raw energy of the seed to create life

The Heart-Genital connection or
Chinese Duality—two pole expression

Figure 39: Heart-Genital Connection

The energy from the genitals is the vital energy. Freud called it libido, and Reich named it Orgone. The free flow of vital energy is the full expression of the life wish. Any blockage or suppression of this aliveness manifests in the death wish.

Reich viewed the genital blockage as a belt of tension right above the pubic bone. This ring closes in the genitals and holds in on the bladder. The first layer of its rigidifying tension affects the flow of energy, and a more focused second tension layer attends specifically to sexuality.

The genitally related bladder in the Chinese five element theory represents psychological control. The repression of control could come from being told to control yourself, and hence, always being in control.

Oscar Ichazo, the founder of the Arica school, viewed the inner triangle of legs, anus, and genital area as dealing with the fear of sex, and the sit bone area representing the fear of conservation or insecurity.

LEGS

- movement through life
- psychological change
- grounding

Legs support the self, which resides in the heart.[109] The legs are the root of the body and, according to Stone, represent the body's negative polarity (positive at the head).[110] Movement in the body and in the psyche are created by the legs. Psychologically, movement is change. As we move through life, we change. Movement is change toward a goal. The goal of the legs finds a basis in their grounding energy. Nourishment is the goal of the legs.[111] The goal is to go out into the world and obtain all that is required to satisfy the needs of the body and psyche.

Legs literally support the weight of the body, and the alignment of the foot, ankle, knee, and hip determines the degree of physical security or insecurity felt by an individual.[112]

In general, the legs ground us to the earth and the earthly realities, especially that of gravity. The term grounding, often used in Bioenergetics and Eastern practices, refers to one's alignment or orientation to the earth. This is always accomplished in terms of gravity or the duality of forces pulling up and down. The legs quite literally move us toward goals. They enable people to get what it takes (i.e., one's needs in life) and to obtain that sense of nourishment.[113] It is a life-or-death issue both on a physical and a psychological basis. The legs get you what you need in order to survive. Legs give us the ability to take action and provide the strength and security required to take that activity. Our movement and change toward our evolving higher consciousness are rooted in the legs. Movement in one's inner world is also reflected in the legs.

Movement holds the psychological significance of the legs. The positive aspect or movement of the legs for right action denotes uninhibited energy flow through the entire body. The negative element represents a fear of moving to be oneself or procrastination by not taking the right action.[114]

Three general types of legs describe their appearance: thick, muscular, and thin. These types correspond to the three centers of physical (endoderm), thick, heavy, or fat; emotional (mesoderm), muscular or medium; and mental (ectoderm), thin. Two subtypes of each type are categorized according to a passive or active lifestyle. Thick leg subtypes are soft (fat, underdeveloped) or toned (muscular, although they may have a layer of fat on top of the muscle). The subtypes of the medium-build muscular legs are the soft (underdeveloped), often covered with a layer of fat, and the toned (defined development to highly developed muscular). Thin leg subtypes are soft, weak (underdeveloped), and tight or toned (strong muscular). Like the arm, the types in the three centers of round, muscular, and thin have subtypes of the body parts with numerous variations.

Each of us as individuals has the decision about how to live, even though we are driven by unconscious drives from unresolved conflicts, possibly making good choices difficult. A person can keep as fit as possible or be passive with little activity and all the variations between. Thus, someone with a very thick or high endomorphic body will easily gain weight but can decide to exercise or do hard work to keep the legs and body as toned as possible, which may still appear somewhat heavy with a fat covering on top of the muscle. They can also be passive, enjoying the good life, or through psychological issues like depression and grow an abundance of fatty tissue.

A muscular person with a high level of mesomorph may be active and show their muscles and even aggressively body build to bring out muscle definition, or they may have created a highly muscled body (over-muscled). The individual could also decide (consciously or unconsciously) to be passive and gain weight, which results in a more fatty, underdeveloped look. Similarly, a thin person could exercise or work to maintain a fit, thin, muscular body or be passive and have a thin, underdeveloped body with saggy skin. Thick, undeveloped, fat legs look puffy or heavy; the active heavyset is more muscular, but there is still some excess padding due to the natural body type.

There are six categories based on having two subtypes (active and passive) for each of the three body types. Put below in graph or box

Leg types with active or passive lifestyles:

Thick body	Muscular body	Thin body
Active: muscle with fat	Muscular to highly muscled Developed to overdeveloped	Thin, tight with muscle
Passive: Fatty tissue abundant	Muscular covered with fat	Thin, loose tissue w/o muscular appearance Undeveloped to highly underdeveloped

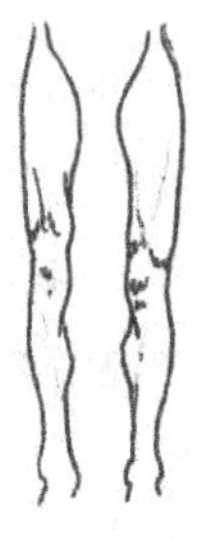
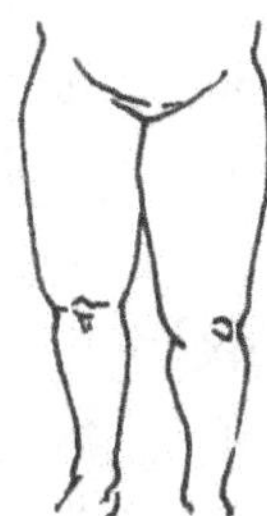

Thin, Strong Legs **Thick, Fat Legs**

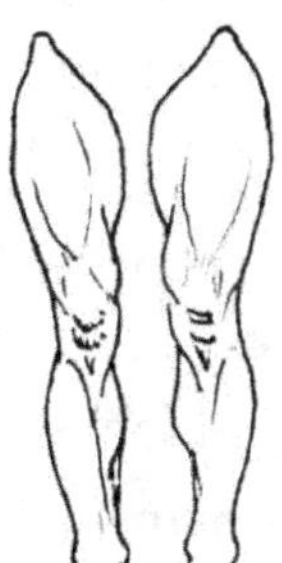
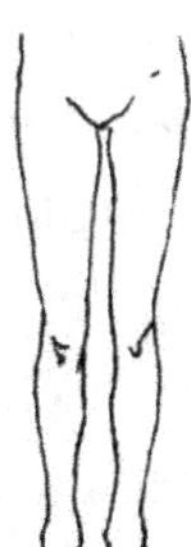

Muscular Overdeveloped Legs **Thin, Underdeveloped Legs**

Figure 40: Leg Types

1. Thick legs with subtypes of soft (fat) and toned (muscular): Our legs carry us through the world, and their shape generally corresponds to the rest of the body, such that a leg that is either soft or muscular is connected to a body that is more soft or muscular. Our legs literally connect us to the reality of the earth with variations between the very soft fat and the more toned muscular. The soft leg appears underdeveloped due to a general lack of movement and exercise and perhaps over-consumption of food, characteristic of a high endomorphic body style. The soft legs appear like the burdened, submissive, masochistic character structure type in Bioenergetics. This physically sluggish look reflects on both a physical and psychological level as a stress reaction to not taking the necessary action. Rather than taking the necessary steps, this person seems burdened by the distress of not initiating what they know (at least unconsciously) they should do. The sluggish posture becomes a defense for not acting and a sign of their feelings of failure. As if with weighted feet, these individuals feel so heavy as to lower their ability to pull themselves up and face the issues of life. The toned or muscular type tends to watch their appetite and move about or exercise.

2. Muscular legs with subtypes of soft or toned (developed or highly muscled): People with the genetic disposition of the mesomorphic quality more often have a more muscular body structure, but without the movement and exercise they tend to crave, the muscle turns to fat and looks soft. Nature and nurture are the hereditary and environmental qualities. There is a little more to it, but in general, people blessed with a high mesomorphic body structure can keep their body toned by movement and exercise or sit on their cognitive laurels and, through lack of movement, become soft and maybe chubby.

Most people are in the average bell-shaped range, but some people strive to become massively muscled, which has been called muscle dysmorphia. The body, including the legs, looks out of proportion, often with the head. Dychtwald considers highly toned muscular legs that become massive to be overdeveloped and over-muscled, which denotes a defensive survival reaction to the unstable environment of "holding on." Not knowing whether or when food or love (nourishment) would appear again, this person spent a lot of time "holding on" to whatever they could to survive. It would not be uncommon for a torso-limb split to appear in which the limbs are oversized for the body. The chronic "holding on" from the panic of survival develops a physical and psychological rigidity reflected in a compulsive, overdeveloped sense of self-control. Rigidity in the personality inhibits spontaneous responses. The person needs and, in fact, desires structure in work and play as an unstructured activity or event may be uncomfortable. Psychological growth and change may be impossible until the rigidity issues and the panic of "holding on" are dealt with. This individual may work out with weights and become so "muscle bound" that movement becomes restricted. But psychologically, the strength to hold on has priority to grace the fluidity of movement.

3. Thin (soft or toned subtypes—weak, underdeveloped) legs: Thin legs are a hallmark of the genetically high ectomorphic or thin-framed body. This thin-framed individual usually has a strong genetic disposition for a slender, often tall body structure, i.e., skeleton. The major subtypes are a thin, weak leg and a thin, strong leg. The subtypes depend much on the environment and social setting. When the environment as survival depends on moving and getting things done to survive

physically or psychologically, a person gets stronger and forms the strong, thin subtype. When the person does not have strong environmental demands and an overly supportive social situation, it's easy for them not to move or exercise as much and have a weaker, slender frame. There are exceptions, of course, depending on disease and handicapping conditions.

The thin weak are usually characterized as underdeveloped, and legs may be seen as the Bioenergetic oral type. It represents a poor self-image and, perhaps a self-inflicted low position in life. This person may feel so dependent that they need others for the support that their legs are inadequate to offer. They become easily dependent on others for the confidence they so dearly lack. This type finds it hard to stand on their own two feet and may need to compensate with the use of arms, neck, and head.[115]

The thin, strong legs are described by Dychtwald as the go-getter leg with intense energy, which comes and goes and flows in spurts, making it erratic and inconsistent. At times, this person has smooth and flowing movements, yet in other situations, the clumsy, graceless efforts bring distress to the occasion. Both the grace and lack of it are the behavioral manifestations of the inconsistent flows of energy due to the blocking and unblocking of energy flows. The energy conflict may play a role in the difficulties and diseases often present with this leg type.

THIGHS

- strength to be yourself and resentment when not
- fear of inadequate capacity (strength)

Thighs represent the strength to be yourself and the fear of helplessness. Strength from this powerful human muscle comes in energy and power. The thigh's strength lies in the ability to physically move oneself and psychologically to be oneself. Thighs psychologically want to be adequate in producing sufficient energy to be able to "get the job done." In physics, the thigh's power is measured by strength over resistance. In metaphysics, psychic resistance becomes ego or negative thoughts.

The thigh stores resentment. The bulge of fat around the thigh, especially in the female gender, forms insulation that acts protective of the stored fear, resentment, and hurt in the tissue. However, this adipose tissue overprotects the thigh and thereby undermines the person's need to be himself. The added tissue cuts off and lessens the power or strength of the thigh. In a sense, the extra flab undermines the flow of energy to the knee, lower leg, and foot. The amount of excess fat reflects the quality of power with which we "step forward in the world."

The thighs are the strength of the legs, which, in essence, support the self. Thus, the strength is self-sufficiency, which is the ability to accomplish the next task or master the appropriate skills. It is like a child associating the feeling and the act of elimination with the mastery of achieving the art and skill of excretion. The shape that the thigh manifests depends on achieving a level of competency that comes with support from parents or pressure and a struggle to perform. The holding in of muscles forms rigidity like the Spartan youth with a fox hidden in his cloak and who is eaten away in the night without sound or utterance.

The thighs relate to the support from parents. From toilet training to tying shoes, the issue ensues the support as helpful, loving assistance or critical reminders of our already known inabilities. The quality and quantity of our life-support systems (family, friends, relations) largely mold our own internal self-support system. Physically, the legs reflect the self-support system as they support the self or body and are thus "self-supporting."

Parent-child relationships can also suffer from overly supportive, protective parents, as well as the neglectful extreme. A child's development can be undermined by not allowing the child to act as if "mommy will take care of sweetie." The child is softly rewarded not to act or to do. Well-adjusted women allow their children to grow, while dependent mothers have many psychological needs to satisfy through their children. They act to care for every need that will assure their needfulness. Children not acting or exploring become dependent and less mobile. Fat in the thigh (and usually elsewhere) becomes locked into the muscles and tissue to assist further the immobility of the already freezing body tissue layers.

Psychologically, the person "cannot do, cannot accomplish, or cannot perform" because she or he or they were taught "not to." The negative sense from this experience would be inadequacy. The psyche resenting the lack of strength "to do" or act finds anger from the stored resentment.

ABDUCTORS

- sexually charged
- protection of genitals

An abductor is a muscle that pulls away from the body's midline. Hip abductors include the gluteus medius, gluteus minimus, and tensor fascia latae. Abductors are psychologically significant due to their roles in the rotation of the feet (balance and understanding), rotation of the pelvis (anal-retentive from early toilet training), and proximity to the genitals. Upper inside legs are the recipient of the spreading sexual charge and work according to their psychological orientation. In females, keeping the upper legs tight may indicate sexual rigidity; the extreme fear could be from the trauma of rape. The chronic abductor tension in males could depict a natural primitive reaction for the protection of the genitals and sexual anxieties. With either sex, the high state of energy charge that works to protect the genitals (from real or imagined threats) engages more tissue mass than needed. The quadriceps and the abductors start working (fascia become glued) together to maintain the habitual movements, when in actuality, only the quadriceps are necessary for effortless walking.

Smith has an interesting story about men having a significant sensitivity to touch on the abductors. The upper inside leg is close to the genitals, and men supposedly have an unconscious fear of genital mutilation.

HAMSTRINGS

- self-control
- letting go

The hamstrings psychologically relate to self-control and reflect the difficulty of letting go. Dychtwald reported that the issues are in terms of: "fears of falling, falling over, falling in love, losing touch with reality, losing consciousness, being rejected, being abandoned, being taken advantage of, being controlled, loss of support, loss of self, and loss of life."[116]

KNEES

- fear of the death of the ego
- fear of change
- transmits strength of the thigh into the action of the lower leg
- reflects change and movement in the body-mind

Like all other joints, the knee demonstrates in action the quality of the person's movement and gracefulness as the movement of a joint reflects one's movement through life. All joints have psychosomatic crossroads.

The strength of the thigh goes through the knee and becomes the action of the lower leg. Knees perform as the junction, attaching tendons that carry the energy from the thighs to the lower legs. The function of the knee changes strength into energy. Psychologically, the knee reflects change and movement in the body.

In the Arica system, the knee signifies the fear of the death of the ego or fear of change or movement. One's ability to change is the ability to move, which depends on getting needs met and thereby being grounded. The quest of the energy of the knee is to find out who you are, which can become the resolution of the issue. Fear of change is the ego holding on to the fear of the death of the ego. In fact, the knees shake and tremble in a situation wrought with great fear. The rocking of the knees can symbolize terror, the fear of letting go of the ego mechanism.

Knee problems may arise from two types of issues:

1. Chronic tendon stress pulling the patella from top and bottom
2. Force of gravity and energy flow blockage resulting from an unaligned knee, locked knee (hyperextended), or rotation of ankle, knee, or pelvis inward or outward.

The hyperextended knee reflects the difficulty in moving from one experience to another. The locked knee represents a locked psyche. This knee position remains popular in Western culture as part of the "Great Western Bow," which is the knees locked, pelvis out, shoulders back with the head forward in a frantic attempt to balance the misalignment. A typical example of a locked-kneed heritage stems from a child frustrated by his parents' rigid, puritanical value system. Slowly, the residual tension brought by frustration develops blocks and, entirely unnoticed by the child, transforms his body into an unmoving, inflexible, and unresponsive replica of his parents; the knees are only a part. This fear of change, to upset the holding of energy, rests in the fragility of the patella, which becomes the "weakness of the knees."

Terror and fear are the glue of the locked knee because if the knee goes, "You don't have a leg to stand on." Surrender is symbolic of the death of the ego as exemplified by a person on her knees in prayer.[117] Getting down on your knees could be a humiliating experience or show submission, for instance, in the presence of a king.

Procrastination is a knee issue. It reflects in the difficulty to take charge of or to take action or change. It becomes rather difficult for psychological growth or movement to occur with such an emanation. Psychologically, the accompanying hyperextension inhibits the flow of energies.

The locked knee can be symbolic of someone who rigidly stands their ground. They want to hang on and not give up. Their position matters, and you are not going to easily change their mind.[118]

In Chinese medicine, the knees are related to the kidneys, which relate to the water element, the sex organs, fear, and vitality.

LOWER LEG

- movement toward goals
- fear of taking action

As the controller of the foot, the lower leg reflects on how the foot rests on the ground. Our lower legs allow an action to occur or inhibit the energy. Pulling in or out of the gastrocnemius muscle, along with pulls up or down, reflect different physical defense adjustment mechanisms, which, like all such mechanisms, allow for the psychological and physical survival of the individual. Charges of energy over time result in enlarged or contracted body parts.

In a psychological sense, the patterns restricting action and energy in this area reflect the fear of taking action. Procrastination occurs in two ways: passive and assertive. The passive model or the reactive response to oneself and the environment is not to do what everyone needs to do to move forward in life. This putting off of action, whether for need fulfillment or inner nourishment, is stimulated by the fear of "not getting it" or "it not being there." In the assertive model, one overcompensates by doing what he was afraid "to do."

ANKLE

- balance
- pride and self-satisfaction

The ankle connects the understanding of the foot with the drive and action of the lower leg. This ball-and-socket joint reflects feelings of pride and self-satisfaction.[119] The balance of the entire body rests upon the position of the ankle bone over the midline of the foot. An ankle off-balance to either the inside or outside creates a great strain from the irregular muscular tension necessary to keep the ankle off-center. Chronic muscular tension rigidifies the muscles and acts to inhibit the main energy flow in the body. Chronically held off-center ankles habitually present the feeling of imbalance. Uncertainty is felt about taking a step, as each new step provokes feelings of imbalance, uncertainty, and insecurity.[120] Joints are critical in the body-mind schemata. Like all joints, the ankle reflects the gracefulness in movement or lack of it that the person demonstrates in behavior. The way we move our joints is the way we move through life.

FEET

- goals of life
- grounding on the earth
- understanding, security
- contact with reality

The feet are the body's final connection to the ground. They are our contact with reality (the earth). With our feet firmly planted on the ground, we are able to "make our stand." If the root foundation was present, that is, if satisfying early nurturing occurred, the feet would be straight out and secure (barring genetic and congenital effects), and the person would have a great "understanding." If early needs are satisfied, the ability to be oneself will be easy.

As the "sacred connection" to the ground, the feet reflect many aspects of the personality in their physical form. The feet form the basis or platform for the structure of the body, which is why structural problems with the body are sometimes identified as stemming from problems in the feet. This is why feet as the negative pole (the head as the positive electromagnetic pole) are so important. The feet can be soft and flexible, allowing the free flow of energy. They can also be "bound up" with psychological trauma, or perhaps the feet can have a passive (limp) or rigid (hard) reaction to trauma. Kurtz and Prestera likened the rigidity found in the foot as a reflection of the rigidity found in the body.

According to the Arica system, the fear in the feet came from the fear of being oneself, standing on one's own two feet, or reaching one's goal in life. In the parent-child relationship, the fear is translated into the unconscious expectation of being undermined.[121] The parent who gives negative information or feedback to the child about the child and the world provides little support for the child's psychological growth and, in fact, "undermines" the child. The child may hear, "No, you can't help wash the dishes; you'll probably break one." The child may react internally with, "I'm not good enough," or "They don't love me." And the child wonders and fantasizes about what is wrong with him or herself. The result is the flexor muscle on the plantar surface of the foot grabbing onto the ground as if to say, "I know who I am." The foot clutches onto the earth for security, grabbing onto the ground for the nurturing never fulfilled in infancy. It becomes the clutching foot holding onto the world, frightened and insecure.

The squeezing of the foot is also reflected in the clutching body and personality style. The body-mind compensates with thighs that look quite overdeveloped with a tendency to over-rationalize and use self-control to overcome feelings of needing stability to balance with the earth.[122]

The feet portray our "understanding" of our relationship to ourselves and the environment. Rolf insisted that demands placed upon the arch were instrumental to its formation. The arch forms when a person starts walking by the peroneal muscles of the lower leg. Everyone is born with flat feet and formless lower legs. The person's psychological and physical response to the environment builds an arch and puts shape into the lower leg. To Kurtz and Prestera, a flat foot or collapsed arch was related to a collapse in the entire structure, while the high, rigid arch came from a person's difficulty in being grounded so that they are not in contact with the ground.

The foot reflexology chart (Figure 46) displays the traditional Asian notion of how the soles of the feet reflect the functioning of different body parts. Energy flows out through the feet, and all the nervous and meridian connections end in the feet. Feet are a homunculus through which the body's entire physiology can be diagnosed.

The feet shape themselves along the lines of energy flowing through the entire body. The shape of the foot can usually, by itself, be an indicator of personality. Foot shapes generally agree with the design of other body parts. Yet, an entire body reading is necessary prior to formulating a psychological body history due to the human body variations. Energy flows change from trauma, especially in developmental stages, which tends to change the configuration of the tissue in the appropriate (to the tissue) body part or section.

The following selection of psychologically influenced physical variations of foot shapes is a composite from Dychtwald, Kurtz and Prestera, and from Green.

1. Healthy foot: A healthy foot reflects a balanced personality. The person has a balanced footing from a stable, three-point contact with the earth (Figure 41). This well-grounded contact allows for the free flow of energy through the biosystem. The footing stability shows a sense of personal security and the ability to stand firm in the situation. A healthy, three-point contact goes along with a good understanding.

2. Flat feet: An infant has flat feet, claims Ida Rolf, and develops arches out of the body-mind interaction with the environment.

Sometimes, the child is not allowed to develop a good footing in life. The flat foot may be partially related to Lowen's masochistic character structure, whose central tendency is submissiveness. The picture of the burdened, flat-footed individual has been characterized by Dychtwald as surrendered, passive, and constantly sliding along through life. This individual tends to have a deflated self-image with a face tilted forward and down, perhaps with extreme abdominal tension and a developing hump on the upper back, which shows unexpressed anger in tissue. In allowing for the body to maintain some semblance of alignment, the back, as noted, may have some built-up tissue, as well as the back of the neck and head.[123] The shuffling or sliding along of the feet shows as a sliding along in life, which indicates a difficulty of staying in a relationship. The geomagnetic energy does not flow freely upward, energizing the arch of the peroneals. Other personality characteristics include being easily persuaded and being very gullible.[124]

3. Clutching feet: The feet appear as though they were holding on to the earth for dear life. Developmentally, the individual did not have adequate maternal care or support. The foot reflects the squeezing in or clutching of the whole body and psyche by attempting to hold on to the earth for stability and self-support.[125]

   Often, the thighs overdevelop with adipose or fatty tissue insulating the body-mind from any thought that would detract from the thigh's function of strength. The fat tissue symbolizes rationalizing thoughts and an emphasis on self-control, which is usually never achieved. The clutched foot has a physical imbalance, giving it a floating effect, as shown in Figure 41, making it impossible to find a firm physical balance. This situation leaves the psyche in a continual state of physical imbalance and emotional insecurity.

This tension, which could relate to early unresolved emotional issues, motivates the person to try to prove himself. Physically, the tension pulls on the muscles at the rear of the body, particularly at the back of the legs (hamstrings—the psychological muscle of control) or lower back, which points to a significant issue needing self-protecting (in order not to be hurt) by holding on to survive.[126]

4. Heel-digging feet: They walk with a chronic sense of determination. Arduous walking places the body directly over the heels. Psychologically, this person experiences issues of fear and instability, which they compensate for with feelings of control and determination.[127]

5. Floating or unbalanced feet (floating balance): From the illustration in Figure 41, the common problem of the high pathological need for outside controls (with the actual need for inner understanding and control) can be easily seen as a physical entity but hard to comprehend as a psychological issue due to the over-ability to control for overcompensation. Rather than using the three-point contact, the foot evolves a two-point contact and balance on the middle of the front and rear foot. Often, the front has the more developed callus, and the toes, sometimes curled, are charged with residual tension. This presents a precarious situation because balance is never possible for any length of time. An unbalanced footing adds instability to the psychological self because of the physical impossibility of the situation. A physical imbalance puts stress on the psychological balance. This lack of balance heightens the sense of insecurity. How can someone feel very secure when his very balance to the earth or gravity (which is one's

relationship to reality) is continually back and forth, balanced and unbalanced? It's moving physically and psychologically.

A hardened skin callus on the middle of the front foot pad and on the middle of the heel form the hallmark of this foot. Often, this floating balance accompanies the clutching foot. To clutch with genuine anxiety over basic survival can leave one to wonder where they fit into the world.

6. Rigid high arch: This foot type is also known as the assertive foot. A person with this foot type may have an overly inflated self-ego, and poor contact with the earth is symbolic of their poor connection with reality. The tendency is to be head-oriented, stepping lightly, living out ideation of how the world is supposed to be. Rigid feet may exemplify the Bioenergetic classification of "Rigidity," which may be concomitance with a persistent straight spine and often a psychological overcompensation manifesting intellectual curiosity and academic achievement.

7. Tiptoers: These people are virtually out of contact with reality. The tiptoer floats along in dreamland. Walking on the toes with little weight on the heels, this person may tend to be so out of contact with the world as to be psychotic. However, this person could also have great artistic and imaginative talent. Walking on the toes expresses an uncomfortableness with reality (the earth). The mental center dominates the physical center, keeping the person in the clouds.

8. Lead feet or thundering step: Imagine sitting peacefully, then feeling the ground or floor tremble, and you feel the vibrations that seem like a herd of buffalo. But a quick glance up shows no wild animals, only a determined person. This individual is so weighted down that it is as though he is fearful of losing his relationship with the earth (reality). This loud-walking person

is very determined about what they want and maintains an unbending approach to preserving the stability of what they think they should have.

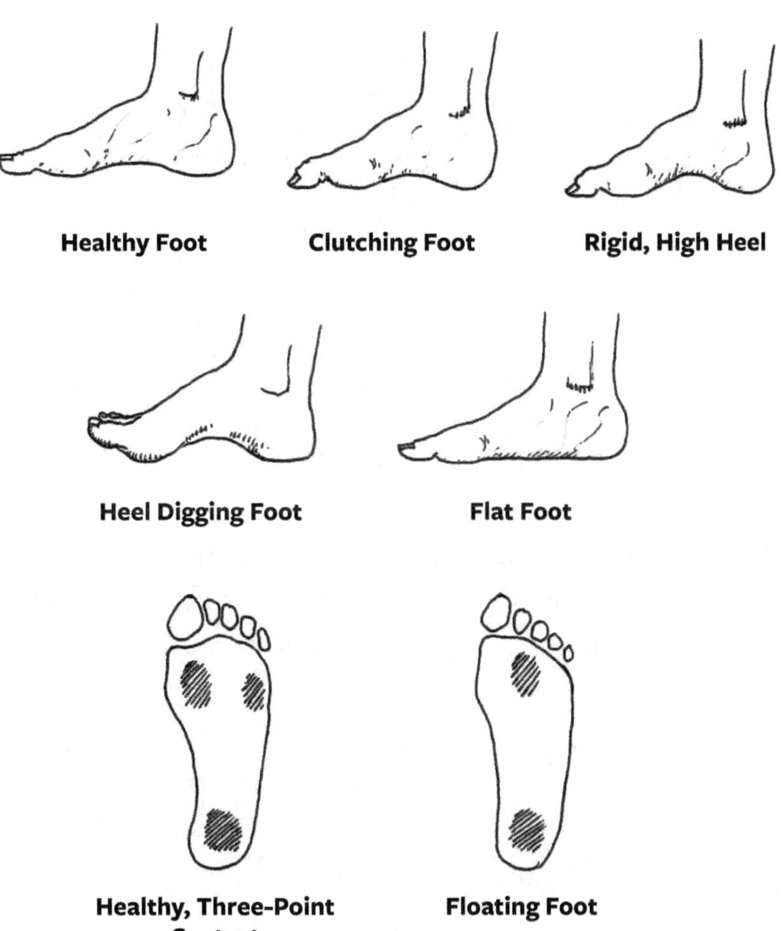

Figure 41: Foot Types

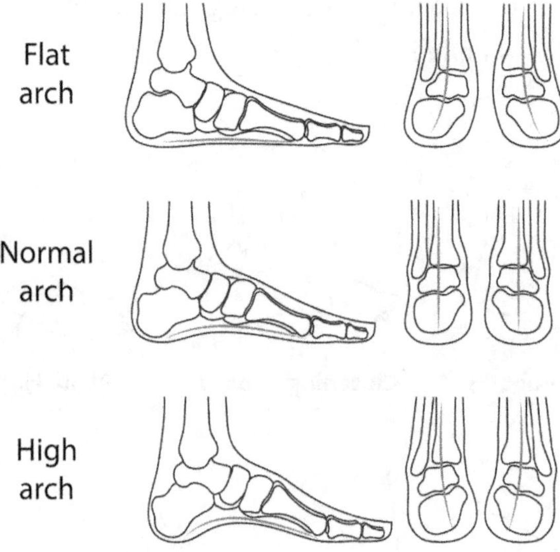

Figure 42: Foot Arch Types

It should be pointed out that the arch is in a normal range, according to science, whether the arch is flat, high, or in between. The main difference is the tendency to get ailments due to use or overuse.

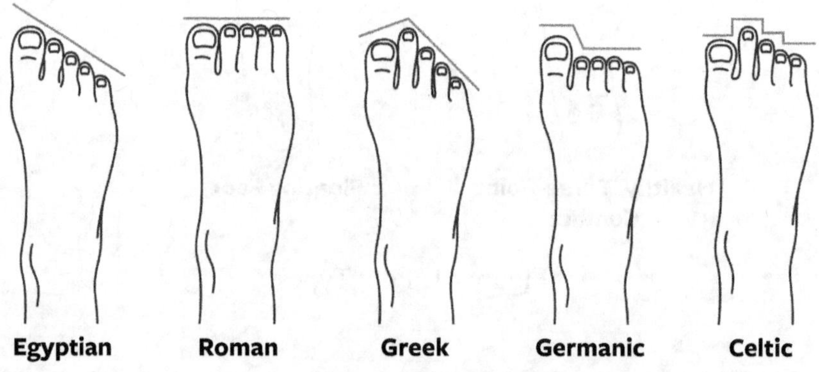

Figure 43: Foot Shape Ancestry

Other classifications of the foot and toes include the Egyptian, Roman, Greek, Germanic, Celtic, Peasant, and Aboriginal. The feet type is based on their appearance, but the personality characteristics are from traditions or assumptions and not scientifically based, although interesting.

1. Egyptian feet have toes at a 45-degree angle and are the most common; taller and narrower. They tend to belong to people who enjoy a private life, perhaps moody with a royal air and want extra pampering. They are also friendly and have an eye for aesthetics.
2. Roman feet have the first three toes that are the same length and a common foot for about 20 to 25 percent of people. They are social with people but can be arrogant; well balanced with proportional body shapes.
3. Greek feet have a second toe that is longer than the big toe. They are also called flame feet or fire feet (or Morton's toe), as these people are energetic, athletic, creative, artistic, highly motivating, encouraging, impulsive, and fun but do stress out.
4. German feet are square with a long big toe, and the other toes are the same size. They tend to show devotion, forgiveness, and compassion.
5. Celtic feet are the most complex. They are thought to reflect a powerful dynamic personality.
6. Peasant (square or European) feet have all toes the same length with a square appearance. These people are balanced in decision-making as they want to look at both sides; pragmatic and honest.
7. Aboriginal feet are rare, with the second and third toes larger than the big toe.

The Polarity Therapy movement formulated by Randolph Stone contained a theory of energy that postulated an electromagnetic flow up and down the body. This electrical current across the skin can be measured by a galvanic skin response (GSR) meter and represents the empirical basis for electromagnetic vibrations and the associated color of auras or our natural-emitting electromagnetic energy, as shown in Kirlian photography. This energy flows up and down the body, predominantly escaping through the feet, hands, eyes, and head. The energy finally releases its final residue from its trail of biological electrochemical reactions out of the feet. The feet and toes are the last depositories of the residual tension that is repressed and unreleasable. According to Stone, the feet and toes reflect the personality.

Feet tell the tales of body life. Every body part that had a lack of balance resulted in tissue changes in the feet and ankles.[128]

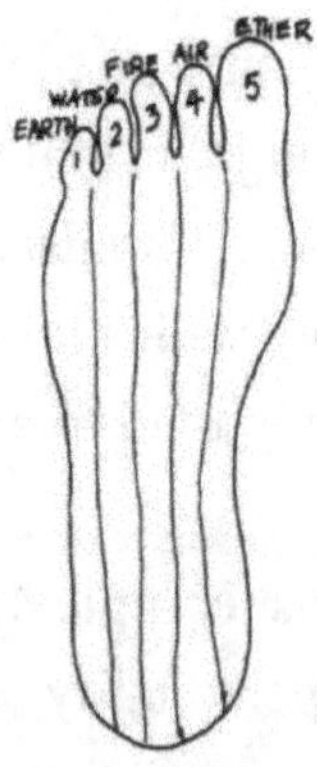

Figure 44: Polarity Therapy – Feet and Toes
(Reprinted by permission of the publisher)

The foot chart of Polarity Therapy is basically the same with reversed numbering as that of Reflexology or Zone Theory.[129] Polarity Therapy's five elements—earth, water, fire, air, and ether—come from a mix of the Chinese five element theory and the ancient Greek and Egyptian theories of essences.[130] The Western five element theory was passed on in occult, underground, alchemy, and Freemasonry social organizations.[131]

TOES

- homunculus
- energetic reflection of personality

The system of toe diagnosis developed by Stone may at first appear unusual. However, the author's experience has shown the system to be seemingly accurate for personality diagnosis. The Polarity Therapy method relates one of the five Western elements to each toe and the corresponding foot area, which is very similar to Zone Therapy. The Eastern theory of acupuncture and the Chinese five element theory are also related in the toe descriptions, although they have some differing relationships to body functioning.

1. Little toe: The little toe represents the earth element or root chakra. The earth's functions are excretion and reproduction by the actions of giving out and letting in. It shows the condition of the rectum. Stone found that the energy prana was a current going downward that had an effect on the rectum, bladder, and elimination. Relatedly in acupuncture, the bladder meridian ends in the little toe; however, Eastern theory assigns the water element and the emotional pole of fear.[132] In Polarity Therapy, the psychological meaning has more to do with life and life energy. The toe reflects how one cares for his life in diet, exercise, living space, career, and relationships.[133]

2. Second toe: This toe was assigned the water element, which deals with the emotions and feelings of the pelvis. The pelvis is both emotionally generative and creative and is thought of as the prana of creative functions.[134] In Polarity Therapy, the genitourinary organs are functionally reflected. In acupuncture theory, this toe is the end of the gallbladder meridian with an element of wood and an emotion of anger.

3. Middle toe: The element of fire reflects in the physiology of the middle toe. Contained in the abdomen, the fire element psychologically means action, vitality, or the spark of life with which one puts oneself out in the world to receive power and demonstrate action. Stone recognized the functions of the abdomen, digestion, and assimilation as the prana of the fire of digestion working on the abdomen and the caloric energy.[135]

4. Fourth toe: The element of air reflects the desires and passion of the chest. Stone identified this as the chest that reaches out with heart, touch, and circulation. The lung and chest function to circulate what Stone called the prana as the energy in the air. The stomach meridian in Asian/Oriental theory ends in the third and fourth toes and has the earth as the element and sympathy as the emotion.

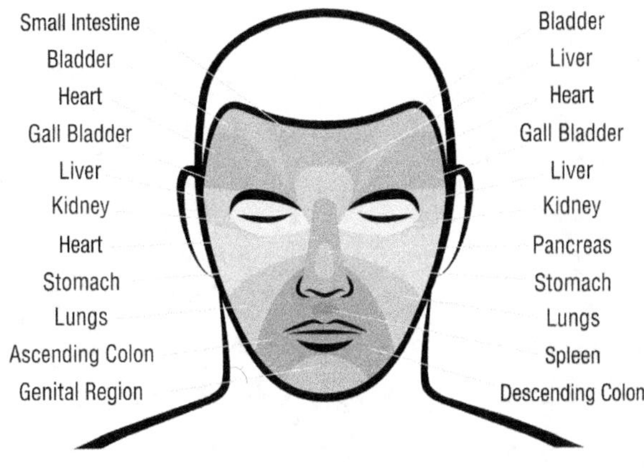

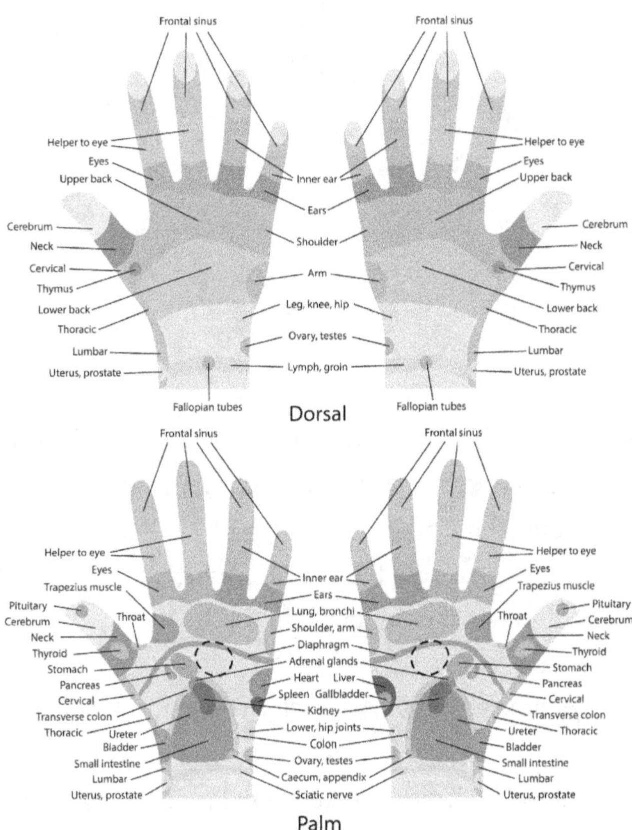

Figure 45: Zone Chart for Reflexology

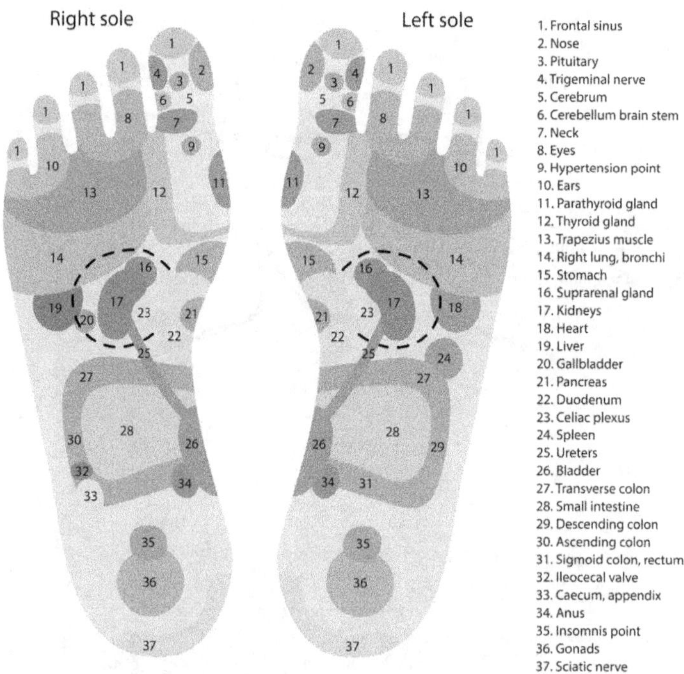

Figure 46: Foot Reflexology Chart

5. 5. Big toe: The largest of the toes has the element of ether, which, psychologically, stands for communication and discrimination in relationships. The head and neck are the areas that the prana, as the sound ether, passes through.[136] Both the spleen and liver meridians transverse the big toe. Earth is the symbol for the spleen, and wood is the element for the liver.[137]

Other toe characteristics from Polarity Therapy include:

1. Straight toes: These represent a balanced body-mind system.
2. Crossed toes: One toe partially or fully covering another shows the crossing toe as dominant with influence over the other. An

example would be the water toe over the fire toe, meaning that water (emotions) drowns out fire (passion).

3. Toe split: An open space between the toes means a split between the appropriate elements. For example, a fire and air toe split on the left (female, receptive side) would denote the split or separation between desires (air) and not letting the need be satisfied or not allowing the need to be known (fire). The right male side is active (rather than receptive), making the split between the desire and giving it out or letting it be known (air) and having the desire satisfied (fire).

4. Bending toes: Toes can bend toward other toes, which attracts the lesser dominant toe.

5. Enlarged top of toe: A ball or heaviness at the top of the toe represents an energy flow block in the head area. With the fire toe (middle toe) as the example, the significance would be that the person thinks a lot about desires but does little to manifest them. Toes without the enlargements show a person who has better contact with his desires and can actualize their satisfaction.

The lower parts of the toe, as shown in Figure 46, represent the neck and shoulders. An enlargement in one of these areas shows a body-mind difficulty in the corresponding area of the body and mind.

The theory relating to toe psychology is that the bioenergy travels down the body and escapes through the toes and feet. Energy also travels up and out the head, face, arms, and hands. The unreleased residual tension or blocked energy deposits in the feet and toes form crystals. The toes' positions in relation to each other and the configuration of each toe relate to the quality of energy flowing out on, in essence, the "person-ality."

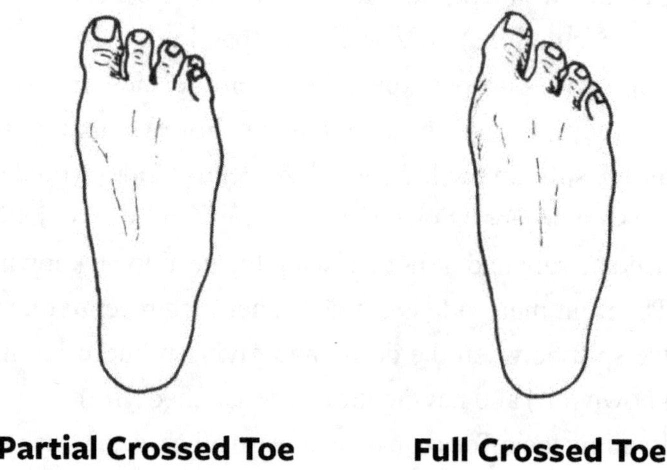

Figure 47: Partial Crossed Toes

CHAPTER 6
Body Splits

SOMETIMES, THE SHAPE OF THE BODY looks odd, as if it has two different shapes put together as one. The term *dysplasia* means a disproportion of body parts, and the term *dysmorphia* means a malformation or abnormality of shape, and both are relevant in discussing what is known as body splits. When one's body seems disproportionate to the person, the worry, stress, and activities to mitigate the perceived body-shape problem can become a psychological dysmorphia. The body shapes relating especially to the top-bottom splits can have a variation of a somatotype with genetics, psychological stress, and trauma as causal agents. Powerful social pressures may result in psychological trauma or stress accompanying an unusual appearance. The body can become even more morphed out through the process of chronic or complex stress, emotional repression, and habitual body positioning with tissue adaptation primarily involving trauma, inflammation, and induration, creating a type of psychophysical tissue dysmorphia.

The body splits, tissue or anatomical dysmorphia, involve the main body sections, including the three centers of sensation, emotion, and thinking; the conscious and unconscious; and the being, doing, and moving in life. All people have some issues in their lives, and the body splits occur to the extent they are present and habitual. We all have some, if not all, of these body splits going on to some degree. The body splits represent in tissue the conceptual image of psychological issues.

Dychtwald, Kurtz and Prestera, and others, identified significant body-mind splits, including the left-right, top-bottom, front-back, head-body, and torso-limbs. One part of the body split cannot exist without the other, just as the mind does not exist in human form without the body. These splits go together to form body types, which are also investigated.

TOP-BOTTOM SPLIT

- bottom heavy: nurturing, female, grounding
- top heavy: doing, male, creating

Top-bottom splits are primarily visible in individuals with bottom-heavy (endo-ectomorph or meso-ectomorph) or bottom-light body subtypes (ecto-mesomorph or ecto-endomorph) (see Chapter 7 on body types). The top-heavy/bottom light can be seen as a variation with the thick forming at the top, which is set on the bottom part, spawning a thin body (pelvis and legs). The different appearances of the tops and bottoms become more visible through the psychophysical process of trauma or stress, emotional repression, tissue adaptation involving inflammation and induration, and finally, anatomical dysmorphia.

The thin top of the body and either the muscular or thick lower body initiates the bottom-heavy/top-light body split, which tends to become more visible over time due to psychological factors.

Body proportions begin to look significantly like stemming from two different people when the individual's inactivity or health condition contributes layers of fat or muscle and visual bulk to the heavier segment of the body. Thin sections tend not to grow, unlike the thicker sections.

Additional growth allows for the physical center or belly-mind and the emotional center or heart-mind (possibly the head-mind) to somehow come into conflict. Energy is cut off from either the top or the bottom. Typically, an image comes to mind of a big, burly-chested man with little, thin legs and buttocks, or a woman with big hips and little, tiny shoulders.

The bottom half of the body represents contact with the earth as it makes physical contact through the legs. The belly-mind (physical center) consciousness seeks nourishment. It cares about survival, sex, and eating. The physical center keeps the flow of the vital force moving. Here resides the Mother Earth principle of grounding, stabilizing, supporting, and balancing the body.[138]

The top half signifies the doing in life: expressing, breathing, and extending the heart into social situations. Tops represent the male element. Mouths, sensory organs, and the brain do the speaking, thinking, and sensing of the environment. Top-half dominance or top-heavy types can be pictured as the man with a large barrel chest that rests on skinny buttocks and legs. Chests are overcharged from the social need to deal with issues of the heart and, to a more limited extent, the head, where physical issues are not so important. The growth period did not lack physical necessities; instead, the emotional interactions brought out a reaction to hide the heart, forming a large cage with ribs as pillars to protect the hurting, perhaps rejected, heart.

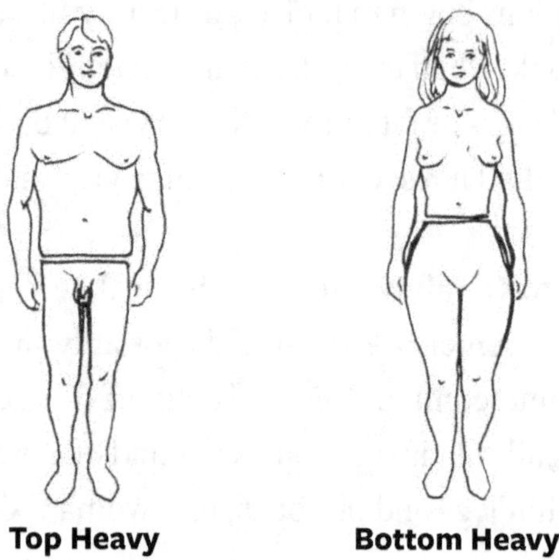

Figure 48: Top-Bottom Split

The reaction was assertive rather than introverted, as in the collapsed or constricted chest type. The less-mature lower body lacks the female principle that allows the male principle, which is oriented to the external, to dominate. Perhaps this vacuum of one essential element reflects in top-heavy men tending to form relationships with bottom-heavy women.[139] One balances out what the other lacks. Small bottoms show the energy flowing upward, providing ample charge for developing the higher center's assertive qualities but without the necessary downward flow of energy. Energy was trapped somehow in the chest. Possibly from a tightness in the lower abdomen, which gave the head added control over the sexual charge. This outward social being, not having tasted sufficient downward energy, cannot fully have a sense of grounding or connection to the world. Instead, without a sense of place, the charge brings out a lack of support and contact with the earth (reality).[140] This person tends to lose touch with their internal needs and work themselves to death.

The bottom dominance or bottom-heavy type can be pictured as the woman with large maternal hips with little shoulders and breasts.

Lower, grounding, stabilizing parts of the body and the personality have "filled out." This person knows what they want physically and nutritionally as they are finely tuned to the belly-mind and have a keen sense of "gut awareness" for other people and the environment.

Underdeveloped tops represent a lack of growth from a lack of charge, as the energy is locked in its upward flow. Undercharging produces a contraction of the communication and socialization aspects of behavior, creating inertia or the feeling of not having the ability to do anything.[141] Needs for privacy and introspection are felt, which becomes psychosocially oriented toward needing support and emotional stability.[142] Our belly is the connection to the umbilical cord, which, psychologically, is severed; thus, the person forever longs for someone to take care of them. Development of extra flab in women may reflect sexual repression by protecting the area and making it unattractive to ward off potential lovers.

HEAD-BODY SPLIT

- head: intellect, insensitive, orientation to the environment (syntony)
- body: emotion and sensation, overly sensitive, nourishment issues

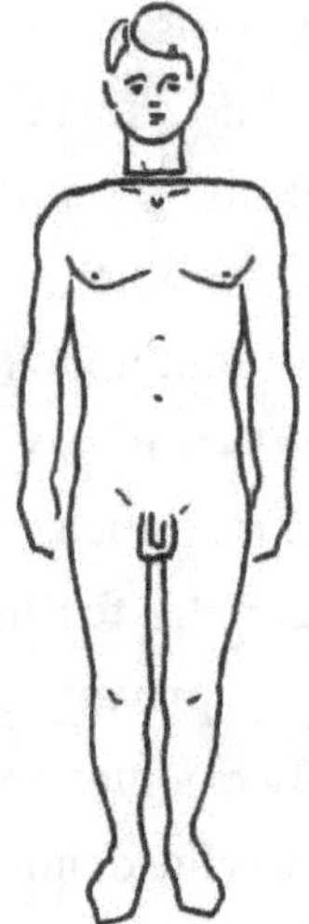

Head-Body Split

Figure 49: Head-Body Split

Heads are the center of intellect, and the body has centers of emotions and physical sensations. Issues of the head can overrule the needs of the body. Conflict takes place in the neck, which is the battleground between the thoughts of the head and the emotions of the heart. Tightening in the throat can be caused when the heart feels pushed by the intellect to say things that are not true or difficult to say out of fear of rejection or some consequence.[143] Their head may appear too small or large or otherwise fragmented from the body, looking like it is resting on the wrong body. Tension manifests in the neck and produces rigidity. In some cases, the author has witnessed large globules of tissue on either side of the neck, which looks, in miniature form, like the steel rod of Frankenstein's monster or like screws holding the head on.

This split represents the classic body-mind separation. Thoughts are devoid of the evil of passion, and reason is uncluttered by the needs of the flesh. However, head dominance can also show reason with little sensitivity to intuition, which itself may be a vibrational sense detected through the emotions. In fact, Presman reviewed scientific evidence that showed that the thalamus and hypothalamus are directly affected by magnetic fields, which are the energy we feel as vibrations.

The face remains undressed and open to the world to see, so we try to "put our best face forward" in presenting ourselves. A face usually shows the personality in a microcosmic manner. A split in the neck can literally be "a pain in the neck." All the tension in the body from emotion and sensation attempts to dress itself up to hide for protection. Hiding the body, which is to hide passion and sensation, reflects in the tension of the fascial muscles and the drawing back of the eyes in an attempt to pull back and hide in the orbital sockets. Heads will demand control, but the heart and tan tien (physical center), not cut off from the earth's energy (reality), disagree. A head is not capable of taking on both the heart-mind and belly-mind when the chest and pelvis agree on an issue. Control may go to the neck, where the head can demand control and perhaps cut off energy flow. Excess residual tension may form globules on either side of the cervical vertebrae, which signifies which aspect, assertive or receptive, is blocking more energy.

Heads may be held forward, seemingly trying to "get ahead" of the body, as it were.

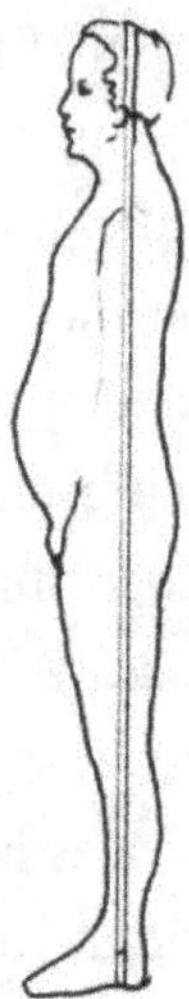

Front-Back Split

Figure 50: Front-Back Split

FRONT-BACK SPLIT

- front: social, out front, intellectual, conscious
- back: unconscious, repressed memories, hidden issues

The front of the body forms over time as our "front" in life. The front is shaped as the persona's facade or what we put "up front" to show the world. This is, in a sense, what we want the world to see. It is the self shown in the social arena, the conscious self, and the one we use to form our conscious self-image. A soft front resembles a smooth, receptive approach to life or to the social environment. A hard, rigid front is grown to defend the self from the abuses of the world and functions with a blunt but somehow restrained and rigid attitude.

The backside of the body is the unconscious. It is the place where the consciousness dumps unwanted thoughts and feelings. Backbone areas become the "garbage pail" or depository of much unleashed emotion or residual tension. The backside contains the repressed emotions and thoughts encapsulated in negative or painful experiences.[144] Degrees of tension in the back reflect the degree of openness of the unconscious. A hard back maintains tension to keep memories repressed.

A difference in the quality and degree of softness, skin texture, muscle tone, and tension of the front and back depicts the amount of a front-back split. As the body usually is not symmetrical, we have all the body splits to some degree, just as we are all in conflict with head, heart, and pelvis issues, conscious and unconscious representations, and trouble being ourselves in a world that demands movement and doing.

Right-Left Split (right-dominate: assertive / left-dominate: receptive): This very common split runs down the middle of the body. The opposite brain hemisphere connects and largely influences each side. Aston and photographers insist that bodies are asymmetrical. The right-left split occurs as an overdevelopment of one side, usually at the expense of the physical matter of the opposite. Most people have one slightly more developed side, reflecting a greater abundance of those characteristics in the personality. Kahn thought that over 90 percent of people exhibited more of a developed face on the right side than on the left. The right-left split characteristic for the dominant side includes:

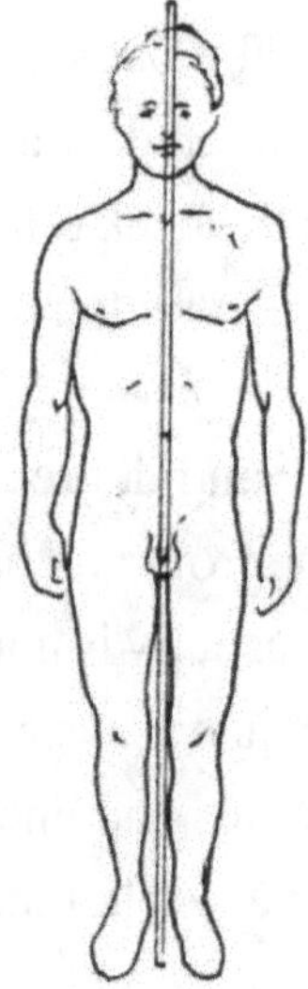

Right-Left Split

Figure 51: Right-Left Split

A. Right side: masculine, assertive, yang (created force) focused energy

B. Left side: feminine aspects, emotionality, passivity, creative thought, yin (receptive) diffused energy

TORSO-LIMBS SPLIT

- body: being, inner self
- arms and hands: doing, manipulating the environment
- legs and feet: moving through life
- Torso Heavy, Limbs Heavy

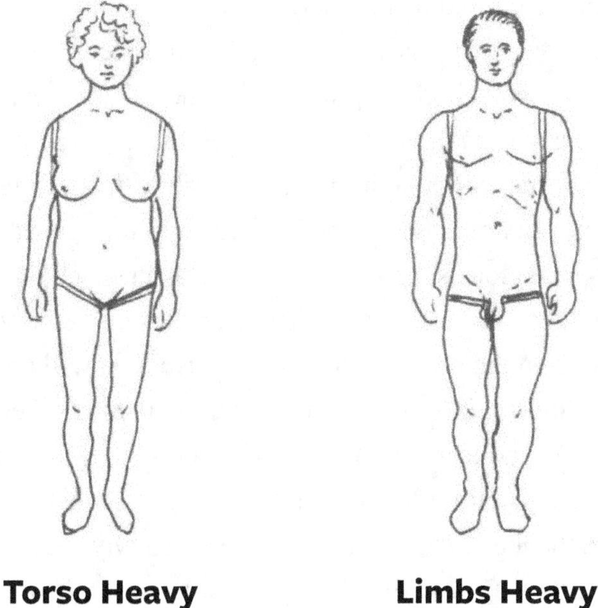

Torso Heavy **Limbs Heavy**

Figure 52: Torso-Limb Split

The torso is the body, the being, or the core of the self. Arms and hands are the doers of life, and the legs and feet move us through life. An issue here is the wish to be authentic or in tune with the inner feelings (the pure being) and the societal demands about how we do or function in life (or effectively move) according to our expectations of what life is to be.

A person with a strong torso and weak limbs has all the energies bottled up and has a fear of outward expression or doing or moving in life. The strong desire to take hold of life and run with it (the impulse from our natural need for mastery) has in opposition the conflict of a fear of the unknown or fear of the world. It is better to stay inside than to risk venturing out and "being hurt." Dychtwald said that migraine headaches are common with this type due to the bottled-up emotions and expressions. Lowen indicated that with the peripheral structures cut off by tension or holding the energy, which, according to the second law of thermodynamics, dissipates heat, the limbs become colder than the body. This results in the saying "cold hands, warm heart."

The person who has a thin torso and overdeveloped limbs becomes a "doer" and a "mover." Imagine being in a crib with uncertainty about the consistency of nourishment, perhaps fed by a time schedule rather than a biological clock schedule. The young arms reach out, grab the bottle, and hold on for dear life, even when it becomes empty, because who knows when the next selection of nourishment will appear. The installments are not in tune with the infant's natural schedule. The person holds on and learns to manipulate. In life, they become a doer and a mover. This individual uses the arms to arrange the world for survival and the legs to move through life externally value-oriented.

In the same way that the strong torso, weak limbs person was internally or "being" oriented, this type has a predominantly extrinsic locus of control; they always are "doing" to the environment. Getting in touch with the inner self or inner feelings may be difficult as the person has little time to be still and little patience for quietness.[145] The inner qualities do not mature at the expense of the overdevelopment of the appendages, and a feeling of emptiness brings out the fear of self-expression. The need for holding on to the environment becomes so strong that the limbs are over-energized at the body's or torso's expense.

CHAPTER 7
Body Types

ALL BODY TYPES ARE COMBINATIONS of the three centers or the three main types: thick, medium, and thin. Explaining how the biomatter adapted to obtain differing proportions has been progressively advanced, but we will look closer into the theories of body typing. Body types obviously have a genetic component, but the lifestyle of thoughts and feelings interfaces and renders the final product over time. Over- and under-energized areas suffer from chronic emotional, physical, and mental blocks. Energized areas with the lion's share of energy had more fuel for growth. These more developed sides tend to influence the personality and manifest increased characteristic muscle and emotional holding.

The incredible effects of gravity and the person's alignment to gravity over time slowly manifest. This is to say that someone with hunched-over shoulders with chronic feelings of depression and lack of self-worth would have the power of gravity literally pulling them down in maintaining that posture. The fascia, tendons, and ligaments, as the body's connective tissue, create structure. Over time, it forms that shape with the habituation of posture and movement in an idiopathic or personalized way.

Part of alignment involves tissue induration (hardening from within), and that process has multiple causes. It may stem from the body's method of eliminating, defusing, or containing metabolic wastes or toxic residue. Calcification is an example of the calcium buildup in the interstitial tissue (fascia) and basement membrane (blood vessels). The tissue indurates or hardens, primarily affecting flexibility and the alignment to gravity.

We talk about chronic stress from thoughts and emotions. To simplify, thinking and feeling release several substances, which results in the release of neuropeptides and hormones into the bloodstream and, hence, the lymph. The sticky (highly bonding molecules) and leftover residual chemicals and matter in the tissue (interstitial), blood, and lymph vessels then congeal and indurate over time. These physiological processes provide for the habitual standing, sitting, and movements over time to become the person's habitual holding patterns. Thus, thoughts and feelings slowly change the body. The lifestyle of thinking, feeling, sitting, standing, and moving becomes your body style. As you think and feel, you become, rings the Eternal Law of Life.

An interactive approach to body typing says that the interaction between heredity (physical constitution) and the environment creates the personality and the body type. This interactive view is espoused in the Triune Theory and the Bioenergetics of Alexander Lowen. The triune view stems from the Three Centers Theory, which states that the interaction between the three centers of the human's constitution (physical, emotional, and mental) and the social and physical environment produces body types. This view is clearly supported by others, including Lowen, Johnson, and Dychtwald.

Lowen's body typing stems from how the individual became armored during his growth through Freud's psychosexual stages, which are explored later. Johnson viewed the body's shape as stemming from our personal history of upbringing, traumas, sickness, culture, gravity, and our intention of what we want to do. Dychtwald viewed the body's shape as stemming from heredity, emotions, activity, nutrition, and environment.

Table 2: Body Types Outline

BODY TYPES OUTLINE

I. TRIUNE THEORY
    A. Physical Orientation: living, eating, being in relationships
    B. Emotional Orientation: feeling, doing, moving
    C. Intellectual Orientation: thinking, planning
    D. Composite Orientation: most people are a mix of the pure types

II. SOMATOTYPES: SHELDON
    A. Endomorphic: thick, maybe fat, enjoy life
    B. Mesomorphic: muscular, movement
    C. Ectomorphic: thin, nervous-inhibited, intellectual

III. DOSHAS: AYURVEDIC
Kapha: heavyset, calm
Pitta: decisive, forceful
Vata: thin, quick
Mixed Kapha, Pitta, and Vata

IV. BIOENERGETICS: LOWEN
    A. Schizoid: body-mind dissociation, fragmented
    B. Oral: dependent, needy

    C. Psychopathic: control

    D. Masochistic: submissive, burdened

    E. Rigid: control, rejection

V. ROLF'S BODY MODEL

VI. ASIAN PHYSIOGNOMY: GEORGE OHSAWA

    A. Mental Type: thin, frail, delicate, and reserved

    B. Wood Type: long body with broad shoulders, often meticulous and patient

    C. Earth Type: balanced body structure, flexible, adaptable, and calm

    D. Water Type: usually fat, attracted to food, the good life, jovial, and humorous

    E. Fire Type: red complexion, well-developed musculature, hot temper, and dynamic

I. TRIUNE MODEL

The Triune Theory is more fully presented in Chapter 8 on the Three Centers. This summary is used to compare with the other approaches listed.

Body Types and Characteristics within Triune Theory

    1. Physical Orientation: living, eating, being in relationships, thick, overweight

    2. Emotional Orientation: feeling, doing, moving, muscular

    3. Intellectual Orientation: thinking, planning, slender

    4. Composite Orientation: most people are a unique mixture of the three pure types

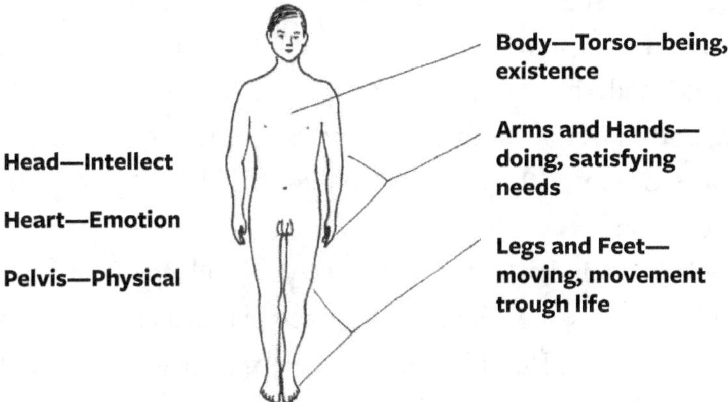

Figure 53: Triune Psychology Body Model

The Triune Psychology body model adds to the significance of the other body models by showing the relationships between the torso and limbs. A detailed description of the Three Centers Theory is in Chapter 8.

II. SOMATOTYPES

Sheldon represents a modern approach to body typing called Constitutional Psychology, in which he believed that the physical constitution influenced temperament and personality. His work was further enhanced by Carter and Heath and others. The idea of having certain body types came many years before Sheldon.

Sheldon developed a rating scale of 1 to 7 for each of the somatotypes to show how much each person had of the characteristics of the triploblastic or three germ cell layers of the endoderm, mesoderm, and ectoderm. He labeled these characteristics as endomorph, mesomorph, and ectomorph. These characteristics are based on the function of the triploblastic three germ cell layers. The endoderm develops into the digestive system and related organs, commonly called the gut, which Sheldon designated those with thick or fat bodies as endomorphs. Mesoderm grows into the bones, muscles, and circulatory system, and muscular bodies were named mesomorph. Ectoderm essentially becomes the nervous system and skin; thin people are called ectomorphs.

Sheldon concluded that the physical body and temperament were two aspects of the same thing. He based temperament and personality on these body types. He had a good amount of evidence to support his somatotype characteristics. Still, he could not meet the statistical and academic analysis of the times for the psychological aspects of temperament and personality, which left his body typing outside the gate of psychological academia. It was not that his theories were disproven, as is commonly reported, but that his model did not demonstrate the statistical analysis needed to win approval in academia at that time.

However, somatotyping continues with research in sports and physically oriented studies and classifications, without the concerns of temperament and personality, as shown by Carter and Heath and others.

The idea of making sense of the different body types can be traced back in Western culture to Hippocrates, who identified thick and thin people as susceptible to differing ailments. Historically, many people had previously developed methods of body typing.

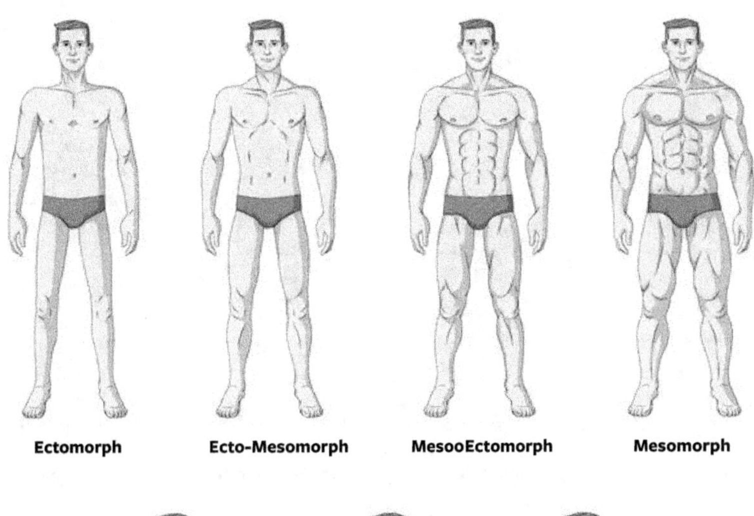

Ectomorph
Ecto-Mesomorph
MesooEctomorph
Mesomorph

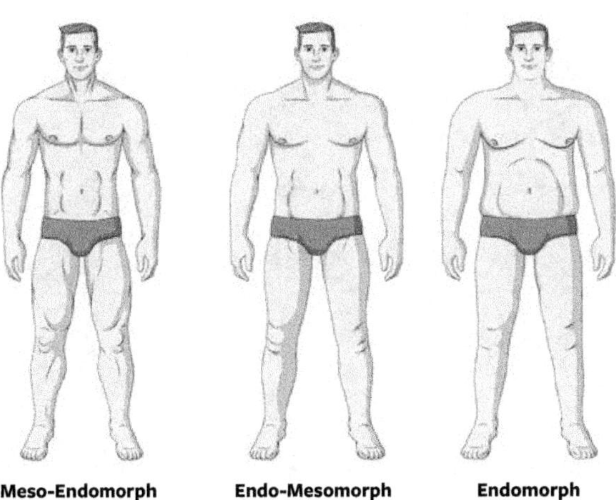

Meso-Endomorph
Endo-Mesomorph
Endomorph

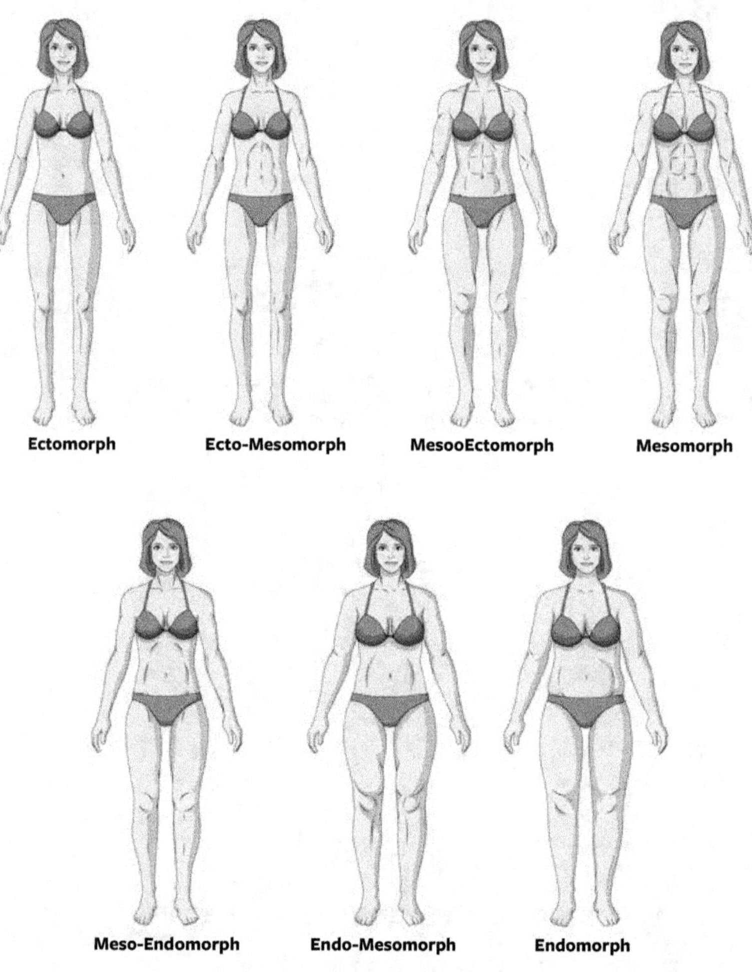

Figure 54: Somatotypes

Table 3: Somatotypes

Somatotype	Temperament	Traits
Endomorphy	Viscerotonia	Highly developed viscera: tend to be overweight, social-emotional orientation
Mesomorphy	Somatotonia	High muscular activity, action and power
Ectomorphy	Cerebrotonia	Controlled the functions of inhibition and attention of the cerebrum

Sheldon showed three types of people: overweight endomorphs, muscular mesomorphs, and slender ectomorphs. Every person has all three germ layers composing the physical makeup; thus, each individual is a mixture of the three somatotypes. Sheldon used a one-to-seven rating scale for each category, showing that each person is a composite of each somatotype. The purer types rate high on one scale and low on the others. Most people are not pure types but have some of each scale. For example, an extreme endomorph would score 711, mesomorph 171, and ectomorph 117. The average on all three might be 444.

The thick endomorph (gut); medium, muscled mesomorph (heart and vessels, muscle and bone); and thin ectomorph (nervous system, brain, skin) are part of the basis for the somatotypes or body types. As everyone has all three systems rated 1 to 7 each, a high number in any of the three indicates a predominance of that body system. It is more apparent when you look at someone to see if they are heavy and fat, medium and muscular, or skinny with a skin-and-bones appearance. But when people are a bit of each, say muscular and heavy fat, they are mesomorphic endomorphs. If part thin and part thick, they are ectomorphic endomorphs or ectomorphic mesomorphs.

There are many combinations, and Carter and Heath listed twelve different endo-meso-ectomorphic combinations plus one central classification for those who differ less than one for each (on a 1–7 scale).[146] Each of the three has a balanced type, with one type dominant (for example, endomorph) and the other two less than the dominant but equal to each other (such as mesomorph and ectomorph). There are combinations of each, such as endomorphic mesomorph or ectomorphic endomorph, making nine combinations, plus three balanced types and one central type. The three, six, nine, or twelve types and combinations have an interesting geometrical pattern that relates directly to sacred geometry.

Then there are the somatotypes considered anatomical or postural dysmorphia, where a certain part of the body appears disproportionate or out of proportion with the rest of the body. This aspect of the somatotype theory seems to explain, at least, the initial entry into the body splits of top/bottom, head/body, right/left, and front/back split. Much of the bottom-heavy split could be identified with the ectomorphic-endomorph in the somatotypes. A larger question has to do with the environmental and social effects, especially of early childhood and to the degree that social conditioning propels the developing body into anatomical or postural dysmorphia as a reaction to trauma or excessive stress, which is the rationale of theorists such as Dychtwald, Rolf, Kurtz and Prestera, and others.

The somatotypes of Sheldon are similar to the personality types in Triune Holistic Theory, as shown in Chapter 8.

III. DOSHAS – AYURVEDIC

A. Kapha: heavyset, calm

B. Pitta: decisive, forceful

C. Vata: thin, quick

D. Mixed Kapha, Pitta, and Vata

Kapha is the container for the doshas, as pitta is energy and vata is heat. The stomach is the primary site for kapha. Kapha is a heavyset body that seems calm and relaxed. Pitta is the medium body that can seem forceful, intense, or angry. Vata is a tall, thin body that can be anxious or unpredictable. As with the other models of body types, most bodies are a mixture of the purer triune types.

IV. BIOENERGETICS

The predominant body-mind-oriented school of psychology known as Bioenergetic Analysis was founded by Lowen, Pierrakos, and Walling, who were students of Wilhelm Reich.[147] Reich studied Freud's concept of libido and found it in the body and renamed it orgone, which means organismic energy or energy from the organism. Reich found that the energy or orgone became blocked in certain areas, which he mapped out. Seven areas or segments were identified where bioenergy was most likely to become blocked. The process of energy blockage was described as body armoring. The body armors or defends itself much like the ego with defense mechanisms, protecting itself against the threat of the environment. Armoring occurs in the physical area related to the psychological issue. Each thought or intent produces sufficient energy to perform the associated action.[148] Anytime the free flow of energy is inhibited, that frustrated desire or thought actually becomes residual tension, which forms with tissue, fascia, toxins, and other wastes to become energy blocks or armoring.

Lowen's body typing stems from how the individual became armored during his growth through Freud's psychosexual stages. Lowen found in Freud's psychosexual stages the keys to the development of armoring. Each body type is described as coming from the self-protective adaptation that the child makes to the environment, especially in parental interaction. Childhood adaptations manifest physically in the tissue and psychologically in thought formation and social interaction in interpersonal drama. Many of Lowen's character structures or body types relate to the issues of the body splits and body-mind parts as previously outlined.

Lowen presented a sequence that involved reaching out or attempting to gain pleasure with an inability to do so, bringing deprivation, frustration, or punishment and the resulting anxiety that evolves into a defensive reaction as a general scheme for explaining the entire context of personality problems. To Lowen, the character represented behavior patterns in which the person attempted to deal with their striving for pleasure. The character was the psychological component formed with the body's character structure in adapting to the environment. Humans have a primary orientation to go for pleasure, which is felt like the flow of energy, and to avoid pain, which is to close off and withdraw. Withdrawal causes coldness in the body by cutting off energy, while pleasure increases the body's warmth. Cutting off or inhibiting energy from the body has two forms, according to Lowen. The first is by withdrawing energy from the muscle in the form of chronic muscle contractions. Armored muscles no longer feel the inhibition and, in fact, suppress any flow of energy, which actually begets feeling. In this way, the physical shapes the person's thinking. The second inhibitory function is to cut down body metabolism by constricting the diaphragm and thus decreasing air, which lowers the energy level.

The schizoid character comes from schizophrenia and designates a body-mind split in which thinking is disoriented from feeling. Physically, the character has an uncoordinated and segmented muscular system. Lowen speaks of energy being cut off from the peripheral area of the face, hands, feet, and genitals, which looks pretty similar to the torso-limbs and head-body splits. The person develops a survival defense by withholding energy in an effort to hold the personality intact.

This fragmented type may have a definite right-left body split, which may display as a mask-like face from the head-body split and cold hands and feet from the limb-torso split. Their body is usually narrow and contracted; however, the more paranoia present, the fuller and more athletic the body becomes. An inadequate sense of self is felt due to a lack of body identification and tending to avoid intimate-feeling relationships. The cause of this character was an early maternal rejection so hostile that the infant saw it as a threat to survival and reacted with a fear of reaching out or demanding.

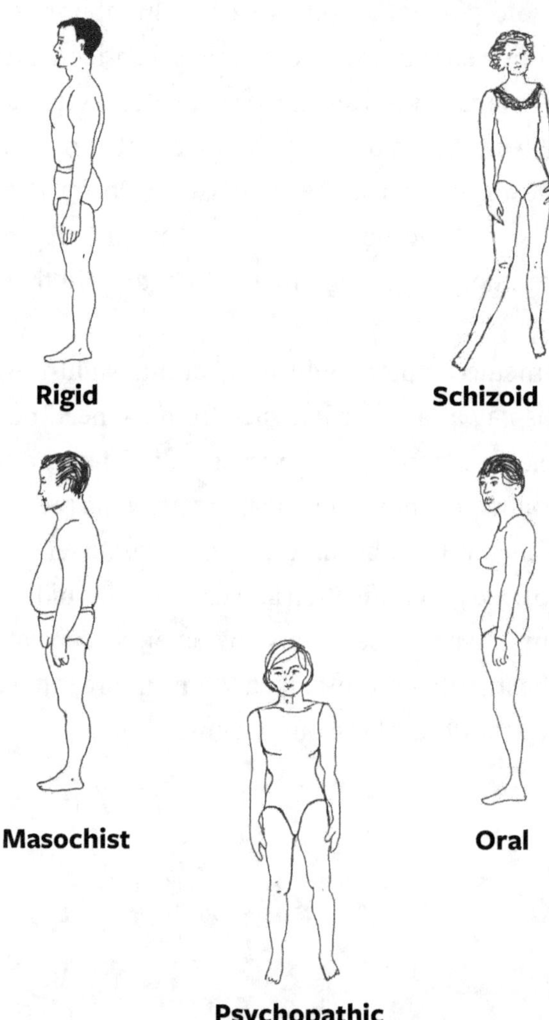

Figure 55: Bioenergetic Analysis Character Structures *(Artwork by Pam McCormick)*

The oral type is characterized by dependency, weakness, clinging to others, and passivity. The muscles are underdeveloped, and the energy flows out weakly to the periphery. Lowen saw the long, thin body developing from a delay in maturation that allows longer bone growth. This body type has been related to Sheldon's ectomorphic somatotype. This person has shallow breathing that keeps the metabolism and energy low. Psychologically, the oral type stems from a mother who was physically absent due to death, illness, or working, or who was psychologically withdrawn with her own depression. Thus, the oral either clings to others or proclaims an exalted air of independence yet is unable to be alone due to the trauma of internal emptiness.[149]

The masochist is trapped in suffering and in feeling trapped, complains and perhaps whines, yet cannot break out of their self-imposed submissive.[150] This short, thick, muscular, overdeveloped body has a pelvis pulled forward that is collapsed at the waist from its psychological burden. The head is shortened with a pulled-in appearance. The masochist type was raised by a dominant mother who let her sacrifice be known, while the submissive father remained distantly passive. Exploration or letting the child do for himself was not allowed, and the focus was on eating and excretion. Guilt feelings started for any self-assertion, and the child was forced to give up temper tantrums.

A psychopath denies feelings, especially sexual, and forms the need to control or dominate by either bullying and overpowering or seducing and undermining. By overpowering another, the person rises above, in a sense, which is reflected physically by the energy displaced to the upper half, which reduces it in the lower half. This results in a top-heavy, top-bottom split.

The second type (seductive) does not become top-heavy but usually has a hyper-flexible back. Their eyes are distrustful, and they have a high fear of being controlled. The control issue, in fact, is the cause of the problem. The child was sexually seduced (energetically rather than physically) by the opposite-sex parent and then rejected because of the parent's fear of the energy. This renders the child, who must cope with a denial of the feeling, to rationalize the denial of need.[151]

The rigid type has a stiff holding of the back. This character was due to frustration in the genital stage of development. Rigidity becomes a defense against giving in or yielding and fear of being used. This body has integrated proportions, but rigidity can be seen in movement, skin tone, and eye energy. Psychologically, the person is worldly and aggressive, as passivity is a vulnerability that cannot be tolerated. Rather than manipulate, the person will maneuver to gain the closeness desired. The person is very sensitive to the rejection of love because love is tied to pride and self-worth.

Three sub-categories of rigidity are compulsive, phallic-narcissistic, and hysteric. Compulsives include both males and females frustrated at the phallic stage and who regressed to the safer anal phase. Energy is anchored in the anus and at the top of the head, producing orderly behavior and ruminative thinking.[152] Phallic-narcissistic types are usually male with athletic, confident, and aggressive tendencies. Hysteric rigid types are usually a feminine type and are afraid of sex but have constant sex as their defense.

V. ROLF'S BODY MODEL

Ida Rolf viewed the body from a physical rather than a psychological orientation.

The Rolfer's body is a model of a stack of building blocks set to a plumbline. Rolf visualized a body that was correctly vertical in its alignment with gravity and would be without the strain from the pull of gravity. This is the model that Rolf devised with the building blocks. She developed this model from a physical approach to restructuring bodies.

Rolf displayed cephalic indices of broad-headed (dolichocephalic), middle-width (mesaticephalic), and long-headed (brachiocephalic), showing their significant correlation to endomorphic, mesomorphic, and ectomorphic somatotypes (Figure 7). The cephalic index used by Rolf has added marvel when viewed side by side with the faces from the three basic shapes: round, square, and triangle. These are, so to speak, the pure forms of shape, and most faces fit in between as oval and oblong.

VI. ASIAN PHYSIOGNOMY

Eastern philosophy, as described by George Ohsawa, tells of a method of diagnosis he called "Oriental physiognomy." From this method, Ohsawa claimed that one could diagnose a person's current symptoms and condition with an understanding of conditions in the future, as well as the embryological life of the person. Five physical and personality types are distinguished, which are on a spectrum from yin to yang.

1. Metal Type: This is the most yin type. The person has a frail constitution with a long face and head and with long, delicate hands. These people tend to have a lowered right shoulder. Personality characteristics usually manifest as shy, timid, modest, and reserved. This Asian or Eastern type seems most like Sheldon's ectomorph or Lowen's oral type.

2. Wood Type: This is less yin-oriented but still basically yin. The person has a lengthy structure with wider shoulders proportionally to the body. These people are usually characterized as meticulous in their endeavors, making them conscientious workers, and they tend to be patient with other people.

3. Earth Type: This person has an equal amount of yin and yang and is, therefore, balanced. Their structure is usually well-proportioned, and their actions are smooth and harmonious. This is a person who can adapt easily to new situations, and their flexibility in life reflects

in their more open and loose body. The earthy person is characterized as usually calm and agreeable and tends to make stable relationships.

4. Water Type: This type has more yang. The good life is an attractive goal. They love to cook and then easily become overweight. They bloat themselves from a high quantity of yin food and look even heavier than they are because their tissue tends to retain water. This person may be small but with strong bones. Characteristically round and jovial, the water type is fun, loves pleasure, and likes to tell stories and jokes. In comparison, the water type is closest to Sheldon's endomorphic and Lowen's masochistic type.

5. Fire Type: This is the most yang type. This type has a fire-red complexion with hot, red hands. The person may be small and thick but very strong with well-developed musculature. They may not have a lot of body weight. This proud person tends to be dynamic, always moving and doing, and therefore, accomplishing goals they set out for themselves. However, they can easily be angered.

The Bioenergetic model of Lowen is compared in Table 4 with the ones presented by Kurtz and Prestera, which is an adaption of Lowen's, and the models of the Triune Theory, Sheldon's somatotypes, and Asian physiognomy as described by Ohsawa. The models are arranged to best picture their similarities.

Table 4: Body-Mind Personality Types

Bioenergetics	Somatotypes	Triune Theory
Oral—depen[153]dent, needy Masochist—submissive, burdened Psychopathic—control, manipulation Rigid—control, stiff, fear of rejection Schizoid—fragmented, body-mind dissociation	Ectomorphic—thin, nervous, inhibited Endomorphic—overweight, emotional Mesomorphic—physical, muscular	Intellectual Orientation—thinking, planning Emotional Orientation—feeling, being in relationships Physical Orientation—doing, moving

Kurtz and Prestera	Body-Splits	Oriental Physiognomy
Needy type - tired slump Burdened Type—squeezed down Top or Bottom — Heavy Types Rigid Type—stiff body	Front-Back Split—conscious front vs. repressed back Head-Body Split—conscious (pseudomoral superego) head vs. instinctual body Top-Bottom Split—heart vs. abdomen issues Torso-Limb Split—moving and/or doing vs. being Right-Left Split—logical vs. intuitive	Metal Type—thin, frail and shy Water Type—over weight, cooks and eats, humorous Wood Type—long body with wide shoulders, patient Fire Type—red complexion, well-developed muscles, dynamic, hot temper Earth Type—balanced body structure, flexible, calm

CHAPTER 8
The Three Centers Theory

THE FOUNDATION OF THE EMPIRICAL BASIS of the Triune Theory of body psychology rises from its evolution according to the three centers of the brain. MacLean's Triune Brain Theory provides scientific validity for this approach. The Three Centers model is the overall conceptual network that ties human evolution to psychological functioning. Each of the three centers is analyzed to better ascertain their constitution.

PHYSICAL LIFE

The physical center forms the foundation for the other centers:
- Intellect
- Emotion
- Body

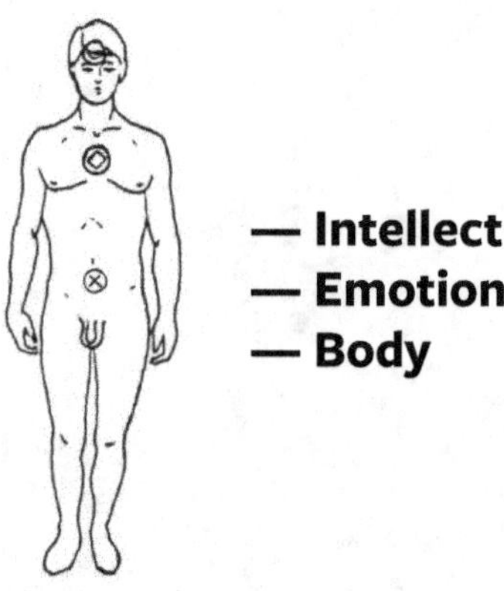

Figure 56: The Three Centers

Physical self is the initial life-force with digestion, elimination, and procreation functions. The physical or life center also compromises the old hindbrain or reptilian complex of MacLean, which assumes responsibility for all the essential survival functions. Physical self regulates all the autonomic functions, including breathing and blood flow. Mother represents early physical survival on a deep behavioral and cultural level (social and physical recapitulation). East Indian first, second, and third chakras represent life, survival, and procreation. The physical self is the primordial self.

Yet the physical self represents more than blood and tissue, survival, and mother; the gross body is symbolized as holding the body's center of gravity. Sufis call this center the kauf; the Japanese call it hara; in Aikido, the one-point; Taoists call it the tan tien; and Carlos Castaneda spoke of it as the center of the will.

Actually, the Kauf is the physical center of gravity, and it resides at the sigmoid flexure of the colon and continues to the rectum and anus. It is the survival instinct from the alimentary canal, which can be linked to the first worm.

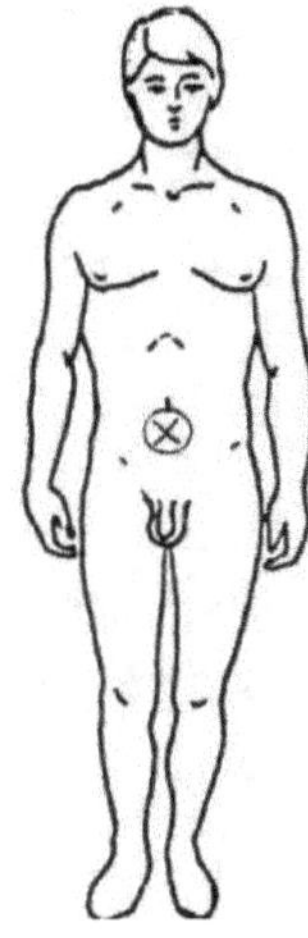

Figure 57: Physical Self

This one point is the center of the body's gravity and the space of physical consciousness. It is the physical part of each person; its life is movement, its duty action, with the instinct of conservation and the question, "How am I?"

The physical process has many parallel expressions in a fascinating variety of theories and philosophies. The Eigenwelt is the person, him or her, including the body.[154] It is the body and the body's world of needs, the part of human nature that needs to meet its own needs. The physical center is a top priority and fundamental to survival, for nothing else exists without meeting basic physical needs. Eigenwelt signifies the importance of getting one's own needs met. Concerns are on survival functions: where to eat, when to sleep, and, in essence, how to survive.

Binswanger's Three Worlds

*Eigenwelt: body-world of own needs, their satisfaction,
behavior necessary to meet needs, such as eating.*

*Milwelt: with world interested in whom I'm
with, social relations with other people.*

*Umwelt: world around being in the world, world of
understanding how it fits together, being oriented,
knowing it's okay to be here, the being*

Aikido uses the concept of the one-point to ground or orient the self to the universe.[155] Aikido movements are made possible by leading the body movement with the one-point in the same way that the Taoist follows the tan tien for exact flowing movements. Castaneda recalled that his mystical Don Juan often had him hold the area, called the center of will, to protect the self during drug experiences.

Carl Sagan connected with Freud's theory as he related MacLean's R-complex, limbic system, and neocortex to the id, ego, and superego. Freud's id, consisting of instincts from the body's biological requirements, accurately reflects the reptilian behavior of survival and selfishly satisfying one's needs. As William James put it, instincts are the "further development of reflex action and ... as forerunners of intelligence."[156] The Three Centers Theory is also ancient knowledge of both Eastern and Western cultures. The *Yoga Sutras* described by Misha speak of the cosmic forces or gunas (binding rope):

1. physical (tamas) 1. Tamoguna, force of inertia, mass-stuff, matter
2. emotional (rajas) 2. Rajoguna, electronic force, energy-stuff, motion, change

3. intellectual (sattva) 3. Satoguna, protonic force, intelligence-stuff, mind-stuff

The physical center is the creator of the human cosmic force, as seen in tamas, which is the force of inertia of matter in motion. The physical system bears the responsibility for the awareness of balance and of movement through space.

The ancient Bhagavad-Gita says it thus:

"Threefold the faith is of mankind, and springs from those three qualities, becoming "true" or "passion-stained" or "dark" as thou shalt hear!"

Plato embodies the Western root of philosophy and body-mind knowledge. In *Timaeus*, he wrote of the physical center or the abdomen as:

" …the part of the soul which desires meats and drinks and the other things of which it has need by reason of the bodily nature, they placed between the midriff and the boundary of the navel, contriving in all this region a sort of manager for the food of the body, and there they bound it down like a wild animal which was chained-up with man and must be nourished if man was to exist."[157]

Plato had a three-part gradation of soul represented by a little Kosmos in each of the centers. The spinning Kosmos were "rotary spheres" with inner (body) and outer (soul) parts that may represent the Western similarity to the yin and yang of the Eastern Tao.

Plato's Little Kosmos[158]

1. Cranium: rational (active) and immortal soul (receptive)
2. Chest: energy, courage, anger, etc.
3. Abdomen: appetite

Perhaps in another form, the Tao of each part may be:

- The Tao of Cognition: rational versus intuitive
- The Tao of Emotion: love (positive) versus hate (negative)
- The Tao of Physical: relaxation versus contraction (flexion versus extension)

Aristotle said that the "nutritive soul, the basis of all the others, the first constituent of the living individual, the implication of form with matter in a body organized as a nutritive body; the soul of digestion, nutrition, and propagation of the species."[159]
Aristotle's three-part soul appeared as:

1. Nutrient: "digestion, nutrition, and propagation of the species," plant level (soul of plants)
2. Sentient: animal level or sense, sensation (animal soul)
3. Noetic, Nous or intelligence (human soul): two-part (yin-yang); receptive intellect, "Intellectus Patiens," and active or constructive intellect, "Intellectus Agens"[160]

The famous church theologian St. Thomas Aquinas held the following position to compare:

A. "Vegetable or nutritive soul—incorporates an immaterial part, although unconscious

B. Animal soul—has an immaterial part, with consciousness
C. Intellect—purely immaterial"[161]

EMOTIONAL

The second psychological process that reflects the need to detect danger from a distance and respond quickly was named the limbic system by MacLean in his three-part brain system:

- R-complex—Physical
- Limbic system—Emotional
- Neocortex—Cognitive

This emotional, psychological system was, to MacLean, the generator of powerful emotions, best represented by love evolving at the mammalian level of recapitulation.

MacLean described the limbic system of his triune brain as the emotional mind that reacts with feelings to direct the body's responses. This emotional system and social relationships evolved hand in hand with the change from the cold-blooded reptile to the mammal. Fundamental changes at this level were based on warm-blooded physiology with the mammalian glands that provided nursing for the young and maternal caring for offspring. A rise of the emotional system some 180 million years ago was the essential physical ingredient for what Ichazo termed the relations instinct. Families made possible the basic social unit of survival.

Refined hearing, also a mammalian development, was significant in the mother-child bond with group interaction and cooperation. Parental care and family affiliations were made possible by the development of the limbic system.[162]

The emotional body, called the Oth in Sufism, has the traditional metaphysical position of the heart as its location. Scientific argument against the heart being the center of emotion was that the heart is not wired for sensation. Yet phenomenologically, the experience is of emotion in the heart. Endocrine glands secrete hormones into the bloodstream that spread into the tissue. Intellect consciously or unconsciously interprets the spreading reaction of the tissue as emotion. The heart holding this vast blood supply also holds feelings (the hormones and neuropeptides). Triune understanding of the heart or circulatory body as the emotional center is consistent with intuitive knowledge and is metaphysically believed down through the ages in Eastern and Western philosophy and religion.

The heart is the seat of the emotions, as far as our experience of it. This is why the emotional system has been referred to as the "circulatory body." The glands, the limbic system of MacLean's triune brain, and the circulatory system form the emotional center.

Emotions are the powers of passion that emote or motivate the mind and body to act.

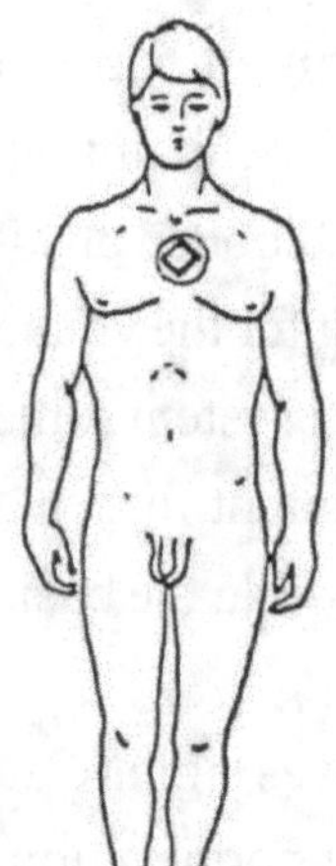

Figure 58: Emotional Center

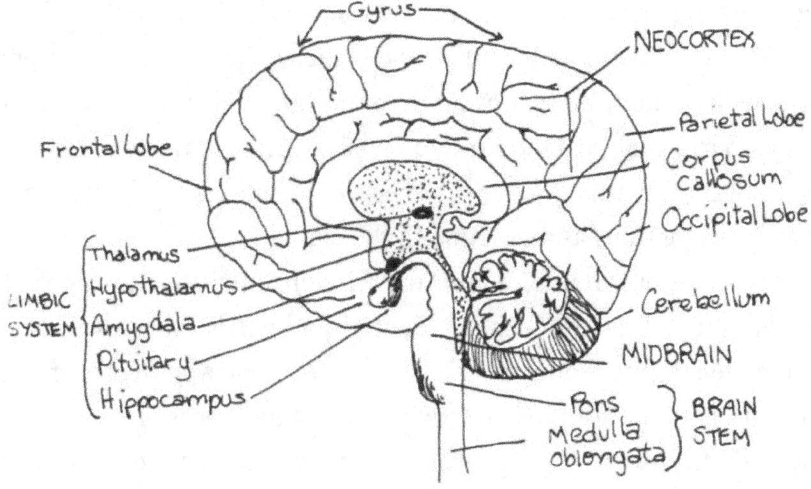

Figure 59: Limbic System

Plato, in his ancient wisdom, saw the connection of the emotion and circulatory systems, which he described as:

The heart, the knot of the veins and the foundation of the blood which races through all the limbs, was set in the place of guard, that, when the might of passion was roused by reason making proclamation of any wrong assailing them from without or being perpetuated by the desires within, quickly the whole power of feeling in the body, perceiving these commands and threats, might obey and follow through every turn and alley, and thus allow the principle of the best to have the command in all of them. But the gods, foreknowing that the palpitation of the heart in the expectation of danger and excitement of passion was caused by fire, formed and implanted as a supporter to the heart the lung. . . .[163]

Emotions are the feelings that indeed seem to be the battleground between thought and the physical or instinctual. Freud, unable to find a physical entity for thought and instinct, labeled them the superego and id. The circulatory body moves; it emotes glandular energy charged by the fourth chakra at the cardiac plexus. As a system parallel to the triune brain, the id, ego, and superego elements fit nicely, as Freud described emotions as a function of the ego.

The emotional body contains the relationship instinct, which acts as a vibrational radar of others' feelings and needs. This body-mind system detects the feeling states of others from, in a sense, the meshing of the aural bodies or electromagnetic biospheres. This form of telepathy transforms energy from one system to another, and it is a common occurrence, especially for more evolved beings who "pick up on others' vibes." The fundamental inborn question at the emotional level is, "Who am I with?"

To Binswanger, the Mitwelt was the human environment interested in social relationships with other people, or the "Who am I with?" in this world question.[164]

Physician-psychologist William Sheldon developed the idea of the interrelated personality and body type. Physique and temperament, he claimed, were two aspects of the same thing. The emotional self directly relates to Sheldon's mesomorph, who is viscerally oriented, tends to be overweight, and loves people (social relations) and comfort.

William Sheldon's somatotypes:

1. Endomorphy: heavy-fat, physical life orientation
2. Mesomorphy: muscular, emotional, and sensation orientation
3. Ectomorphy: slender, nervous system, intellectual orientation

Interestingly, Plato's concepts of a rotary Kosmos and the Tao both have sets of spinning and opposing forces for each of the three centers.

This theme can also be found in a more subtle or more refined form, further defined as the Hindu chakras. In Plato's system, the two parts of the intellect are represented as assertive (logical) and receptive (intuitive). The duality of the emotional center can be seen as love (positive) versus hate (negative). There are other conceptions for the explanation of the affective system. Rado speaks of a two-part model of welfare and emergency emotions:

WELFARE EMOTIONS:
love, joy, pride, pleasurable, desire

AFFECTS:
Emergency emotions: fear, rage, guilty fear, guilty rage

Dahl and Stengel presented an interesting
dualistic classification of emotions:

Specific (Emotions)

IT

Attraction	to	— love
	from	— surprise
Repulsion	to	— anger
	from	— fear

General (Emotions)

ME

Positive	passive	— contentment
	active	— joy
Negative	passive	— depression
	active	— anxiety

The seventeenth-century philosopher Descartes identified
six primary passions, which were:

Admiration—	Desire
Love—	Hate
Joy—	Sadness

Figure 60: Emotions

MENTAL – COGNITIVE

Cognitive systems, which Freud called the primacy of the intellect,[165] form material representation by the forebrain or neocortex. Intellectual apparatus provide the activities of thinking and memory that raise the need to think and make accurate perceptions of the world. Memory systems have the need to operate to the best of their abilities and interact with moment-to-moment conscious awareness. This is the gestalt to give what is called "an intelligent view."

The second function of the cognitive body involves orientation to one's self and the environment. This orientation represents the third instinct, syntony, which is knowing what's happening, as opposed to being out of syntony and not knowing what is happening and not knowing where to fit into the world.

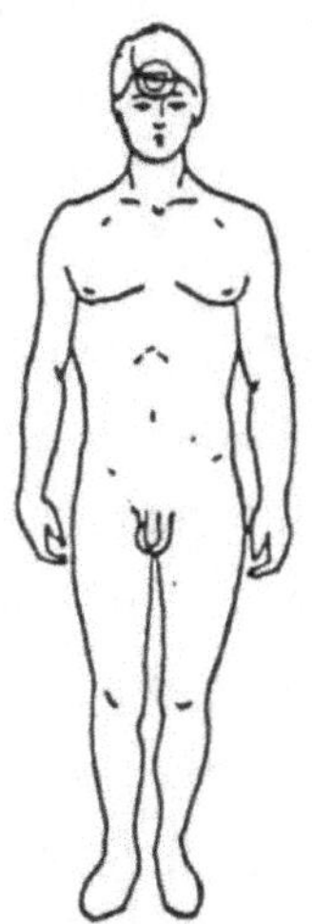

Figure 61: Intellectual Center

The orientation function is literally in the head due to the head's sensory modalities (eyes, ears, nose, taste), which act for distance orientation and perception.

Cognitive systems evolved from the emotional, just as the emotional built upon the physical center. The beast was not as vulnerable to the environment with the more highly developed cognitive system. Danger could not only be detected at a distance as with the emotional (fight-flight) system, but now impressions and experiences could be put into a bio-computer for later referencing. Animals now could "figure out" (think it out) or anticipate and plan for the future.

Functions of intellectual communication can manifest themselves in the forms of talking, gesturing, or writing. The psychophysical need to express thought is the motivator of human communication.

Unexpressed thoughts or thoughts not communicated can come out psychically through the natural processes of dreaming and hallucinating. The repressed thought or desire attached below this level of psychic expression must then be expressed in body tissue or psychosomatically. The functions of dreaming, visualizing, and hallucinating are unknown, uncharted alleys of the psyche. Freud was classically educated and seemed to relate his clients' symptoms to the characters' behavior from Shakespeare's plays and other literature. Erik Erikson suggested that Freud understood the plight of his patients' unconscious, inhibited motivations and used the characters from Shakespeare's *Hamlet* or *Oedipus Rex* to explain their symptoms.

Jung looked into the collective unconscious and found fundamental archetypes of human personalities, which evolved like issues out of primordial experiences. In his Eight Ages of Man, Erikson found that the crisis in each stage was related to some part or function of society. Much like Plato and Aristotle, Erikson viewed a person's life cycle and society as intertwined as both evolved together.

The evolution of humanity is reflected physically, socially, culturally, behaviorally, and historically. The drama is repeated with the birth of each child. Children go through each developmental stage just as a society evolves and becomes more aware over time.

The Eastern parallel is the chakra system. This system traditionally has seven successive stages of psychic development. In embryology, the recapitulation of our ancestors can be seen in very striking physical dimensions. The progressive stages of human evolution may be what philosophers and scientists have been searching for in attempts to classify the systems of life. Freud had a glimpse of the developmental process and created the Psychosexual Stages of Development. Erikson called life's progression the Eight Stages of Man or the Psychosocial Stages. Maslow understood the essential order of life and called it Maslow's Hierarchy of Needs. The Hindus viewed the stages as physical entities of spinning energy centers (chakras) flowing life up the spinal column. Using an adaptive form of Ernst Haeckel's biogenetic principle, modern biology shows that the development of the person, in an embryological form, is a brief, telescoped recapitulation of the history of the entire genus.

The Three Centers Theory is based on the physiology of humanity and the biology of evolution. The Triune or Three Centers model is presented in Table 5 with apparent similarities to a vast array of psychological theories and ageless philosophies.

Table 5: A Comparison of the Three Centers in the Triune Theory and Other Psychological Theories and Philosophies

Theory	Physical	Emotion	Cognition
Triune Theory	The physical self being, life needs, eating, digestion, balance, kinesthetic sense, sensation, bioregulation, relationships	The emotional self, "limbic system," feelings (emotions), movement, vibrational sense, glandular reactions, relationships	The intellectual self, neocortex, thinking, memory, orientation to self and world, syntony, dreaming
MacLean's Triune Brain	R-complex	Limbic System	Neocortex
Aristotle's Three-Part Soul	*Nutritive:* "digestion, nutrition, and propagation of the species," plant level, soul of plants	*Sentient:* animal level or sense, sensation, animal soul	*Nous* or intelligence: two-part human soul: *Intellectus Patiens,* receptive intellect *Intellectus Agens,* active, reproductive, constructive intellect
Sigmund Freud	Id: primitive needs	Ego: emotional, balance of id and superego	Superego: values, social restraints
Sheldon's Somatotypes	Endomorphic: physical life, overweight	Mesomorphic: muscular, sensation emotional	Ectomorphic: slender, nervous, intellectual

Theory	Physical	Emotion	Cognition
Biorhythm Analysis	Physical: 23-day cycle	Emotional: 28-day cycle, relates to passion or will	Intellectual: 33-day cycle, thyroid gland, rational reasoning
Yoga Sutras	Tamoguna: forces of inertia, mass-stuff, matter	Rajoguna: electronic force, energy-stuff, motion	Satoguna: protonic force, intelligence-stuff
Plato's Little Kosmos	Abdomen: appetite	Chest: "energy, courage, anger"	Cranium: "rational" active and "immortal" receptive "soul"
Polarity Therapy	Urine, excretion	Circulation and lymph	Nervous system
Binswanger's Three Worlds	Eigenwelt: body	Mitwelt: with the world	Umwelt: world around
Sufi	Kath	Oth	Path
Jerome Bruner	Actions	Emotions	Thinking
Consciousness / Bioenergetics	Body process, sensations	Emotions, feelings Ego, self-image	Thinking principles Ego, self-image
Three Centers	Belly-Mind: drives	Heart-Mind: emotions	Head Mind: thinking
Three Centers Approach	Physical	Emotional	Intellectual
Three Fields or Centers, R. Stone	Life and motion	Speech	Intelligence

Theory	Physical	Emotion	Cognition
George Gurdjieff	Instinctive Moving	Emotion Moving	Thinking
Huna	Unihipli: low, subconscious, inner mind, center at solar plexus or gut, in charge of physical body and movements	Uhane: middle conscious, outer mind, emotional functioning	Aumkua: superconscious, higher self, intuition, inspiration
Chinese I Ching	Earth: below consciousness	Man (Humanity) will, emotion	Heaven: above
	(Each part has a yin and yang, making six possible relationships or stages or steps of transformation for each hexagram)		
Three Main Body Systems Macrobiotics	Digestive: yin digestion	Circulatory: in between	Nervous: yang
Structure Determines Function (Rolf)	Intricate Gut	Cardiovascular system: circulation	Musculoskeletal system: movement
Living Love System	Reticular Activating System	Limbic System	Cerebral Cortex
Rebirthing	Touching	Breathing	Thinking
Three Centers	Gross body: muscles, bone, body	Circulatory body: heart	Neuro body: head

Theory	Physical	Emotion	Cognition
Ashish's Cosmic Levels	Physical Level: physical of human, hominid, and animal	Desire Level: subtle animal body	Lower Mental Level: mental ego Higher Mental Level: individual self
Kahlil Gibran	Pigmy Self	Man Self	God Self
Holistic Tao of the Three Centers	Physical: relaxation versus contraction	Emotion: love (positive) versus hate (negative)	Cognition: rational versus intuitive
Arica Three Centers	Physical	Emotional	Mental
Three "Vestures" or Bodies of the Buddha **D. Tansley**	Dharmakaya	Sambhogakay	Nirmanakaya
Polarity Energy	Inferior (negative pole) generative center provides the total pattern of life as with seeds and flowing as energy currents	Middle (neuter) sustaining principle of life in the heart center that gives the sensory energy of warmth and emotional feeling	Superior: brain (positive pole); the pattern of mind energy
Mandala of the Soul **Alice Bailey** **Esoteric Philosophy**	Sacrifice Petal: sacrifice or will	Love Petal	Knowledge Petal: active intelligence

Theory	Physical	Emotion	Cognition
	Outer Court: generative center: Sagittarius	Inner Court: heart: Leo	Holy of Holies: head: Aries
est	Be	Do	Have
Constitution of Man **Alice Bailey** **Esoteric Philosophy**	Physical	Emotional	Mental Intuitional Spiritual Monadic Divine
Three Stages of life	Birth	Living	Death
Basic Shapes	Circle	Square	Triangle
Germ Layers	Endoderm	Mesoderm	Ectoderm
Three States or Forms of Matter	Solid	Liquid	Gas
Cell Processes	Anabolism	Metabolism	Catabolism
4 Components of Every Action, Feldenkrais	Movement Sensation	Feeling	Thought
Ayurvedic **3 Doshas** **3 Mixed**	Kapha heavyset, calm	Pitta decisive, forceful	Vata thin, quick

P.S. Ouspensky, who became known for reporting the work of Gurdjieff, lists these qualities of humans:

1. Physical Man: instinctive
2. Emotional Man: feeling level
3. Intellectual Man: concepts and words
4. Self-developed: knows oneself
5. Self-conscious
6. Objective conscious
7. Permanent "I" free will

William James's *The Genesis of the Elementary Mental Categories*

1. "Elementary sorts of sensations, and feelings of personal activity;
2. Emotions; desires; instincts; ideas of worth; aesthetic ideas;
3. Ideas of space and time and number;
4. Ideas of difference and resemblance, and of their degrees;
5. Ideas of casual dependence among events; of end and means; of subject and attribute;
6. Judgments affirming, denying, doubting, supposing any of the above ideas;
7. Judgments that the former judgments logically involve, exclude, or are indifferent to, each other."[166]

A final Three Centers story is ready to unfold. From Manly P. Hall, this one concerns the ancient pagan priests of Europe. They viewed the solar system as a Grand Man with three centers of activity analogous to the human's three main centers of life: the brain, the heart, and the generative system.

Grand Man	of pagan priests	Christian Trinity
1. generative system	body	Holy Ghost
2. heart	love	Son
3. brain	rational	Father

The 3 bodies in 1: If man (kind) is made in the image of God, which is 3 in 1, then man (kind) must also be made 3 in 1.

CHAPTER 9

Triune Psychology: The Evolution of Consciousness

HUMAN EVOLUTION

Humans evolved through an evolutionary process that simultaneously manifested itself on physical, psychological, social, cultural, and metaphysical levels. In East Indian philosophy, such a measure of reality exists as the chakra system. The seven spinning, vibrating energy centers, or chakras, reflect reality in their energy ascent from the lowest form of life (the primordial force, as it were) up the spinal structure, or backbone of the body, to the crown of the head (which represents the unity with all things). According to the chakra system, the human psyche, reflected by the group or collective consciousness of the culture, travels through a succession of seven stages. Starting with life, survival, and functions for living; then sex and procreation of the species as the basic primitive needs; and spiraling upward to power and love; and then higher to the functions of communication, insight, and spirituality.

In comparison with Maslow's Hierarchy of Needs, the progression of the human through the chakra system appears much like human development. In a Western sense, the significance of evolution is change. An energy principle in physics can be stated simply as $E=MC^2$, which means energy changes from matter and matter to energy in various ways.

Energy and matter flow from one to the other, neither destroyed but constantly transmuting from one to the other. One walks through a door at the end to enter and begin at the other side. The end of one is the beginning of the other. Yin becomes yang at its crest of potency.

Anthropologically and biologically, creatures change or adapt in accordance with their physical environment. The change occurs on both social and physical levels and assists the animal's survival through natural selection. Food (matter) is eaten and digested; flows to the blood; mixes with oxygen, glandular secretions, and other elements; and is arranged in particular electromagnetic patterns.

We will home in on evolution for this discussion, starting with the phylum protozoa, which is Greek for the first animal.[167] Protozoa consist of only one-celled organisms and have only genetically preprogrammed actions based directly on the type and intensity of energy (stimulus) impinging on them. The one-celled organism moves when touched by pressure, light, chemicals, and magnetic energy and absorbs food when contact is made.[168] It has a basic physical system that responds immediately to direct stimuli and can be identified as a stimulus-response (S-R) system. Thus, we have an example of an organism with the fundamental physical stimulus-response: the protozoa. The "old" physical S-R apparatus remains in animals, including humans, comprising most of the body, spinal cord, and hindbrain. It maintains regulatory and autonomic functions like blood circulation, breathing, essential motor activation, muscle movement, and general body housekeeping.

MacLean identifies the physical brain control mechanism as the Reptilian Complex or R-Complex as the first part of the triune brain. The ancient part of the brain evolved with physical survival, and this most basic brain is involved with primordial energy. Yet at its most basic, it remains the foundation upon which the more advanced parts reside.

The simple animal evolved over eons and adapted following the influences of the environment. Animals (matter) developed equipment (redirected energy) to detect the external environment. Sensory equipment slowly evolved, enabling the organism to perceive better and respond. The sensory modalities of the eyes, ears, nose, skin, etc., found their purpose through their function. The new advanced sensors of sight, hearing, smelling, and taste enabled the organism to sense or detect danger at a distance and locate food supply, other animals, the lay of the land, and the abundance of nature.

With the rise of the sensory system, animals no longer had to respond to direct stimuli like touch to survive. Now an animal could react in advance to an imminent foe. The scenario of the protozoa responding to touch changes into a deer seeing a bear or smelling a hunter. In essence, it detects danger at a distance. The sense modalities, except for olfaction, send an electrochemical nerve message to the lateral geniculate of the thalamus that, in turn, goes to the hypothalamus, which stimulates the pituitary gland.[169] The pituitary releases adrenocorticotropic hormone (ACTH) and others that activate the adrenals to produce epinephrine and other hormones, which together create an adrenaline rush. These body functions happen sooner than it takes to read this sentence. It is immediate. It is the flight-fight response.

The protozoa's response to touch is classified as physical, and the reaction of the deer is labeled as emotional. This emotional classification involves the body structures of the limbic system, midbrain, endocrine glands, and sensory modalities such as eyes, ears, nose, and touch.

MacLean's second part of his triune brain was the emotional unit, named the Limbic system, which we have in common with mammals but not as much with reptiles.

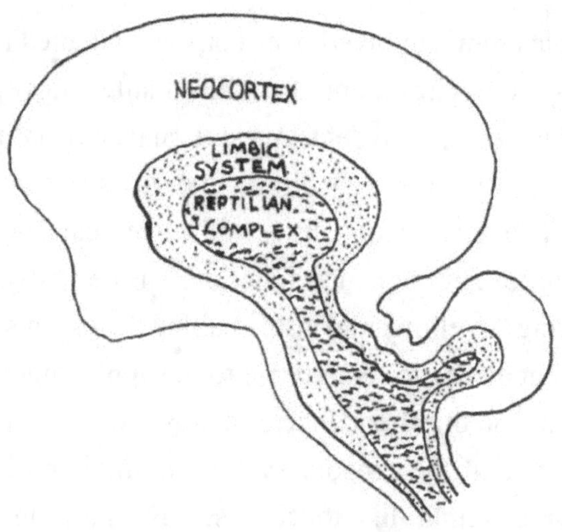

Figure 62: Triune Brain

MacLean developed a model with three systems or sets of drivers in the neurological system. These three sets of interconnected physiological neural systems can be thought of as interdependent computers. Each biological computer system has a separate function with its own specialized intelligence. These three interconnected biological computers have their own memory and sense of time and space. Each of the three brains developed as a major step in evolution and can be identified by their specific neuroanatomy and functions. Each brain differs in the neurochemicals dopamine and cholinesterase. The three brains are labeled as the Reptilian Complex or R-Complex, Limbic System, and Neocortex.

Whereas the R-Complex rests in the hindbrain, the limbic system is in the brain's center and includes the pituitary gland that controls the endocrine system. The emotional control of the limbic system is evident with an endocrine imbalance that can alter moods and affect a person's state of mind. The limbic system includes the amygdala, which is involved with aggression and fear; other limbic productions include rage and sentimentality. The limbic system includes the amygdala and hypothalamus, which drive emotions.

Maternal care and altruistic behavior are also common aspects of the mammalian brain, the limbic system, and the emotional self. One can argue that love, as an emotion, emerged in mammals. However, Sagan contends that all three brains—R-complex, limbic system, and neocortex, are involved with sex. To be clear, the body and its functions work synergistically or holistically. All parts work together, and each affects all others. All structures work together to produce an integrated operation.

The emotional system was built upon essential physical equipment by way of sensory modalities to sense the environment, a glandular network to do something powerful and quick when danger was detected, and the development of the limbic system. Survival value in detecting and responding to danger at a distance is obvious and the next evolutionary step. However, like the initial physical system, the emotional system had the drawback of immediacy; it could only deal with the present.

The forebrain developed as the organism continued to evolve and thinking emerged. The rise of the forebrain anatomically rearranged the long-smelling nose (olfaction) of creatures like dogs. This development meant that animals in relation to their place on the phylogenetic ladder, could classify information into a bio-memory bank and have the information referenced at a later time. The physical and emotional systems previously acted upon this information with quick, innate responses. The thinking structure grew out of the emotional, not replacing it but increasing its functions by its interrelation. Older biological systems tend not to disintegrate but rather become an integral functioning part of the newer ones. Evolution holds on to preexisting structures because it is needed by the new structure.[170]

Thinking is the biomechanism that organizes the emotional and physical systems with the added functions of memory, recall, and understanding into a more coherent way of responding to or acting upon the environment.

Sagan suggests that the data points to an arrangement of the neocortex.

The three psychological systems of thinking, emotions, and body are so intertwined in structure and function that they make an unclear differentiation of where one ends and one begins. Animals' evolutionary development on a phylogenetic scale is likewise so continuous as to make it difficult to clearly distinguish between the three systems. First, the protozoa on one end of the spectrum and the humans and dolphins on the other are certainly clearly distinguishable animals.

MacLean points out that the triune brain developed up to the reptile with the R-complex or what can be termed the physical system. The mammals developed the limbic system to its zenith. While present in lower animals, the neocortex finds its fullest function (although it still may be evolving) in humans. This three-part mechanism functions as one in a normal human and represents our evolution from the worm to the reptile, the mammal, and the human.

The scale in Table 6 roughly shows the evolution of animals in line with the development of psychological systems.

Table 6: Biological Evolution of Psychological Systems

BIOLOGICAL EVOLUTION PHYLOGENETIC SCALE		PSYCHOLOGICAL SYSTEMS
Human Beings Modern Man (humans) Monkey		Forebrain Cognition (neocortex)
Cat (mammals, birds, social insects) Rat Lizard		Limbic System Emotional (limbic system)
Worm (reptiles) Amoeba		Hindbrain Physical (R-complex)

The case for the psychological system comprising physical, emotional, and cognitive components is compelling because the systems exist. Their structure and function can be determined to an extensive degree by studies of biology and anthropology, such as we see in MacLean's work.

THE BASIS OF PERSONALITY

If these physical, emotional, and cognitive systems are so evident from a biological perspective, why has psychology overlooked them? The answer is that they have not been overlooked; instead, they have been identified differently and defined in other terms. Let us look at some examples.

Table 7: Freud and Triune Theory

FREUD	**TRIUNE THEORY**
Id	Body-Physical Life
Ego	Emotion
Superego	Cognition

Freud's understanding of the organic flow of life energy equated the id with the instincts of the basic animal. He thought that all instincts had their source in the biological or metabolic requirements of the organism.[171]

The first-level systems are the hindbrain or R-complex or the physical body in the system presented. In line with Freud's thinking, the body resembles the id in that it deals with basic biological regulation and maintenance and involves instincts such as the plantar reflex.

The problem with the id, as well as the ego and superego, is that it is a concept without actual substance. They only have a conceptual relationship and not a physical relationship. No actual location is cited. It exists because Freud saw that within one's structure of thinking, we have physical needs that we strive to gratify, and our body does its utmost to tell us about these needs.

The id or the body formed self-preservation instincts for biological needs such as food, water, air, and temperature regulation. Freud thought the id was the primitive mind that later differentiated into the ego and the superego.

During the embryonic stages, the various body parts become differentiated initially into the ectodermic system of skin and nerves and the endodermic system of organs and internal structures. Later, more will be said about this differentiation that is obviously related to Sheldon's Somatotypes. Still, it is sufficient to note that certain anatomical divisions occur as the animal develops. These various divisions give the organism the structure that develops and performs specific functions relative to its survival. In fact, the embryo goes through the entire drama of physical evolution. The embryo develops gill slits, a tail, and fur, and in later stages, uses this matter to develop more advanced systems such as lungs and skin.[172]

Human embryonic physical evolution is essential in several ways. It points out man's relationship with other earthly life. It demonstrates the initial biological basis for one system to grow into or evolve into another system, which relates to Freud's ego and superego developing from the id. It also lends credibility to Jung's archetypes because we do physically pass through all human evolutionary stages as an embryo. On our way to "becoming" human, we may undergo all the learnings of our animal predecessors in the evolution of consciousness.

As the physical systems develop into the next system of higher complexity, so do the psychological systems. Both the physical and psychological systems maintain a symbiotic relationship with each other. Physical development will bring about a psychological change, and psychological development will promote a structural adaptation in the body. This is to say that the mind directly affects the body, and the body, the mind. Their relationship is not separate, as humans are holistically oriented and functioning systems.

As infants, we start with developing essential motor and survival functions. Freud identified the instinctual energy that powered the primary motor and survival functions and labeled it the id, or perhaps more precisely, translated it as the "it."[173] Piaget labeled the first two years as sensori-motor, which seems more of a descriptive term than Freud's id, which is more interpretive. The author would simply identify this initial life period as most concerned with physical development.

After the sensori-motor phase, to use Piaget's term, when our musculature has begun to develop, the tiny person also begins to associate particular objects and events with feelings or emotions. Initially, the emotional responses came from internal stimuli, such as the sensation of hunger or skin irritation. Through experiencing the environment, one learns or associates inner feelings with external objects and situations. A young one smiles when happy and cries when sad. The emotions become more and more reflective of external influences. Although the musculature continues to develop, the emotions become more noticeable and communication with the child takes on this emotional tone. We play with the child and say, "peekaboo." Our reactions to the environment begin to shape the meaning of our emotions. The physical, glandular feeling is set up via living experience to the constructs we learn, which is how we interpret the world. Erikson discovered the initial emotional functioning and termed it trust versus mistrust.

Cognitive functioning arises next in the infant's development and is noted by the use of language. The higher mental process takes the longest of the psychological systems to develop, perhaps a lifetime to fully mature. The emotional system may take until early adulthood to develop, although it can be argued that it never reaches maturity in some individuals. Physical growth is obviously realized in adulthood. The body, emotions, and cognition, as has been discussed, always work together, and although their differences in function and structure are mentioned, these structures are never separated. Even in an infant, all physical, emotional, and cognitive systems are present and in operation, although at an immature level. Each system, in turn, develops, yet not independent of each other but together as a unit. In a predominance of development, the order is from physical to emotional to cognitive, just as developing up the phylogenetic scale.

Freud's superego contains society's traditional values and taboos and makes guilt possible. Values and taboos are conceptual items, and we, as a society, have to think up these concepts. Anthropologically speaking, the values and social mores come over a period of time out of the tribe's relationship to their environment—physical and social—as a way to explain themselves (need to know). We think of how we are to think about ourselves. Only we humans and probably dolphins are endowed with higher cognitive functions, allowing us to deal with a level of values and beliefs. The superego deals with morality and all the stuff of thought. The superego is cognition.

The ego or emotion is also part of the brain, not the primitive physical hindbrain and not the advanced cognitive forebrain. The brain's emotional part predominates in development from six months to one and a half years of age or until pre-language formulates. Its progression starts after the sensori-motor and assists cognition in developing speech, for emotions give speech its power. "I want food. I want that. I want, I want …" goes the emotional outcry of wanting a physical substance that the cognitive process has identified.

Freud viewed the ego as part of the mind active in satisfying instincts. An instinct is usually identified as a need. When such a need strikes us, the feeling is part of an emotional process. In the triune system presented, emotions rely on thought for recognition and memory for sentiment. Emotions have control over the voluntary nervous system and the musculature, as does Freud's ego. In a real sense, emotions struggle between our bodies and our thoughts. Our emotions are torn between what our body wants—sex, for instance—and what our thinking tells us, such as that we shouldn't do it, it's wrong, or not until marriage.

Although some Freudian subconstructs may not fit as well into the physical, emotional, and cognitive triune reinterpretation of the id, ego, and superego constructs, the psychological systems are otherwise interchangeable in many ways. The psychological systems of body, emotions, and thinking have the advantage of scientific validity related to real matter present and accounted for. This differs from words arranged in ways to develop logic. The non-empirical logical theories have meaning, as they are attempts by intelligent people to define human behavior. Much can be gained by studying the logic used to develop systems of thought, as can be gained from the logic in mathematical formulas. However, each theory needs to be connected in some manner to the other theories in psychology and their relationship displayed. If theories are not connected together, each system fails to benefit from the knowledge derived from other points of view.

The Triune Theory displayed in Table 8 is easily related to other theories. The following is an outline that diagrams some relationships:

Table 8: Personality Theories

TRIUNE THEORY	Freud
1. Body-physical (R-complex) —life, being, body regulation, and balance —sensation 2. Emotion —limbic system glands —feeling from glandular response —quick reactions to danger, movement 3. Cognition —forebrain, neocortex —intellectual — thinking, memory	1. Id —primitive needs 2. Ego — balancing Id and Superego 3. Superego — values — social restraints

BERNE'S TRANSACTIONAL ANALYSIS	SHELDON
1. Child - Archeopsyche —natural —adapted 2. Parent - Extereopsyche —nurturing —controlling 3. Adult - Neopsyche —computer —objective	Somatotypes 1. Endomorphic —heavy, overweight —physical 2. Mesomorphic —muscular —emotional 3. Ectomorphic —slender —nervous —intellectual

OUSPENSKY	BIORHYTHM ANALYSIS
Levels of Man 1. Physical Man—instinctive 2. Emotional Man—feeling level 3. Intellectual Man—concepts and words 4. Self-developed—knows oneself 5. Self-consciousness—unity 6. Objective Consciousness 7. Permanent "I"—free will	1. Physical —23-day cycle 2. Emotional —28-day cycle —relates to will or passion 3. Intellectual —33-day cycle — thyroid gland —rational reasoning

KHALIL GIBRAN	GORDON ALLPORT
1. Pigmy self 2. Man self 3. God self	A. Opportunities functioning (influenced by the world) a. Needs for food, water, etc. Propriate Functioning (influences of the world) a. Sense of body b. Self-identity c. Self-esteem d. Self-extension e. Rational coping f. Self-image g. Propriate striving

The relationship of the Triune Theory to Freud's psychoanalysis was previously noted, and in the same vein, the connection to Berne's Transactional Analysis relates on the same level. This is consistent as Berne derived his concepts from Freud's model, although he adapted the terminology to appeal to non-professionals. The parent represents our cognitive processing with morals and understanding of appropriate behavior. The adult (ego) faces the conflict between rational knowledge of right and wrong versus the impulsive desires of the child (id). Kahlil Gibran voices a poetic understanding of the primary aspects of humans. The mystic Ouspensky developed a theme acquired from Gurdjieff of the levels of men, which is similar, in many ways, to the Triune Theory. Sheldon's somatotypes illustrate a version of the three-centers theory using the earliest tissue differentiation in the germ levels: endomorph, mesomorph, and ectomorph. The Biorhythm Analysis is interesting because it purports to show physiological glandular cycles regulating each psychological system. Adherents of this system will chart your cycles based on your birthdate. Unfortunately, little research has been forthcoming to substantiate claims that these cycles regulate or influence psychological systems. Allport was included, not because his model fits well with Triune Theory but rather because his opportunistic functioning relates solely to the body, and appropriate functioning is an interesting mixture of emotional and cognitive aspects.

As discussed previously, the embryo undergoes development corresponding to stages of ancestry, which, in biology, is known as the biogenetic law. [174]Due to its place on the phylogenetic scale, the human is a triploblastic animal, which means we have three embryonic germ layers. The ectoderm becomes the skin and nervous system; the mesoderm forms the muscular, skeletal, and circulatory systems; and the endoderm develops the digestive, elimination, and many internal organ systems. Sheldon, who had a medical background, used these biological findings to build his theory. Sheldon's somatotypes directly support the triune constructs of body, emotions, and thinking. The supporting biological logic he used in creating his theory directly applies to the triune model. He used the character types that seem, in general, to be one's orientation to life from a biological standpoint.

BASIC HUMAN NEEDS AS THE BASIS OF PERSONALITY

The psychological structures of the body, emotions, and thinking have been identified according to the triune brain's biological structures, including the R-complex, limbic system, and neocortex. Each of these systems has a physical base, a physiological function, and a specific need to maintain itself. The triune model's diagram of structure, function, and needs displayed in Table 9 requires fuel (food, air, vibration, and light) put into the body to continue the energy-matter cycle of life.

Table 9: Basic Human Needs

Structure	Function	Needs
Physical Self Hindbrain, R-complex, bulk of body except that specialized for higher senses, internal senses, and primitive senses	1. Maintain proper body functions, regulates autonomic system, keeps energy flowing through the body for vitality or aliveness (regulation and maintenance survival) 2. Responds immediately (S-R) to impinging stimuli (survival) (physical reaction) 3. Orgasmic release, reproduction, and relaxation 4. Kinesthetic sense, orientation, location of muscles and bones, awareness of space, balance and movement 5. Maintain physical life activity, energy regulation	1. Proper nutrition, air, temperature, regulation of their physical needs; sleep 2. Feel sensation 3. Sex and touching 4. For touching, sensing 5. Physical activity to keep motor system active, muscles conditioned, and body toned; balanced system of flexation, stress relaxation, and extension

Structure	Function	Needs
Emotional Self Limbic system, glands, circulatory system, sensory modalities	1. Monitor or sense environment by use of sensory modalities (eyes, ears, nose, skin) and glandular reaction to stimuli; detecting danger and pleasure at a distance, movement 2. Orgasmic release, reproduction 3. Relaxation (from movement and tissue release) 4. Emotional expression; happy-sad, love-hate. desires-depression 5. Contraction-relaxation, flexion-extension	1. To use sensory modalities for glandular reaction (sensation to produce emotion), including that of touching on vibrational and auric levels, movement 2. Sex and social relationships 3. To calm the body and for touch 4. To express emotion, verbally or nonverbally, and to have emotional balance (feel good about self and others) 5. Physical activity to keep motor system active, muscles conditioned, and body toned; balanced system of flexation, stress relaxation, and extension

Structure	Function	Needs
Intellectual Self Neocortex	1. Thinking and memory (frontal lobes) 2. Orientation to self and environment (spatial orientation, parietal), perception and auditory (temporal), visual(occipital) 3. To speak intellectually, communicate 4. Dreaming, visualizing, hallucinating	1. To think, anticipate future, make accurate perceptions 2. Have power, control, mastery 3. To have a stimulating environment 4. To be creative, self-actualization 5. To know, understand the self, have self and world theory 6. To be in balance with all systems, in tune with self and nature

As can be seen from the outline of the structures and functions of the psychological system, needs arise from the system's operation. The needs constitute what humans' essential requirements for living, although the need can be attached to other behaviors and become desires. The lower the need, the more critical it is, and the more energy it will have toward its satisfaction.

Many people seem to function with the predominance of one of the psychological systems. That is to say that some people are highly physical (always doing, moving), many passionate and emotional, and others caught up in thought with little care for the body or for the satisfaction of physical or emotional needs.

Sex was listed as both a physical and emotional need because components of both interplay. Sex may be a need of all three centers, as MacLean and Sagan suggest. An orgasm may be a physical release, yet we need another to care for with mutual pleasure. This shows an emotional component, and this gregarious nature shows the human need for each other, relations, and instincts.

Both relaxation and touch are listed in the physical and emotional areas because we touch and massage the physical being, yet we connect on an emotional level of experiencing. When we express feeling, which directly relates to the need to express emotion verbally and nonverbally, the emotions work with the cognitive functions in speaking and with the physical through body language.

Thinking and memory functions classify past experiences and place them in perspective with present experiences and future direction. When we remember, we are accessing or referencing information stored in the memory. It is information retrieval.

The basic physical system developed into the specialized systems of emotion and thinking, yet they all remain basically physical. Each part is so intertwined with the other that only a few non-connected physical behaviors exist, such as the plantar reflex. Physical reactions can be separate, but all emotional and cognitive actions must include the physical, as it is our basic system. However, two systems can function together with little action from the third. Thinking may not involve emotion unless an emotion has been or is being associated with the concept.

Most behaviors interplay with all the psychological systems, as shown in the examples in Table 10.

Table 10: Behavior Chart

Physical Behavior	Emotional	Cognitive
Crying	Sadness	Referencing date (memory) with present
Laughing	Happy	Same as above
Exercise	Feel good about self	Think positive about self, orient mental patterns associated with movement
Sex, orgasmic release	Feel good about self and other person	Have social relationships

Needs arise from the structure and function of the systems. As outlined, the hierarchy of needs can be related to other theories and philosophies, as shown in Table 11.

Seeing how well the Hindu chakra system, Fromm, and Maslow's Hierarchy of Needs fit into the Triune Body Psychology and the Three Centers Theory was amazing. The needs systems all developed from different backgrounds. The chakras came from ancient East Indian philosophers, Maslow's from his humanistic approach, and the triune needs from the Three Centers Theory. Yet all three virtually have the same categories. All the systems presented can be shown to relate directly to the psychological systems of cognition, emotion, and body physiology.

The needs exist because we have a body and mind that function in an intricate interrelationship with the environment. The psyche's needs are both physically and socially based and evolved from the biological and cultural influences of the past. Like the fuel, temperature, and oil gauges that indicate the automobile's proper functioning, human needs keep us in tune with or appraised of our condition of need satisfaction or regulation. In another sense, what we need amounts to the fuel to mix with the mind and body to create specific outcomes in the biological, psychological, and social arena.

Table 11: Hierarchy of Needs

TRIUNE hierarchy of Needs	Maslow's hierarchy of Needs
1. Need to maintain proper body functions 2. Need for sensations, touch, pain, pleasure 3. Movement, touch activity needs 4. Sex and reproduction needs 5. Emotional expression: love 6. Social relations: love 7. Need to think and to remember, make accurate perceptions, have mastery 8. Need to have a stimulating environment 9. Need to be creative, self-actualize 10. Need to know, have a self and world theory (orientation to self and environment) 11. Need to express thoughts 12. Need for unity, transcendence, resolving problems, and being in tune with the self and therefore the universe	1. Physiological needs 2. Safety needs 3. Need for belongingness and love 4. Need for esteem 5. Need for self-actualization 6. Need for cognitive understanding 7. Need for transcendence

Erich Fromm	Chakras (Hindu)
Animal nature—physical Human nature 1. Need for relatedness—emotional 2. Transcendence 3. Rootedness 4. Cognitive 5. Frame of reference	1. Health, assimilation, nutrition 2. Sex drives and reproduction, primitive energy 3. Power and mastery 4. Feelings of love & affection 5. thought communication, expression self-identification 6. wisdom, heightened self-awareness 7. union with the self and nature enlightenment, experience of self-realization, transcendence

Need satisfaction may be an essential aspect of mental health. Our mind and body can let us know what they need, and it is within the realm of our personal, biological, and social understanding to define the needs and how to satisfy them.

CHAPTER 10
Energy

THE BODY CONSISTS OF VARIOUS body parts as enumerated with each appropriate psychological orientation. Yet, the human is more than the sum of the parts (N+1). The human is a living organism with energy flowing through the system, creating and maintaining life. But what is this energy, and how is it manifested?

This chapter will explore the concept of energy and provide descriptions in Western and Eastern terms. The manifestations of energy are the functions of the structure in breathing, talking, standing, walking, and forming a balance with the pressures of the Earth (gravity, atmospheric pressure). Blocks or limitations in the flow of energy impact the various body functions to produce habitual movement patterns. The very process of growth is altered by the blockage or limiting of energy and/or the free flow of energy to produce changes in the body parts and how the major body segments fit together. In a way, it is analogous to expulsive or retentive in that it floods or dams the energy flow. The body's segments can be split, with one part looking different from another as if they belonged to different bodies.

The growth patterns influenced by the energy blocks formed the body types conceptualized by a variety of theorists.

Helmholtz and Mayer, in 1845, developed the famous landmark in Western thought known as the law of conservation of energy, which stated that energy is changed to matter and back but not created or destroyed. This law basically said that living systems are based on the flow of energy and obey the laws of science with energy.[175] Luigi Galvani of the galvanic skin response meter found in 1786 that an electrical current would contract the muscle in a frog's leg and thus demonstrated "animal electricity." And it was Volta from whom we got the concepts of electrical volts by showing that an electrical current flows.[176]

Western thought embedded in the scientific approach looked at food and oxygen as the source of energy. The energy unit is a kilocalorie, which is the amount of heat required for raising one kilogram of water from 15 degrees centigrade to 16 degrees centigrade.[177] Energy is expended according to each individual's basal metabolic rate, which is the rate at which the metabolism digests food and consumes oxygen. All organisms consume substances, and the body's process of metabolism converts the matter into energy. Einstein wrote an equation of a life-sustaining function as $E=MC^2$: energy equals mass times the constant of the velocity of the speed of light, squared. The process of life itself, on one level, is an absorbing substance that is changed to energy. Energy production is life-sustaining.

The two Western laws that govern the relations of energy are the conservation of energy, stating that energy changes but is never created or destroyed, and the law of the degradation of energy or the second law of thermodynamics, which shows energy going from useful to non-useful forms (entropy) and back with substantial heat loss. Biological units constantly change potential energy to kinetic, and the reverse.

To create a method of explaining the energy function (growth and tissue shaping) in body psychology, one must obey the Western laws of science but with reverence to the Western philosophical roots (pre-twentieth century medicine and science) and Eastern knowledge. Energy and matter unite in life, flowing one into the other like yin and yang in internal and external functions.

But energy is more than food and oxygen because the pressures from the earth, geomagnetism, and the air (gravity, atmospheric pressure, ionic balance) affect the organism. The yin and yang of it are that energy goes in and out. During the last seventy years, research, especially in Russia, has conclusively shown that magnetic fields play a physiological role in regulating the body. Presman extensively reviews the literature in this area. In a sense, we live in a sea of energy, and we find movements to shape our way through this force field that is so strong yet so subtle that only a few notice it. Barnwell and Brown conclude that all living organisms have a sensitivity to magnetic fields, and reactions or actions by plants or animals depend upon the strength of the magnetic field. Snails, flatworms, fruit flies, and unicellular paramecium were found to be sensitive to magnetic force fields. Magnetic fields act to orient or reorient body positioning.

Energy as a concept has evolved with virtually every religious and early philosophical system of planet Earth. The names vary from the lee of the Kahuna, ki of Japan, qi or chi of the Chinese, prana or kundalini of the Hindu, or the chiram of Hermes.

Stone produced charts illustrating the body's flow of energy. These charts are duplicated as Figures 65 and 66.[178] The idea of bioenergy flows is consistent with virtually all the world's religions and a fundamental conceptual cornerstone of Eastern thought and Western metaphysical tradition. The energy theory of acupuncture is now a reality in Western science. Although not explained as yet in Western scientific terms, it is a reality because it works. Open-heart surgery using acupuncture as the only anesthesia cannot be easily dismissed.

But where do these energy flows reside physically in the body? Where are the meridians, the Western mind inquires? Stone provides an interesting perspective in his answer. Electromagnetic currents flow through the muscle and fascia. Muscles and fascial planes, Stone suggests, are the carriers of the "holy" energy. The fascia itself may be established as the primary carrier of bioenergy. Body (massage) therapists often encounter a large clump of tissue, mostly fascia, around the right side of the neck adjacent to the backside of the cervical spine.

Miller said that the clump was fascia gathered due to an energy block. Specific deep tissue strokes (Rolfing, Chua Ka, etc.) are often used to "break up" the energy blocks. These deep strokes are much like, although deeper, what in acupressure is known as running the meridians. What is the relation between meridians and fascia? Ida Rolf thought that an organized, balanced body would have a balanced electromagnetic field. This indicates that energy patterns can be altered by changing the fascial network. Stress or residual tension (as hormones, peptides, residual byproducts, and toxic waste) causes the fascia to thicken and "glue" muscles together as a sort of armoring to protect the body-mind from perceived threats. Wilhelm Reich developed the concept of body armoring to explain developmental psychopathologies especially related to sexual fears and inhibitions.

Developing the theme of the muscle fibers and fascia as transmitters of electromagnetic energy, Stone displayed a chart, reproduced as Figure 67, showing the relationship between the polarization of the muscle fibers and the electromagnetic circuits. Stone also described many diseases or physical symptoms as abnormal muscular fibers due to electromagnetic blocks in the muscular structure. The energy field contracts as the muscle contracts. The quality of muscle extension and contraction depends on one's psychological state: the moment-to-moment expression or gestalt or blend of intellectual, emotional, and physical components.

The idea exists that blocks in the electromagnetic flow through the body cause disease (dis-ease; not at ease). The lack of being at ease or dis-ease (non-relaxation) is the cause of energy blocks. Before energy blocks are discussed, other energy systems need definition.

The meridians are the lines of bioenergy used in acupuncture for healing. The relationship of acupuncture points to the viscera and other body parts starts to develop a logical picture when viewed in embryonic development, as shown in Figure 13. It is in the embryo that the anatomical designation of acupuncture points occurs. In studies by Reichmanis, Marino, and Becker, the acupuncture points resembled power lines with a series of resistors. There was an actual decrease in the skin's resistance (electrical) at acupuncture points or increased skin conductivity.

Another energy system, the chakras, is a "gate" in Chinese anatomy where energy is generated for the meridians. Chakras are parallel to the Western anatomy and physiology with the cerebrospinal and sympathetic nervous systems. It is of interest that the caduceus, Figure 64, long the sign of physicians, reflects the same design as the chakra system. The sushumna runs through the spinal cord having dual aspects, Ida (feminine, negative energy) and Pingala (masculine, positive energy), that twist around like a snake or serpent from the pelvis to the lower medulla oblongata. Chakras influence the nerve plexus and glands (and organs) located in their vicinity (see Figure 63). It may be that this swirling concentration of energy exists due to the anatomy of the nervous and glandular systems.

It is noted that the chakras are the landmarks of the spine. In the chakra chart, the location of each shows a downward direction from the back nervous system to the front of the body. The chakras are levels of experience in the body and in the recapitulation of evolved levels of existence.

Seven levels of existence seem as pervasive in the world's philosophies as the Three Centers Theory. In describing esoteric philosophy, Alice Bailey informs us about the existence of seven great rays in which all of existence is part of one of the rays. Everything at any stage of existence is part of one or another of the seven rays.

Storm, teaching the Native American way, spoke of the medicine wheel with seven stones that were the seven stars and the seven arrows. These represent the seven natures of the human and of the universe. Love and fear are two, but the others need to be searched out as part of our learning process.

Stone suggested that the totem pole of the early Native Americans contained the same symbolism and mystery as the sign of the caduceus and the chakra system.[179] Reich's system of seven segments of body armoring relates to the chakras, as does Maslow's Hierarchy of Needs found on the chakra chart (Table 12).

Chakras may be centers of magnetic energy in the body due to the electrical charge of nerves and tissue and the polarity arrangement of the body parts. The vibrational rate set by the body is influenced by geomagnetic, atmospheric, and planetary forces, as well as the magnetic fields of other organisms. The relationship between nerves and glands to chakras is an influencing trade-off that forms an ever-changing or transforming balance or homeostasis.

Chakra comes from Sanskrit, meaning wheel of light, and it is the name given to the body's energy system that arose from ancient Indian and other Asian cultures. Chakras are considered a primary part of the energy systems that include prana and nadis and are related to acupuncture points and meridians. The more well-known chakra systems include the Hindu, Tibetan, and Buddhist systems. Depending on the system, these energy systems have either seven, five, six, nine, or twelve chakras. Other chakra systems are energy systems found in Mayan, Cherokee, Incan, Egyptian, and African cultures.[180]

As people, we live in our body system. Our body has a biological energy system because we are alive. This bioenergy system can be explained as the anatomy and physiology of cells, organs, systems, and the body as a whole. Nerves act as the primary system to conduct nerve energy, but there is bioenergy in all the cells and tissue from nerves, chemical changes, and electromagnetics.

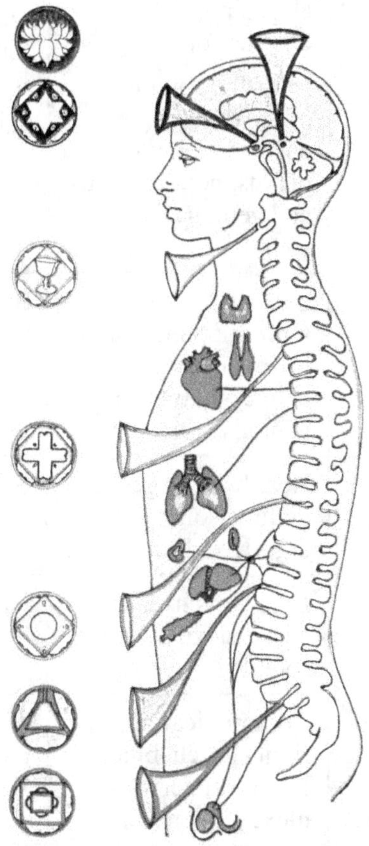

Figure 63: Chakras, Glands, Nerves

Table 12: Chakra Chart

		Endocrine System
The dominant Hindu-based kundalini has the seven-chakra system.		
1. Muladhara root or sacral chakra, kundalini chakra	Life Basis of physical life cleansing, elimination starts the spinning of the chakras, red; coccygeal nerve plexus, between anus and genitals, Lam sound	Base of spine bringing Ida and Pengali (Pingala) female & male aspects Root: spine/ glandular system
2. Svadhisthana	Sex and reproduction, orange; lower abdomen between navel and genitals, Vam sound	Sacral: ovaries, testes
3. Manipura	Health and digestion, yellow; solar plexus, digestive; Ram sound	Spleen: spleen/liver
4. Anahata	Love, green; cardiac nerve plexus, Yam sound	Heart: thymus
5. Vishuddha	Communication, right speech, blue. laryngeal nerve plexus, Ham sound	Throat: thyroid/ parathyroid
6. Ajna	Insight, perception, self-realization, violet; point between eyebrows, Om sound	Third eye: pituitary

		Endocrine System
7. Sahasrara	Union, spirituality, white; top or atop of head, cerebral cortex, Visarga (a breathing sound)	Crown: pineal
Chakras that exist outside of the body.		
8. Above the head[181] Holds Akashic records, shadow records, and Book of Life	Place of karma connecting with all of time, dimensions, and parallel or alterative realities	
9. Above head at 1½ feet; Seat of the Soul	Create energy healings, access life path and future decisions, genetic repair with symbology	
10. Under feet at 1½ feet; Grounding Chakra	Connects to nature's energy, anchoring, healing	
11. Around the body Mainly at Hands and feet	Transmutes physical and supernatural forces, can make instant change to interior and exterior	
12. Surrounds all body; outer bounds	Connects body to thirty secondary chakras, channels spiritual energy	
13. Energy Egg	Three layers, connects physical and spiritual	

HIMALAYAN BONPO CHAKRAS

Tibetan Tantra (six chakras)[182]

1. Secret
2. Right/left foot
3. Navel
4. Heart
5. Throat
6. Crown

BUDDHA (FIVE CHAKRAS)

Tantras

Basal chakra—Earth: Lam
Abdominal chakra—Water: Vam
Heart chakra—Fire: Ram
Throat—Wind: Yam
Crown—Space: Kham

ENDOCRINE CHAKRA CONNECTION[183]

- First chakra—Gonads: male testes, female ovaries
- Second chakra—Peyer's patches (in the appendix and interstitial
- cells in the intestinal wall, or lymphatic)
- Third chakra—Adrenal (or splenic)

- Fourth chakra—Thymus
- Fifth chakra—Thyroid (parathyroid)
- Sixth chakra—Pineal
- Seventh chakra—Pituitary (hypothalamus)

Bruyere makes a case for the root chakra housing the functions of sexuality and life, which is consistent with some Tantric philosophies. The twisting snakes of Ida and Pingala, or female and male energies, form at the base of the spinal cord and twist up like DNA to the top of the head. This creates a spinning action that results in vibrations that the human is thought to be able to perceive at some level of developing conscious awareness. The spinning is like a small cyclone or whirling vortex of energy.

The ideas of life and sex are intertwined. In mammals, sex is necessary for natural reproduction, although artificial insemination has brought about the possibility of reproduction without sex. Yet humans and mammals are wired for sex, as sex is the strong impulse or drive that makes for the continuation of life.

It is of interest that "in the beginning" within Hindu cosmology, there was a unified oneness with a single consciousness, which was space, Shakti (like the Chinese Yin), and time, Shiva (like the Chinese Yang). When the separation happened, perhaps a big bang or a birth, there was a separation between matter and consciousness in things and people. Shakti in everyone is coiled in our root chakra in the guise of a snake but is the power at rest (Kundalini Shakti) until she moves and becomes manifest. She wants to rise up through the denseness of the body to rejoin Shiva in the seventh chakra and create supreme consciousness.[184]

Kundalini rises through the sushumna composed of the three main nadis: central sushumna, Ida, and Pingala, rising up in a DNA-like spiral, crossing the central sushumna four times and activating each chakra one at a time. This raising of kundalini energy is what also provides the spiritual physical powers or siddhi to the practitioner.

The (central) sushumna is the central nadi and comprises three separate nadis: vajrini nadi, chitra nadi, and brahma nadi, and it is the primary channel for prana to the chakras.

Through the power of meditation, the bioenergy kundalini is moved up the spine, energizing the chakras that are connected to the nerve plexus and endocrine glands. This movement of bioenergy assists the person to reach a higher level of physical, emotional, and mental functioning and, ultimately, to a higher level of self-actualization and enlightenment.

From *The Subtle Body* by Cyndi Dale:

Before Manifestation, the *param bindu* (supreme consciousness) assumes a threefold character that appears as a triangle. Each point of the triangle is represented by a *bindu,* or force that interacts with the other bindus, to lead to enlightenment. These three bindus are red (rakta), which represents Brahmi, the energy of Brahma the creator (also called Bindu); white (Shavit), which represents Vaishnu, the energy of Vishnu the preserver (bija); and a mixed color, which stands for Maheshvara the destroyer, or Shiva himself (nada).

The param bindu (which creates the three triangular bindu forces) forms kamakala, the principle of actualizing energized consciousness (Shakti) in the form of subtle sound frequencies. The param bindu, now seen as three separate shaktis, flows through three different nadis to represent three types of consciousness. The vama nadi transforms into knowing; the jyeshtha nadi into feeling; and the raudri nadi into doing. When the kundalini raises to unite with the supreme consciousness in the kameshvara chakra, the three bindus mix with three gunas (sattva, ragas, and tamas), which are the qualities of energy. These newly merged energies now form supreme bindu and three qualities necessary for enlightenment: truth (satyam), beauty (sundaram), and goodness (shivam).[185]

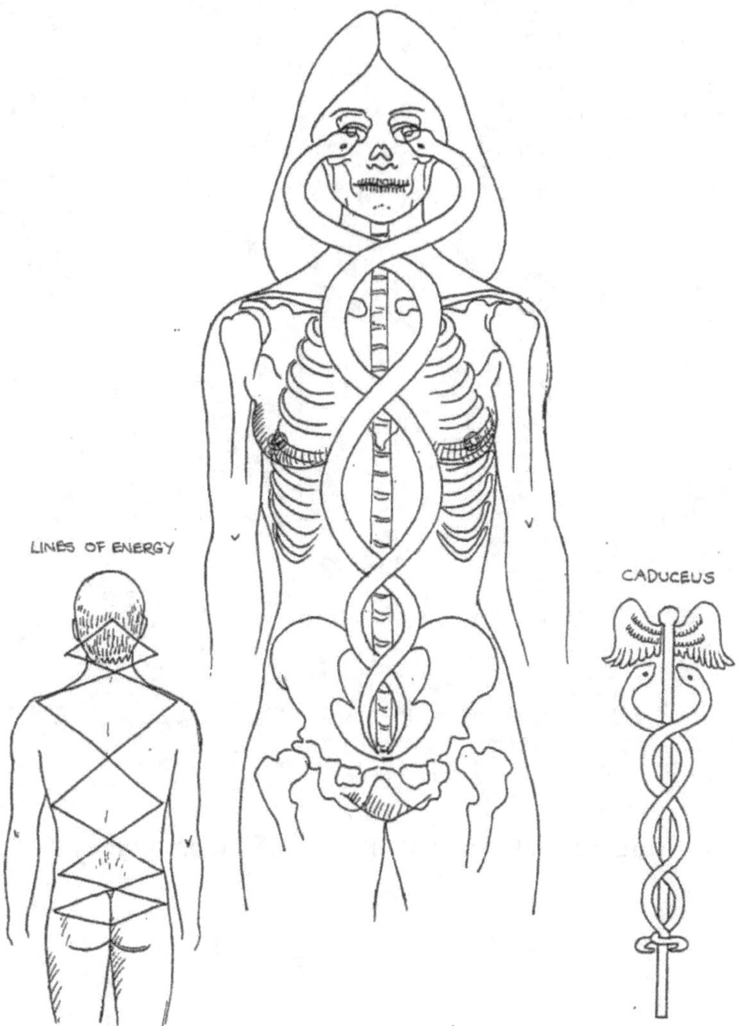

Figure 64: Caduceus in Relation to Chakras

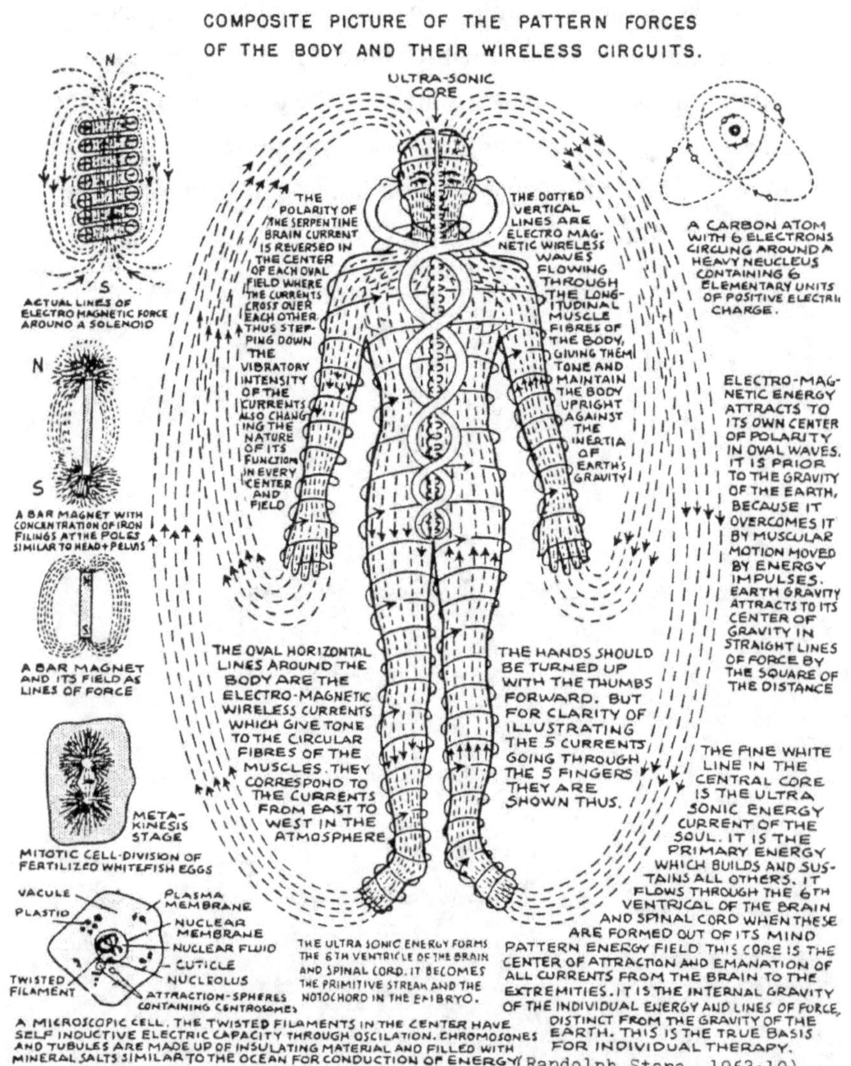

(Randolph Stone, 1953:10)

Figure 65: Composite Picture of Pattern Forces

COMPOSITE PICTURE OF THE PATTERN FORCES OF THE BODY AND THEIR WIRELESS CIRCUITS

The body, like any object or organism, has a magnetic force. Any electrical charge has magnetic radiation. The electrochemical charges down the nervous system and the possible energy charge of the fascia system set up the auric field. The pattern of the myofascial planes may determine the structure and power of the external energy field, as the internal energy system sets the basic pattern (actually influences each other) for the external energy. Discussing the field theory of atomic particles, Hickman said that Einstein and the theory of relativity theorized that the fields surrounding everyone or even a particle were real.

The aura was photographed by a Kirlian (electrophotography) process studied at the University of California at Los Angeles by Dr. Valerie Hunt and others. In the metaphysical tradition of most cultures, the aura is represented in philosophy, art, and religion. A light sphere often accompanies the pictures of Christ, Mary, and the saints. Tansley pictures Buddha with three auric bodies. These three auric bodies and the seven chakras connect to each other, according to Motoyama, and are in both the astral and causal dimensions, yet function directly on the physical body.

As outlined in the Three Centers Theory of Triune Psychology, the three auric bodies represent the human's three-part physical and psychological systems. The aura concept has an extensive history worldwide and represents one central tenet that all major religions agree upon: the existence of the aura. McDougal spoke of Epicurus, who "taught that the soul is a fine substance distributed through the whole mass of the body, and most resembles the air with an infusion of warmth."[186]

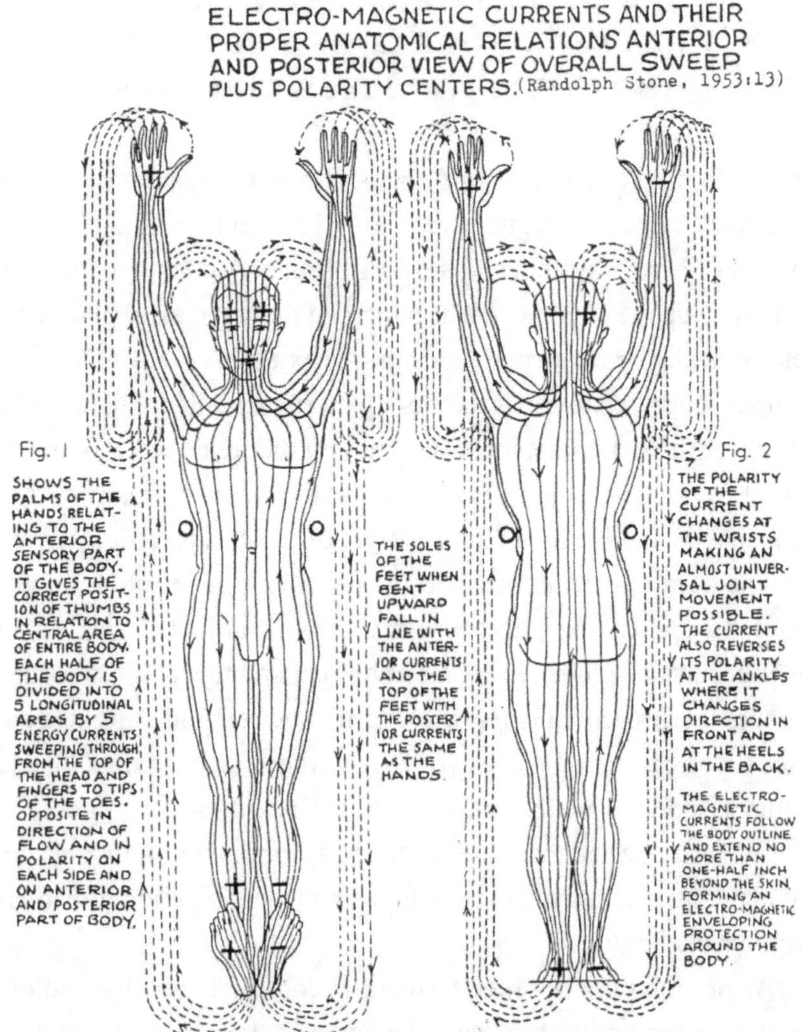

Figure 66: Electromagnetic Currents

The ancient esoteric principle that energy follows thought encompasses a fundamental concept in all martial arts, metaphysical philosophies, and modern mystics. When a person reaches down to pick up an object, the very thought or intent stimulates the creation of enough energy to complete the task. If inhibited from its intended action, the unused energy becomes residual tension. The residual energy becomes unorganized at the body-mind part that its power was meant to motivate and tends to adhere to that part in which the charge was initially attracted. Because of the disorganization of the inhibited or repressed energy charge, the tension dissipates into surrounding tissues. Other residual tension travels through the fascia, muscles, circulatory system, and nervous system and becomes attached to various systems. The mechanisms of speaking, gesturing, and otherwise communicating get an extra charge. This means residual buildup occurs in the voice, mouth, nose, eyes, ears, hands, feet, and lastly, the spinal column, which has been known as the "garbage pile of residual tension." Electromagnetic charges develop as a force field from the electrical and chemical charges of the nervous and circulatory systems and the fascia and muscles. Energy charges attach to tissue and collect in an energetic cobweb of various fascia, toxins, lactic acid, other chemicals, and energy charges flowing through the body. Most noticeably, the energy charge blocks up with fascia.[187]

These blocks change the tissue and gradually lead to body armoring, as Reich described. As the most basic of instincts or senses, the need for survival forms the primordial background for the body's reaction to a perceived threat. The degree of the threat in the environment and the degree that a child successfully learns to deal with that threat (real or imagined) constitute the indicators of the amount of armoring the body builds. Life's progression can show armor building and movement impaired due to the tissue becoming more rigid. Time could also become a measure to describe qualities of lengthening and of releasing residual tension. Is it a painful life to be led with struggle and sorrow or one happy and fulfilling?

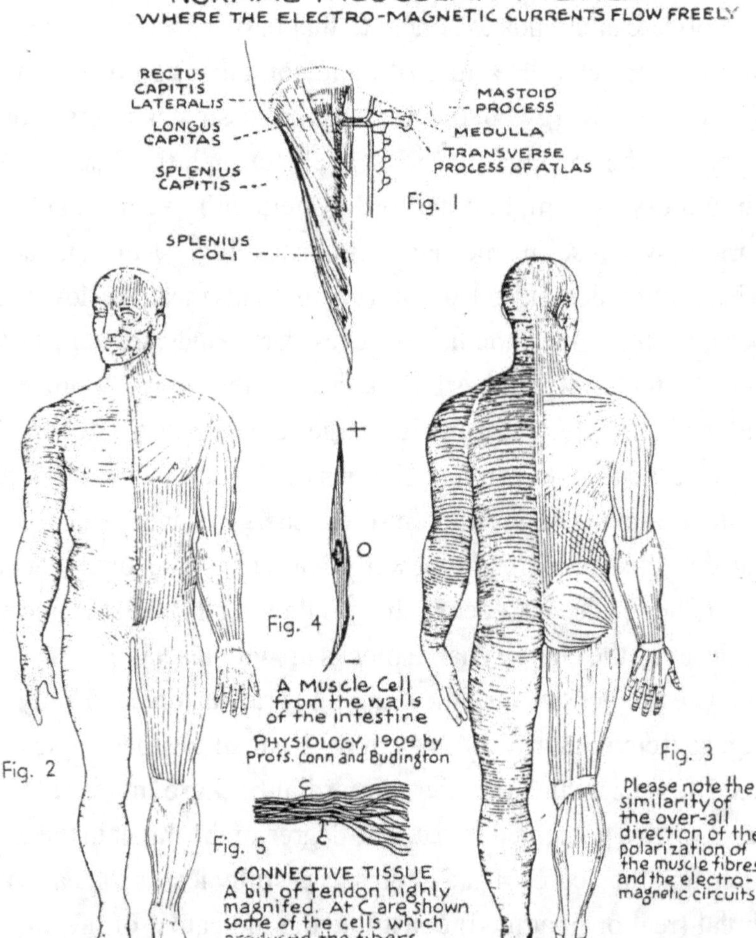

Figure 67: Normal Muscular Fibers

This is the pain or pleasure drama of mind-style and emotion-al-style that is written in tissue as the body style. Tissue armors as if to defend against the environment. Psychological issues of defense are manifested physically. An osteopathic thought that the structure determines the function transforms into a duality dance of either doing both. The functioning of the organism determines the structure in a dynamic sense linked physically and psychologically with growth and development. An inhibited function cannot build its ultimate structure. Blocked energy overcharges some areas and undercharges others. Overcharged areas expand and grow larger while undercharged parts contract and wilt.

Organized energy increases all levels of organismic functioning, which also better balances the structure. Thought manifested in an organized, knowledgeable manner will organize or focus energy. Aikido extension of ki, along with yoga and tai chi, all require the development of the organization of energy. It is accomplished by movement or the use of the physical to influence and alter the emotional and intellectual. Perhaps this is why therapists describe progress as "movement in therapy."

Often, the mystical part of every culture has concepts about extending energy out of the body for particular reasons. Kahunas of the Hawaiian tradition can send out "Lee." The Russian sensitive, Nina Kulagina, has been photographed moving objects by shooting out rays of luminescence from her eyes. Kahunas develop the ability to project a thread or finger of aka out from the eyes.[188] Carlos Castaneda's character, Don Juan, talks about the body as a cluster of luminous fibers that have awareness. Organized thought can project energy, but if thought says, "Can't do it," the energy blocks off, and only a trickle of the normal river flows through. Without proper sustenance, life wilts and becomes underdeveloped. Again, the metaphysical concept at work is that thought follows energy.

The systems theorists (Bateson) have developed an energy concept of negentropy to explain social interactions. The principle of the second law of thermodynamics or entropy shows that energy breaks down or becomes disordered and unorganized. Negentropy is the system integration with increased patterning, organization, and structure. This concept was hailed as the difference between the open and closed systems.

ENERGY BLOCKS

As the residual tension vibrates increasingly slower, it becomes more solid until form manifests in conjunction with fascia, toxins, lactic acid, and other biomaterials. In a sense, the body is energy housed in matter. The body circulates energy as blood and cell nutrients, an electromagnetic energy field, the nervous system, and oxygen. Energy flows in and out of the biosphere.

Ida Rolf explains in physical terms the blockage of energy. Stress causes the fascia to thicken, perhaps due to increased amounts of residual tension. Thickened fascia glues the muscles together, making independent movement difficult. Energy blocks are created from this interplay of fascia and electrical tension. The gluing that Rolf speaks of becomes Reich's personality armoring as the body builds up its defense mechanisms out of tissue to protect itself. The more precarious the perception of the environment, the greater the armoring necessary for protection. Character armor is muscular tensions manifesting from energy into matter. This process of the armoring growing is, in a sense, the body script coming out of the life script.[189]

The energy-fascia interplay may also cause the creation of small lumps from toxins, diet, or, as Rolf thought, dried-out substances, perhaps from a virus, which could be in the muscle or tendon.

Perhaps any overcharge of energy, electrical or chemical, can cause the lumping effect. Selye injected air into fascial sheaths and formed globules. The energy fascial attachments can be explained as a change from energy to matter or from a higher vibration rate to a lower one. This is scientifically plausible. Hickman points out that the kinetic theory of matter has matter as noncontinuous rather than as molecules in a constant state of motion. Three states of matter, solid, liquid, and gas, are known by the relative distance and velocity of the molecules. Molecules closer together, as in solids, have a slower velocity. Molecules in liquids are further apart, and velocity is increased. In gas, the molecules are even further apart, and velocity is faster.

The undissipated energy slows down over time to become mixed with fascia and crystalize into glued muscles or lumps. These globules were of particular interest to the ancient Mongolian warriors, according to Green, who claimed to have extracted the information from a lecture by Oscar Ichazo of the Arica system. These Mongolian warriors believed the body was filled with little globules from blocked energy. The globules had a painful memory, thus developing fear in the body. The body has the memory of all fear, which is the subjective history of pain in the body. "Chua Ka" was the deep tissue method of release the warriors developed to get the fear out of the body before and after a battle in order to become fearless warriors. Psychologically, hate actually stiffens every nerve and muscle, according to Maud Williams. The Hawaiian Huna agree that the energy of hate destroys the body with the power of the magnetic field.[190] Not only fear and hate but all unspent emotional charges become chronic muscle tension.

Stress can originate from diet, physical injury, or emotional trauma. Regardless of the source, the body reacts to stress with a general adaptation syndrome, as Selye outlined. Lowen talked of the three phases of the defensive reaction to stress. In the initial phase, an alarm reaction occurs as the body reacts to stress and secretes adrenal medullary hormones that mobilize body energy. The body undergoes an inflammatory process. In phase two, with stress continuing, the body tries to adapt or contain tension by secreting the anti-inflammatory adrenal corticosteroid hormones. The last stage of exhaustion sees the body unable to deal energetically with stress, and it breaks down from energy to matter and becomes part of the physical reality. At a very empirical level, the tension in the body causes physical dis-ease or being not at ease from tenseness, rigidity, or unbendingness physically, emotionally, or mentally; the manifestation of contraction is non-relaxation.

GRAVITY AND ANTI-GRAVITY

Ida Rolf considered the Earth's gravitational field to be the most potent physical influence in any human life. Humans have the vestibular apparatus for space orientation primarily to the forces of gravity. Yet, gravity exists as the force that many fight against, for it is, indeed, the force of the Earth. An un-erected, unbalanced posture brings the added pressures "of the world." Literally and figuratively, gravity on all parts of the body that are not in alignment, thus not in harmony with the forces/energies of the earth, brings added pressures. Whereas gravity or the electromagnetic matrix of the earth upholds a body in alignment with its forces. Balance brings fluidity and fulfillment, while being off-balance must be a precarious situation that breeds physical and psychological insecurity. The image of the self reflects its degree of balance and security through the body's energy. The bioenergy has an electromagnetic frequency that radiates called the aura, and it displays the color of that balance.

The person's relationship with gravity, according to Rolf, was in adjusting to the flexor and extensor equilibrium. Each body part flexes and extends to find a fit to the mighty force.

The "antigravity" forces include the intrinsic muscles, atmospheric pressure, air buoyancy, and, perhaps, even the process of cognition.

Atmospheric pressure exerts weight on all life at 14.7 lb./in.² at sea level, or approximately fifteen pounds for every inch of surface.[191] The further up one travels, the lower the atmosphere. A full 50 percent of the atmosphere rests below 3.5 miles above sea level. Thus, one weighs more at sea level than up in the mountains. The antigravity function of air pressure comes from the function of joints. Joints form a mechanism for the transmission of energy and movement from bone to bone. This is due to the hermetically sealed joint capsule, which does not contain air. Yet each joint, like the body, is under the pressure of the atmosphere.[192]

One theory holds that the joint created a vacuum through its action or movement, making the body proportionally lighter with that action.[193] A leg's weight feels much less when the atmospheric pressure is high, and more weight is felt when the pressure falls. Air pressure in joints, like the hip joint, would be read like a barometer if it could be installed in that joint.[194] This is why people can "feel" the weather change from the feelings of pressure changes in the legs.

Air buoyancy affects the body's attitude toward gravity. Carter presented a view that the body is in density between the Earth and air, so we float in the air on Earth. The amount of air in the body does lighten it. Kahn described the specific gravity of water and the body as being similar. When floating in water, the trunk has gas-filled intestines and air in the lungs, which floats, as does the head with the air-filled nasal cavity and sinuses, but the arms and legs, devoid of air, sink. The greater the rate of air intake, the greater the buoyancy, in general, in water. Air is, in physics terms, a form of matter with a greater rate of vibration than liquid or solid. Thus, greater air capacity creates more buoyancy in water and, while floating on Earth, in air. The shallower the breath means less air and more feelings of heaviness and depression. Rolf believed that the air spaces in the skull could be designed to reduce the weight of the head. If Reich were correct about orgone, an interesting possibility would be the energy created in the skull bone from organic and inorganic (salt deposits) layers of matter. Energy emanating from the head influences the balance of the entire body.

Food intake alters gravity and antigravity forces. The rate of vibration of the food affects that of the body functioning, making the body heavier or lighter. A lot of fruit has a lightening effect, while heavy meat diets produce a weighted-down, more earthy feeling. The effects of the amount of food producing more or less weight on the body can be seen with over- and under-eaters.

In aikido class, we were instructed to stand on either side of a person and attempt to lift him off the ground using his hands and arms. The subject was told to think "light" the first lift and "heavy" the second. On the first attempt, the subject rose lightly, but my partner and I had to struggle to pull his weight off the ground on the second lift. This researcher does not claim to know how thought can be an anti- or pro-gravity force, only that it was phenomenologically proven to him. Perhaps "heavier" people have a denser energy pattern reflected in the lower colors showing up in their auras and the more primary psychological issues in life.

The importance of the concepts of external energy forces relates to their impact on the body. Randolph Stone considered the internal gravity lines in the human to be the patterns of energy, which may run along the myo-fascia.[195] Rolf described a symmetrical body as wasting less energy in needless tensions and movements. A better balance created a more efficient magnetic field, which brought on heightened awareness and improved perception from greater sensory modulation. Reich thought that energy had an antigravity quality that Lowen insisted came from the energy flow at the two poles of the body. In Stone's concept, the polarity created a higher energy charge that Lowen saw as enabling humans to have and maintain an erect posture.

Man's relation to gravity is manifested in the alignment of the body. To Rolf, this was through the pelvis and its relationship to the gravitational field.

FUNCTIONS OF THE STRUCTURE:
HOW THE ENERGY MOVES US

The way the body moves is determined by its relationship to internal and external energy forces, as well as past history. The way every movement occurs becomes the history of how the function and structure progress in time. Children establish movement patterns early in life, and upon this foundation rests adult interaction. The tai chi teacher often tells students that the movement of the ancient form reflects one's movement through life—smooth or uneven, graceful or clumsy.

The breathing process represents what ultimately occurs as a wave-like motion filling the stomach diaphragm up to the chest. Known as the "breath of life," this action fans the life-force with oxygen to mix with blood and absorb nutrients to create energy. Restrictions with breathing may stem from fears. It is incredible how many people have shallow breathing. Improved breathing can usually enhance one's appearance and health. Kurtz and Prestera suggest that the use of hatha yoga in assisting people to fully breathe air and prana would help eliminate many diseases. Reich noted the shallow breath and found that many people had emotional releases by breathing fully. Leonard Orr and Sondra Ray discovered this therapeutic principle and established "Rebirthing."

With breath comes speech, and the entire social and intellectual culture of humans is based on speech as part of human physical communication.[196] The voice expresses a person's well-being and psychological functioning in the tone and pitch. Talking reflects the relationship between thought and emotion.

Standing is how we meet the Earth. The relation to the Earth, usually called grounding, represents a solid connection. It is how we "make our stand" in life that reflects our values and thoughts. Our "standing in life" actually depicts our lifestyle in the form of tissue adaptation and becomes our body style. Our "understanding" is essential so that we "know where we stand." Lowen describes standing as action and reaction, so when a person presses down on the ground, the ground pushes back and holds us up. In this way, we can say that the person "stands up" to a situation of stress or difficulty.

The body's polarity (head and pelvis or head and feet) creates much antigravity energy that seeks to maintain the erect spine. Bellies always move forward from the locking of the knees (for stability). Heads may also reach out forward in an effort to "get ahead." The critical psychological factor is a lot of put down or criticism. Green suggested a standing pattern called the Big Bow stance, which had a pioneer or American look with everything going forward in the body.

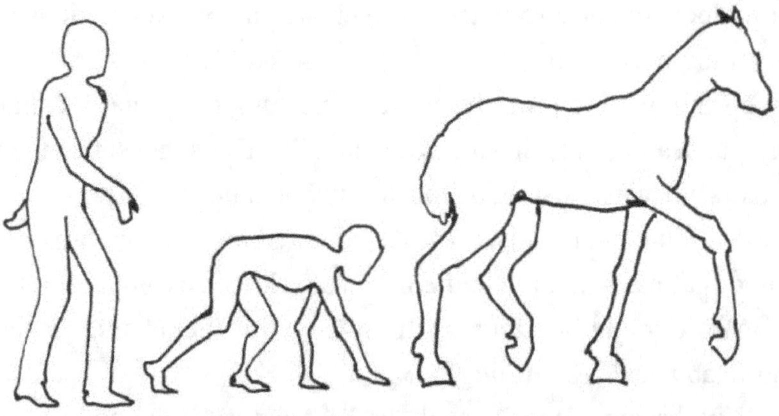

Figure 68: The Cross-gait Walk

Energy flows freely up and down the chakra system if the back is erect. Any significant deviation from the perfect shows a body-mind defense reaction or posturing to a physical, emotional, or mental trauma.

How we move through space is how we move through life. The way we walk reflects the way we move through life's situations.

Naturally, our walking can be effortless, although age and physical limitations or disabilities can show interesting variations. Kahn described the act of the human walking like a pendulum machine.[197] Legs swing like a pendulum with atmospheric pressure pushing on the hips and gravity as a counterbalance. The cross-gait walk shown in Figure 68 remains the human's most efficient manner of movement, as it evolved with man and connects humans to our animal heritage. Kahn considered the way people walk as inherited with the arms swinging in a certain rhythm and said people would have a hard time differing from that rhythm while walking.

But walking styles significantly differ as they manifest our movement through life or through earth-gratifying needs. The heavy, lead, thudding step shows rigidity in the person and in the foot and a lack of personal security to go with the flow or an inability to bend with the world.[198] The tiptoer has all the energy in the head, usually daydreaming, and has little contact, physically or psychologically, with the world, which is reality. A confused walk wanders around and reflects a lack of personality organization and goal projection. Lowen describes a "floater" as someone who moves along with little contact with the environment. This floating can accompany an alcoholic high, a feeling of being in love or receiving exciting news, or the schizoid individual—all of whom float along with little sensing of the earth under their feet.

Humans learn to walk due to hereditary consequences, teachings from the environment, and the influence of patterned motion from role models. In most cases, the person's walk can be significantly improved; often, an awareness of walking patterns brings a shift toward greater efficiency. Rolf pointed out that one significant problem in walking and with injuries to runners is when the feet, ankles, knees, and hips are not lined up in a forward, straight direction. If any one of these joints is everted or inverted, the upper body becomes unbalanced. The psoas-rectus balance, says Rolf, is essential to the mechanics of walking and standing. This balance is necessary for proper weight and energy distribution between the legs and torso. An overdeveloped stomach or thigh muscle can make for patterns of restrictions in walking, an early onset of arthritis, and more.

According to various martial arts and Rolf, the initiation of movement comes from the torso. Specifically, the center of the second chakra, hara or one-point, is the physical center of gravity. Castaneda called this location of grounding energy the center of will. In a balanced body, movement starts at this point and transmits energy to the legs via the psoas. The legs follow rather than lead.

SUMMARY

YOU BECOME THE WAY you think and feel. The way you think about things and how you feel become your way of interacting with others, and through DNA and alignment with gravity, your tissues evolve into your persona body-mind.

This book tells the story of the wonderful, incredible variety of life manifesting physical tissue changes. Obviously, the more marked the change, the more visible, thus easier to see.

The way we function in our habituation of activities moves our lifestyles into our body-styles. You can especially see it in older people—showing, for example, the happy life, sad life, or depressed life. You can see it in their bodies as their bodies have habituated their thoughts, emotions, decisions, and biases.

Our habituated body style is typically unconscious. We become more aware of our body style when people comment about it. Otherwise, we remain primarily unconscious but identify the body style as part of the self. The observer may think, "That guy is cocky or arrogant," but the self thinks, "Yea, I'm cool, man."

PSYCHOSOMATIC CHANGES
AND VARIATIONS

Psychosomatic changes and variations (types) "naturally" occur in tissue due to social and environmental conditions. These factors manifest alongside the genetically endowed characteristics of physiology, and they include emotions, stress, thinking patterns, movement, posture with its alignment with gravity, health issues, and injury or accidents.

Our decisions, actions, and consequences determine our relationship to the environment, including family and community. To some degree, the adaptation to stress, which is biochemical, interpersonal, and psychological, is psychosomatic in nature.

Our choices and interactions with people at home, work, or play bring a certain amount of stress hormones, neuropeptides, metabolic byproducts, and toxic waste. Biochemical reactions spew through the circulatory and endocrine systems and, at some point, infuse the connective tissue. Forms of energy flows can be characterized physiologically as the nervous system energy, blood, and the intercellular interstitial fluids moving in tissue. Degrees of energy flow can be described in Western terms as reactions in connective tissue, especially the fascia.

Inside the body, the residue of stress, metabolic byproducts, and toxic residue remains in the connective tissue. Fascia raises and lowers viscosity (thickens and thins), enabling both inflammation and induration through numerous factors such as heat and cold, chemical interactions, emotions, or abrasion. Specific molecules latch on to connective tissue, which provides it with the role of storage and compartmentalization. This is especially evident in adipose or fatty tissue. Now, these two critical functions of storage and cellular movement can interact. That is why we get lumps, abrasions, and bumps in tissue, which are the more visible blockages of energy flow, significantly if the tissue hardens. These hardened areas could be described as energy blockages, as they limit the amount of energy flow, nerve energy, circulation, and endocrine flow.

The root causes of stress or biochemical imbalance are partially genetics (you are made that way) and interacting with environmental pressures and social choices of family, friends, community, job, posture (alignment with gravity), and diet. Over time, while living life, we naturally begin routines—morning routines, evening routines, and dinner routines—and by our repeated activities over time, we habituate the activities and live our emotions.

Eventually, although contingent on genetics, each body-mind part, body section, and body type demonstrates the changes from psychological adaptations to the social and physical environment. These changes show up in the psychological significance of body sections being joined together by physiological and psychological issues. The character with the various body parts and body types leads up to the whole body's variations.

THREE PSYCHOPHYSICAL CENTERS OF LIFE

Human existence evolved in a three-step process recognizable by its anatomy, physiology, and structure. Life itself created the body form with the first primary level, physical center, or R-complex. Sense modalities of eyes, ears, nose, etc., had the advantage of the ability to detect food and danger at a distance. These senses naturally developed with body systems, such as the nervous system, endocrine system, and circulatory system. Animals could sense, feel, and respond quickly or emote through the second primary level or the emotional center (limbic system). The advantages of emotions are to emote or to react—move, respond, or fight or flight.

Specialization of the nerves from the notochord to the brain's cerebral cortex brought with it the more specialized form of communication and information storage that we referred to as intelligence. This is the third level or the mental center (neocortex). Thus, we have the three major systems of the body: the physical, emotional, and mental. Each center primarily grew out of the previous ones.

Three Centers can be represented as a triangle, and a triangle becomes a tetrahedron in three dimensions. The tetrahedron and the other Platonic solids form the structure of existence, as can be seen in the design of carbon and the essence of quantum physics. The human body has three major skeletal systems: the pelvis, the chest or thorax, and the skull or cranium. Legs hang down as appendages to the pelvis, and the spinal column begins at the pelvis and connects the three systems. Arms are appendages to the chest, and the spinal column finally connects to the head. From the pelvis through the chest rests most of the organ's function for the requirements of living. The head, skull, or cranium form the third primary part of the skeletal system.

Paul MacLean detailed the triune brain as the reptilian complex (R-complex), limbic system, and neocortex. In physiology, three germ cells create the entire body: the endoderm, ectoderm, and mesoderm. Endoderm is the essential gut that allows for life by eating or absorbing nutrients, elimination, and other functions to support life. Mesoderm provides the muscle and bone, circulatory system, and other systems to provide for endocrine communication, the ability to quickly emote or move, and the meaningful communication that we think of as "feeling." Ectoderm branches into the nerves, the brain, and the skin (and more), which comprise our system of speedy communication.

This book explores the various ways people embody the many environmental, cultural, and social pressures. Body types are the living culmination of the psychophysiology of the many body parts and tissues. Body types could be called psychosomatic alterations. Based on the person's physiological adaptations to these many environmental and social issues, various models were given based on theoretical body typing. The ways the body adapts were explored, and theoretical explanations were presented.

We think, understand, and have perspective for interpersonal communication, morals, ethics, and being at the highest level of life form that we know of on earth. Although this brief outline depicts information relevant to our Triune Body Psychology inquiry, much more scientific evidence exists.

The Three Centers model was discussed, compared, and contrasted to other theories as related by Randolph Stone's Polarity Therapy, Ken Dychtwald's Bodymind, Ida Rolf's Rolfing, Sheldon's somatotypes, Misho Kushi's Asian/Oriental physiognomy, Kurtz and Prestera, Green, Lowen, Reich, Freud, Plato, and others.

This book sorts theories from history and science to give more of a complete guide. However, it is realized that not all of these theories or historical references presented will stand up to scientific investigation or analysis. A natural selection of theories meeting scientific scrutiny or analysis will eventually weed out those without appropriate merit in favor of those with scientific or logical analysis. The study of the alterations of tissue, anatomy, and physiology represents a type of psychosomatic or psychophysiology identified as body psychology. My work is based on the Three Centers model, which I call Triune Psychology.

BIBLIOGRAPHY

Alexander, Frederick M. *The Resurrection of the Body*. New York: Dell, 1974.

Arnold, Edwin Sir, trans. *The Song Celestial or Bhagavad Gita*. Los Angeles: Self-Realization Fellowship, 1977.

Asimov, Isaac. *The Human Body: Its Structure and Operation*. New York: New American Library, 1963.

Aston, Judith. "A Somatics Interview with Judith Aston." *Somatics*. Vol. 3, No. 1, Autumn, 1980, Pp 8–14.

Bailey, Alice. *Initiation, Human and Solar*. New York: Lucis Publishing Co., 1951.

Bailey, Alice. *Ponder On This*. New York: Lucis Publishing Co., 1971.

Bain, Alexander. *Mind and Body: The Theories of Their Relation*. New York: D. Appleton & Co., 1877.

Barker, Sarah. *The Alexander Technique: The Revolutionary Way to Use Your Body for Total Energy*. New York: Bantam Books, 1978.

Barnwell, F.H. and F.A. Brown. Responses of Planarians and Snails. In M. Barnathy (ed), *Biological Effects of Magnetic Fields*. New York: Plenum Press, 1964. Pp 263–278.

"Bioenergetics and Zen." New York, The International Institute for Bioenergetic Analysis, Vol. 1, No. 5 (April 1981).

Blair, Lawrence. *Rhythms of Vision*. New York: Warner Books, 1960.

Boadella, David. *Wilhelm Reich: The Evolution of His Work*. Chicago: Henry Regnery Co., 1974.

Bruyere, Rosalyn. *Wheels of Light*. New York: Simon & Schuster, 1994.

Bucke, R. *Cosmic Consciousness A Study in the Evolution: of the Human Mind*. New York: E.P. Dutton & Co., 1901.

Bunker, Ellsworth. *Man In the Trap*. New York: MacMillan, 1967.

Burroughs, Stanley. *Healing for the Age of Enlightenment*. Kailua, Hawaii: Stanley Burroughs, 1976.

Carter, Paul. *Conversations about Body Psychology*. San Diego, 1981.

Carter and Health. *Somatotyping—Development and Applications*. New York: Cambridge University Press, 1990.

Cassius, Joseph. "Bodyscript Release: How to use Bioenergetics and Transactional Analysis."

Horizons in Bioenergetics: New Dimensions in Mind/Body Psychotherapy. Joseph Cassius (ed.). Memphis TN: Promethean Publications, 1980.

Castaneda, Carlos. *Journey to IXTLAN: The Lessons of Don Juan.* New York: Simon & Schuster, 1972.

Castaneda, Carlos. *Tales of Power.* New York: Pocket Books, 1974.

Dahl, H. and B. Stengel. A Classification of Emotion Words. *Psychoanalytic Contemporary Thought.* 3:273, 1978.

Dale, Cyndi. *The Subtle Body: An Encyclopedia of Your Energy Anatomy.* Boulder, Colorado: Sounds True, 2009.

de Langre, Jacques. *The First Book of Do-In.* Magalia, California: Happiness Press, 1971.

Dychtwald, Ken. *BodyMind.* New York: Jove Publications, Inc., 1977.

Erikson, Erik. *Childhood and Society.* New York: W.W. Norton & Co., 1950.

Feiss, George J. *Mind Therapies Body Therapies: A Consumer's Guide.* Millbrae, California: Celestial Arts, 1979.

Feldenkrais, Moshe. *Body and Mature Behavior: A Study of Anxiety, Sex, Gravitation and Learning.* New York: International Universities Press, 1949.

Feldenkrais, Moshe. *Awareness Through Movement.* San Francisco: Harper and Row, 1972.

Freud, Sigmund. The Metapsychology of Instincts, Repression and the Unconscious in *Theories of Psychopathology*. Theodore Millon (ed.). Philadelphia: W.B. Saunders Co., 1967.

Gibran, Kahlil. *The Prophet*. New York: Alfred A. Knopf, 1973.

Gibson, W. and L. Gibson. *The Complete Illustrated Book of the Psychic Sciences*. New York: Doubleday, 1966.

Goleman, Daniel. "The 7,000 Faces of Dr. Ekman" in *Psychology Today* (February 1981), Vol 15 No 2, 42–49.

Green, Barry. *Body Psychology Lectures at the Institute for Psycho-Structural Balancing*. San Diego, California: May 1980 to December 1980.

Greenwald, Harold (ed.). *Active Psychotherapy*. New York: Jason Aronson, Inc., 1974.

Gunther, Bernard. *Energy Ecstasy and Your Seven Vital Chakras*. Los Angeles: The Guild of Tutors Press, 1978.

Hall, C.S. and G. Lindzey. *Theories of Personality*. Santa Barbara, California: John Wiley & Sons, 1978.

Hall, Manley P. *The Secret Teachings of All Ages*. Los Angeles: Philosophical Research Society, 1969.

Hay, Louise. *Heal Your Body: Metaphysical Causations for Physical Illness*. New York: Louise L. Hay, 1976.

Hickman, Cleveland P. *Integrated Principles of Zoology*. St. Louis: The C.V. Mosby Company, 1961.

Hoffman, Enid. *Huna: A Beginner's Guide*. Gloucester, Massachusetts: Para Research, 1973.

Hushi, Michio. *Introduction to Oriental Diagnosis.*
London: Sanwheel Publications, 1978.

Hutchins, Robert M. (ed.). *Great Books of the Western Society Vol 7 Plato.* Chicago: Encyclopedia Britannica, 1952.

Ichazo, Oscar. *The Human Process for Enlightenment and Freedom.* New York: Arica Institute, Inc., 1972.

Institute of Psycho-Structural Balancing
(IPSB), course lectures, 1980.

Jacques, Bob. Bioenergetic Training Group, San Diego, 1980.

James, William. *The Principles of Psychology.* Chicago: Encyclopaedia Britannica, Inc. 1891.

Jensen, Bernard. *The Science and Practice of Iridology.* Escondido, California: Bernard Jensen, 1974.

Johnson, Don. *The Protean Body.* New
York: Harper and Row, 1977.

Johnson, Mary and John E. Grant. *Blake's Poetry and Designs.* New York: W.W. Norton & Co., 1979.

Joyce, Michael. "The Physiological Learning Process: Source of Our Inner Language and Foundation for a Somatic Profession." *Somatics*, III, No 2. 1981, Pp 40–44.

Kahn, Fritz. *Man in Structure and Function.* Alfred
A. Knopf, Vol 1. New York, 1960.

Kelley, Charles P. Orgonomy, *Bioenergetics and Radix: The Reinhian Movement Today.* Ojai, California: The Radix Institute, 1978.

Keyes, Ken. *Handbook to Higher Consciousness*. St. Mary, Kentucky: Living Love Publications, 1975.

Kulvinskas, Viktoras. *Survival Into the 21st Century*. Yethersfield, Connecticut: Omangod Press, 1975.

Kurtz, R. and H. Prestera. *The Body Reveals*. San Francisco: Harper and Row, 1976.

Kushi, Michio. *Introduction to Oriental Diagnosis*. London: Sanwheel Publications, 1978.

Lao Tsu, trans. Gia-Fu Feng and Jane English. *Tao Te Ching*. New York: Vintage Books, 1972.

Lawson-Wood, D. and J. *Acupuncture Vitality and Revival Points*. Devon, England: Speight, The Health Science Press, 1975.

Lowen, Alexander. *Bioenergetics*. New York: Penguin Books, 1975.

MacLean, Paul D. "Family Feeling in the Triune Brain." *Psychology Today*. New York: Vol. 15, No. 2 (February 1981), p. 100.

Maddi, Salvatore R. *Personality Theories: A Comparative Analysis*. Homewood, Illinois: Dorsey Press, 1968.

Mann, Edward W. *Orgone, Reich and Eros: Wilhelm Reich's Theory of Life Energy*. New York: Simon and Schuster, 1973.

Mann, Felix. *Acupuncture: Cure of Many Diseases*. Boston: Tao Press, 1972.

Margolis, Glen. *Conversations about Body Psychology*. San Diego, California: April 1981.

McDougall, William. *Body and Mind: A History and a Defense of Animism*. London: Methuen & Co., 1911.

Meyers, Martha. "Body Therapies and the Modern Dancer: Dance Trainings New Frontier." *Dance Magazine*, July 1980.

Miller, James G. "Living Systems: Basic Concepts." *Behavioral Science*, (1965), pp 10, 193–237.

Miller, Roberta D. *Psychic Massage*. New York: Harper and Row, 1975.

Mishra, Ramamurti S. *Yoga Sutras: The Textbook of Yoga Psychology*. Garden City, New York: Anchor Press Doubleday, 1973.

Montagu, Ashley. *Touching: The Human Significance of Skin*. New York: Columbia University Press, 1971.

Motoyama, Hiroshi. *Science and the Evolution of Consciousness: Chakras, Ki, and Psi*. Brookline, Massachusetts: Autumn Press, Inc, 1978.

Nathan, Gene. Personal Interview. San Diego, California: March 1981.

Nebadon, Michael. *The Form*. Los Angeles: Institute of the Form, 1980.

Ohashi, Wataru. *Do-It-Yourself Shiatsu*. New York: E.P. Dutton, 1976.

Ohsawa, George. *Acupuncture and the Philosophy of the Far East*. Boston: Tao Publications, 1973.Orr, Leonard. Rebirthing Lecture. San Diego, California: 1980.

Ouspensky, P.D. *In Search of the Miraculous*. New York: Harcourt, Brace & World, Inc., 1949.

Pelletier, Kenneth R. *Mind as Healer, Mind as Slayer*. New York: Dell Publishing Co., 1977.

Peris, Rex. Conversations about Body Psychology. San Diego, California: 1981.

Piaget, Jean. *The Origins of Intelligence in Children*. New York: International University Press, 1952.

Pierrakos, John C. "Core Energetic Therapy: A Functional Process for Integrating Body, Mind, and Spirit." New York: Institute for the New Age of Man, 1980.

Presman, A.S. *Electromagnetic Fields and Life*. New York: Plenum Press, 1970.

Rado, Sandor. *Psycho-analysis of Behavior*. New York: Grune and Stratton, 1956.

Reich, Wilhelm. *The Discovery of the Orgone: The Function of the Orgasm*. New York: The Noonday Press, 1942.

Reich, Wilhelm. *Character Analysis*. New York: Farrar, Straus & Giroux, 1949.

Reichmanis, M, A.A. Marino, and R.O. Becker. "D.C. Skin Conductance Variation at Acupuncture Loci." *American Journal of Chinese Medicine*, (1976), Vol 4, No. 1, Pp 69–72.

Rolf, Ida. *Rolfing: The Integration of Human Structures*. New York: Harper and Row, 1977.

Sagan, Carl. *The Dragons of Eden: Speculations on the Evolution of Human Intelligence*. New York: Ballantine Books, 1977.

Selye, Hans. *The Stress of Life*. New York: McGraw-Hill, 1956.

Sheldon, William H. *The Varieties of Temperament: A Psychology of Constitutional Differences.* New York: Harper and Brothers, 1942.

Smith, Adam. *Powers of Mind.* New York: Ballantine Books, 1975.

Smith, Joseph. "Bodyscript Release: How to Use Bioenergetics and Transactional Analysis," *Horizons in Bioenergetics: New Dimensions in Mind/Body Psychotherapy.* Joseph Cassius (ed.). Memphis, Tennessee: Promethean Publications, 1980.

Spino, D. *New Age Training for Fitness and Health.* New York: Grove Press, Inc., 1979.

Spitz, R. *A Genetic Field Theory of Ego Formation: Its Implications for Pathology.* New York: International University Press, 1959.

Stone, Randolph. *The Wireless Anatomy of Man.* Chicago: Randolph Stone, 1953.

Stone, Randolph. *Polarity Therapy.* Chicago: Randolph Stone, 1954.

Stone, Randolph. *Energy: The Vital Polarity In The Healing Art.* Chicago: Randolph Stone, 1957.

Stone, Randolph. *Evolutionary Energy Series.* Chicago: Randolph Stone, 1959.

Storm, H. *Seven Arrows.* New York: Ballantine Books, 1972.

Tansley, David. *Subtle Body: Essence and Shadow.* London: Thames and Hudson, 1977.

Teeguarden, Iona. *Acupressure Way of Health: Jin Shin Do.* Tokyo: Japan Publications, 1978.

Thie, John, and Mary Marks. *Touch for Health*. Santa
Monica, California: DeVorss & Co., 1973.

Tohei, K. *Aikido in Daily Life*. Tokyo: Rikugei
Publishing House, 1966.

White, Harvey. *Modern College Physics*. New
York: D. Van Nostrand Co., 1966.

Whitney, Pamela. Private Interview. San
Diego, California: March 1981.

Williams, Maud S. *Growing Straight*. New
York: A.S. Barnes & Co., 1930.

NOTES

1   Paul MacLean, 1981, Sagan 1977, MacLean developed the Three Brain Theory after significant physiological research. Carl Sagan reported MacLean's research in *The Dragons of Eden* and other writings.

2   MacLean, 1981

3   Kahn, 1960, points out that the right side is more developed and the left side is the softer and more feminine side, which painters and photographers tend to use.

4   Sheldon, 1942, who developed Constitutional Psychology and popularized somatotypes.

5   Gibson and Gibson, 1966

6   Kushi, 1978. Michio Kushi presented numerous Asian medicine insights.

7   Ibid.

8   Rolf, 1977

9   Gibson, 1966, 322

10 Ibid., 325 shows the face profiles of convex, vertical, and concave.

11 Ibid., 324

12 Ibid., 326

13 Ibid., 327

14 Bain, 1877, in his classic *Mind and Body*, points out the three levels assigned by numerous ancients.

15 Stone, 1959

16 Reich, 1942

17 Lowen, 1975

18 Goleman, 1981

19 Bucke, 1901, *Cosmic Consciousness*

20 Stone, 1953

21 Spino, 1979

22 Kurtz and Prestera, 1976
23 Erikson, 1950
24 Kurtz and Prestera, 1976
25 Rolf, 1977
26 Dychtwald,1977
27 Kushi, 1978
28 Ibid.
29 Rolf, 1977
30 Dychtwald, 1977
31 Ibid.
32 Rolf, 1977
33 Ibid.
34 Dychtwald, 1977
35 Blair, 1960
36 Kushi, 1978
37 Margolis, 1981
38 Dychtwald, 1977
39 Stone, 1953, 79
40 Erikson, 1950
41 Kurtz and Prestera, 1976
42 Montagu, 1977
43 Dychtwald, 1977
44 Green, 1980
45 Dychtwald, 1977
46 Kurtz and Prestera, 1976
47 Ibid.
48 Dychtwald, 1977
49 Gibson, 1966, 325
50 Ibid., 324
51 Gibson, 1966, 327
52 Dychtwald, 1977
53 Hay, 1976
54 Ibid.
55 Lowen, 1975
56 Dychtwald, 1977
57 Ibid.
58 Ibid.
59 Rolf, 1977
60 Dychtwald, 1977
61 Lowen, 1975
62 Lowen, 1975
63 Ibid.
64 Rolf, 1977

65 Dychtwald, 1977
66 Ibid.
67 Rolf, 1977
68 Dychtwald, 1977
69 Kurtz and Prestera, 1976
70 Dychtwald, 1977
71 Reich, 1942
72 Miller, 1975
73 Green,1980
74 Dychtwald, 1977
75 Ibid.
76 Ibid.
77 Ibid.
78 Ibid.
79 Stone, 1953, 11
80 Tansley, 1977
81 Dychtwald, 1977, 179
82 Dychtwald, 1977
83 Ibid., 141–142
84 Kurtz and Prestera, 1976
85 Green, 1980
86 Dychtwald, 1977
87 Ibid.
88 Ibid.
89 Green, 1980
90 Dychtwald, 1977
91 Green, 1980
92 Ibid.
93 Ibid.
94 Dychtwald, 1977
95 Ohsawa, 1973
96 Ibid.
97 Kurtz and Prestera, 1976
98 Dychtwald, 1977
99 Ibid.
100 Green, 1980
101 Ibid.
102 Dychtwald, 1977
103 Erikson, 1950
104 Green, 1980
105 Lowen, 1975
106 Dychtwald, 1977
107 Green, 1980

108 Dychtwald, 1977
109 Green, 1980
110 Stone, 1953
111 Green, 1980
112 Rolf, 1977
113 Green, 1980
114 Ibid.
115 Dychtwald, 1977
116 Ibid., 76
117 Whitney, 1981
118 Kurtz and Prestera, 1976
119 Dychtwald, 1977
120 Kurtz and Prestera, 1976
121 Ichazo, 1972
122 Dychtwald, 1977
123 Ibid.
124 Green, 1980
125 Dychtwald, 1977
126 Ibid.
127 Ibid.
128 Rolf, 1977
129 Kulvinskas, 1975
130 Ohsawa, 1973
131 Hall, 1962
132 Ohsawa, 1973
133 Whitney, 1981
134 Stone, 1953
135 Ibid.
136 Ibid.
137 Ohsawa, 1973
138 Dychtwald, 1977
139 Green, 1980
140 Kurtz and Prestera, 1976
141 Ibid.
142 Dychtwald, 1977
143 Kurtz and Prestera, 1976
144 Dychtwald, 1977
145 Ibid.
153 Sheldon, 1942
146 Carter and Heath, 1990, 406
147 Cassius, 1980
148 Feldenkrais, 1972
149 Lowen, 1975

150 Ibid.
151 Ibid.
152 Jacques, 1981
154 Hall and Lindzey, 1978
155 Tohei, 1966
156 William James, 1891, 890
157 *The Encyclopedia Britannica*, 1953
158 Bain, 1877, 148
159 Ibid., 155
160 Ibid., 155–157
161 Ibid., 181
162 MacLean, 1981
163 *The Encyclopedia Britannica*, 1953, 466
164 Hall and Lindzey, 1978
165 Erikson, 1950
166 William James, 1891, 859
167 Asimov, 1963
168 Presman, 1970
169 Pelletier, 1977
170 Sagan, 1977
171 Freud, 1967
172 Kahn, 1960
173 Greenwald, 1974
174 Hickman, 1961
175 Hickman, 1961
176 Ibid.
177 Ibid.
178 Stone, 1953, 10–13
179 Stone, 1954
180 Dale, 2009
181 Ibid.
182 Ibid.
183 Bruyere, 1994
184 Dale, 2009
185 Ibid., 269
186 McDougal, 1911, 26
187 Rolf, 1977
188 Hoffman, 1973
189 Cassius, 1980
190 Wilkerson, 1968
191 White, 1966
192 Kahn, 1960
193 Nathan, 1981

194 Kahn, 1960
195 Stone, 1957b
196 Rolf, 1977
197 Kahn, 1960, 162
198 Kurtz and Prestera, 1976

ACKNOWLEDGMENTS

I THANK THE SOURCE FOR THE INSIGHT into the Three Centers Theory. This saga began at Boise State when I was a psychology undergraduate, with Dr. William Sickles encouraging my research that culminated with the identification of the three centers.

Studies at the Institute of Psycho-Structural Balancing with Dr. Barry Green and others assisted me in better understanding the Three Centers structure in the human body.

With the encouragement of Dr. Dan Eckstein at the United States International University (USIU) came a master's thesis titled *Body Psychology: The Empirical Basis of Holistic Theory.*

I must give appropriate credit and gratitude to Ken Dychtwald, Ron Kurtz and Hector Prestera, Ida Rolf, Randolph Stone, William Sheldon, Alexander Lowen, Michio Kushi, Paul MacLean, Carl Sagan, Alexander Bain, Sigmund Freud, Wilhelm Reich, William McDougall, Plato, Aristotle, and others for their incredible insight into the anatomy, physiology, or psychology related to the mind-body. Their books are widely referenced as primary source materials.

Many thanks to Edie, Sally, and Pam for beautifully creating some of the artwork.

My gratitude to all the people who assisted me along the road.

With Universal Eternal Gratitude.

ABOUT THE AUTHOR

DOUG PETERSON, PH.D., provides insights about the body and behavior from his experience and training as a psychologist, educator, holistic health practitioner, massage therapist, and social worker.

Any suggestions, comments, and training arrangements can be sent to drdougpeterson3@gmail.com, or tricenterspublishing@gmail.com.

INDEX

Note: Page numbers in italics indicate figures; page numbers followed by "t" indicate tables.